# CHRONIC
# GRACE

# WHAT OTHERS SAY ABOUT CHRONIC GRACE

"Julie Rhodes is the Midge Maisel of evangelicalism: prim, smart, funny, and honest — struggling through faith-shaking hardship with guidance from ancient tradition, and sometimes talking back. *Chronic Grace* is a recipe book for life, offering nourishment for any reader who faces real challenges and knows that real success takes more than a ring light."

Ryan Sanders
Commentary Editor
*The Dallas Morning News*

"In a world where we expect doctors to figure out and fix everything, Long-Haul COVID has stumped even the best of them. Long COVID means "fevers, malaise, racing heart, diarrhea, shortness of breath, cough" – and more. What's it like for **a woman, a mother, a wife, a career-woman** to endure months of no diagnosis when she knows from bones to skin that something's there? Chronic illness requires chronic grace to sustain the fragility of life in the whatever-it-takes quest for healing. Julie Rhodes' soul-open memoir transcends the path of description, though myriads in the world with Long COVID need a companion like *Chronic Grace*. She transparently probes God, the Bible, her prayer life, and some of the greatest spiritual masters as she probes her own "quivery, shivery" heart and faith. What's it like? Julie, in turning her transparent self toward our loving God, provides words for the journey and healing for the heart. *Chronic Grace* is a textbook of the journey of faith."

**Rev. Canon Dr. Scot McKnight**
**Professor of New Testament**
**Northern Seminary**

"Can I be honest? I couldn't put Julie's story down. While enjoyable, beautiful, and compelling – it also took my breath away because it held all my fears. As her unexplainable Long Haul COVID symptoms seemed to unendingly stack one upon another, she didn't give up but leaned in. She did what I hope I would do. She leaned on the cross of Christ and found God's grace. And she leaned on the saints of old to borrow their truth for herself. Part history lesson, part unfiltered inspiration, and part well-placed humor, Julie leads us through her valley and helps us see that the bright light of Jesus is always there. If you are facing uncertainty or fear or need a good reminder that no matter what comes your way, Jesus will be with you, and he is, indeed, enough – read Chronic Grace."

**Jodie Niznik, author,**
**Bible teacher, and host of the**
**So Much More podcast**

# ABOUT THIS BOOK

In a world where thorns pierce the flesh of our lives, one woman's journey through pain, illness, and uncertainty unfolds in a story that is as raw as it is inspiring.

Meet author Julie K. Rhodes, a "non-dramatic" running mother who aspires to keep her acting career afloat and her kids educated during the pandemic. But then something unexpected happens, throwing her into a perplexing struggle with an illness that is still mysterious and stubborn — Long Covid. Julie's world has been turned upside down by the Backpack of Woe she is carrying, which is heavy with fatigue, fever, and ultimately the specter of another thorn: cancer.

A ray of hope appears in the midst of the gloom. Julie learns the power of grace — mysterious, elusive, yet the universe's guiding force — by learning to pray biblically with Christian saints and mystics of old.

*Chronic Grace* offers the opportunity to see a woman's profound journey that reflects the struggles of historical figures like Ignatius, Teresa of Avila, and others. Julie strives to comprehend the mystery of grace and how it may heal even the most broken life with these unusual but wise partners.

However, this is not a solo journey. As a reader, you too will develop a bond with the author's colorful cast of characters. These historical figures experienced the pain of thorns and sought comfort via their own individual paths of prayer. Their teachings will shed light on the possibilities of acceptance and healing in a way that will connect with you personally.

Join Julie on this soul-stirring journey through deep canyons and unexpected insights — with a big dose of humor thrown in for good measure. By the time you've finished reading this memoir, you'll have met people who share your struggles and learned about the transforming power of grace — a force that can sustain you even in the most difficult of circumstances.

You'll leave knowing that grace, not thorns, defines our true essence.

# CHRONIC
# GRACE

## PRAYERS, SAINTS, AND THORNS THAT STAY

# JULIE K. RHODES

LEADERSHIP
Thoughtful, Relevant Leaders From Around The World
BOOKS

# ACKNOWLEDGMENTS

Thank you to every friend or family member who brought a meal, Starbucks drink, or random item from Target when I couldn't function.

Thanks also to my friends in the medical field whose advice and practical help during the maelstrom were literally lifesaving. Rich, Katie, Chad, Adam, and Sis-in-Law Katy, I'm looking at you.

To Mike, Faith, Jerry, Joseph, Simone, and the rest of the Leadership Books team: thank you for taking a chance on this first-time author. Your belief in me and this book has spurred me on. Jerry, Editor Extraordinaire: can you come to sit at the table across from me as I write my next book? Your encouragement is utterly life-giving, specific, and motivating.

To Victoria and Lee and everyone at MadeWorthy Media, thank you for the opportunity to share my story early on when it was more of a cry for help and less of a cohesive narrative.

To Katie of VivaWise Functional Wellness: you counted my fevers right alongside me, monitored my supplements, and tracked every last blood test metric. Most of all, you believed me. I wouldn't be well today without you, and I recommend your practice to everyone I meet, even if they are not sick. I forgive you for making me stop with the cheese.

To Katti, who has coached me through auditions and roles over the past decade, and then through the harrowing vocal struggle that was Covid and surgery: I love you. I know you were even more worried about my voice than I was. That's the mark of a true friend.

To my friends who read and re-read all or portions of the book: Sarah, Susan, Suz, Kendra, and Dr. Carolyn Lee, especially. Thank you. There is almost nothing worse than being asked to "read a thing I wrote and see what you think." You all rival St. Francis in your willingness to suffer for Jesus. To Carolyn: your challenge to flesh out the prayers I wrote with more context was a critical step in the process. And Sarah: your challenge to flesh it out even more into a memoir was just the boost I needed.

To my parents, Dr. Andy McQuitty and soon-to-be *Dr.* Alice McQuitty (amazing, ma!), for your invaluable contributions. You painstakingly read drafts of *Chronic Grace*, first when it was just a bunch of prayers, then when it was a devotional, and finally when it took its current form. You loved its many iterations, just like you've loved me through all of mine. Dad, thanks for shepherding me as I entered the business of being a published author!

To my in-laws Jim and Peggy Rhodes and Reagan and Eric Bourassa (and kids Madison, Parker, and Kennedy): your constant support and help made my thorn bearable all those months I couldn't be the mom I wanted to be, and every month since. Thank you.

To my siblings and their spouses and kids: Liz, Danielle, Violet, Bonnie, Jonathan, Andie, Eric, Peyton, Jeff, and Katy: thank you for being born. I love you.

To Dinner Club: I can't think of something appropriate to say here that won't get me in trouble, so I'll give you a wink. (And a big hug for all your love, help, support, food, and laughter over the years.)

To my kids, Drew and Madeline Rhodes, who had the unfortunate assignment of living my thorn alongside me: I don't think I've ever thanked you properly for your endurance during that time. Thank you for the way your eyelashes curl (Maddie) and the way your dimples deepen (Drew). You are the roses.

To my husband, the beard-faced Gordon with the soft eyes: I love you. Thank you for your endless patience as I first wrestled with illness and then wrestled with writing about it. You have brought me a cup of coffee in bed every morning for 18 years. You are an exemplary man.

To Eloise, The Eyeballs, who is currently snoring in front of the fire: you have no idea what a gift you are, and if you did, you would demand more food as compensation.

And finally, to the people who make Jolly Ranchers: this book would not exist without watermelon. The Lord bless and keep you.

# TABLE OF CONTENTS

## Dedication

For Homer and Caroleen Thornton

(Grandaddy and Grandmama)

true saints

# FOREWORD

Possibly the most grievous wound that can be inflicted by pain and suffering on a sincere Christ-follower's faith is the loss of hope in a God they fear has abandoned them.

I personally sustained this wound at 2:58 pm on July 14, 2009, when my doctor phoned to say that I had stage IV colon cancer (only 8 percent survival rate) and needed to get in for major surgery immediately. With one terrifying phone call, my life was forever changed, and in that moment, the one thing I "knew" (erroneously, as it turns out!) was that it had changed for the absolute worst.

Job famously declared in his deepest moment of pain:

*"Though he slay me, I will hope in him" (13:15).* Sadly, that's not how I reacted to my cancer diagnosis. Though I had spent nearly four decades as a pastor urging people to trust God in times of trial, my spiritual wound at that moment was a loss of hope: *"I just wanted to know, needed to know: why? Why this? Why now? Why me? Was it something I did? Something I failed to do? Something God failed to do?"* (*Notes from the Valley*, Moody Press, 2015).

Similarly, questions of lament prompted Julie Rhodes in *Chronic Grace* to engage with God more deeply over His seeming abandonment during her painful season as a Covid Long-Hauler: *"As an actor, I know that sometimes it's best to have a script to follow, especially when it comes to talking with God about touchy subjects like why he hasn't delivered us yet or what his plans could possibly be" (xxiii).*

Though Julie and I may not have known it then, challenging questions in our seasons of pain and suffering were merely twenty-first-century expressions of an ancient spiritual conundrum known to theologians as "The Existential Problem of Evil." This "problem" is usually formulated as a question such as, "Lord, if you are all-good and all-powerful, then why do you allow your children to suffer?" (This proves that Julie and I are entirely unoriginal in our "challenging" questions to the Almighty recorded above!)

No believer escapes this sin-broken world without experiencing loss, pain, and suffering. When it's your turn in the batter's box of pain and suffering, you will inevitably raise the "problem of evil" question with Julie and me. Good news! Wonderful answers are found in scripture and Christian experience in the form of "theodicy," defined as "explaining the ways of God to vindicate God's ways to man." Theodicy addresses such questions as why our good God permits temporary suffering in this fallen world, how God's children can persevere through suffering, and what good can result from suffering as they respond faithfully to it.

Theodicies can be long or short, whole books or short passages within books, a genre (like apologetics), or just a major theme within another genre, as Julie Rhodes has given us in her magnificent memoir *Chronic Grace: Prayer, Saints, and Thorns that Stay.* (Full disclosure: Julie is my daughter. However, I insist that using the word "magnificent" to describe her work is factually objective...no brag, just fact!).

In *Chronic Grace*, Julie mines not only the scriptures to discover ways to persevere and even flourish while suffering but also the wisdom of eminent saints such as Ignatius, Augustine, Julian of Norwich, Teresa of Avila, and Francis of Assisi. But her most profound insight comes from St. Paul himself, the muse who inspired the title of her book:

*"Although Paul begs God to be rid of his thorn (whatever it was), Jesus tells him, 'My grace is sufficient for you, for my power is made perfect in weakness.' A short, simple reply. There is no explanation of how long the thorn will last, when it might ultimately resolve, or how he might be using it to advance the kingdom further. Jesus skirts all that and serves his grace as a reasonable answer to Paul's every other question" (3).*

Paul here in 2 Corinthians 12:7-10 was asking the "Existential Problem of Evil" question. Jesus' answer was a theodicy of grace, and the result for Paul was Romans 5:3-5:

*"Not only that, but we rejoice in our sufferings, knowing that suffering produces endurance, and endurance produces character, and character produces hope, and hope does not put us to shame, because God's love has been poured into our hearts through the Holy Spirit who has been given to us" (ESV).*

Suppose indeed the most grievous wound inflicted by pain and suffering on a sincere Christ-follower's faith is the precipitous diminishment of hope. In that case, God's healing balm is the invitation to receive and trust His grace.

That's the hard-won place of peace where Julie Rhodes lands after her perilous and suffering-fraught voyage through Long Covid. Whether your present suffering-fraught voyage is also through Long Covid or some other chronic illness or pain, I pray you can join Julie in this prayer to our Good, Good Heavenly Father.

*"Oh Lord, help me to let you set the parameters of my thorn. I've insisted on benchmarks, but you have not agreed to my terms. I've insisted on progress, and you've said to wait. Do I trust that you set its boundaries as you do for the oceans, that you set its intensity as you do for the storms, that you set its duration as you do for each season? Help me to trust your good intentions towards me. Help me to trust that you are committed to my final and everlasting happiness" (247).*

God promises that if you endure in faith despite your thorn, He will restore your hope and build into your life a depth of character and experience of love that no thornless life could ever even hope to produce.

This gift of "thorns that stay" we call grace. May you receive it, be blessed by it, and be forever grateful for it.

- Dr. E. Andrew McQuitty,
author of *Notes from the Valley,*
*The Way to Brave, and Your Best Life Later*

*Even in our sleep, pain which cannot forget*

*falls drop by drop upon the heart*

*until, in our own despair, against our will,*

*comes wisdom through the awful grace of God.*

**- Aeschylus,** 525-456 B.C., the Father of Greek Tragedy (Predictably.)

# PREFACE

We all have our stories, our COVID chronicles. The first case of COVID in the U.S. was reported in January of 2020. As of this writing in January of 2023, the World Health Organization's (WHO) website estimates that over seven-hundred and fifty million people worldwide have tested positive, and over 6.8 million have died. A survey released this month by the U.S. Census Bureau and the National Center for Health Statistics (NCHS) estimates that almost 6 percent of U.S. adults are currently experiencing Long Covid, and over 15 percent of U.S. adults have dealt with it at some point[1]. The Center for Disease Control (CDC) has launched multi-year studies to explore our new national bumper crop of illness. (Side note: women are also much more likely than men to be Long-Haulers[2]. Lucky, adorable us!)

Several months into my illness, in addition to the fevers and malaise and inability to breathe or have a normal heart rhythm, I discovered yet another COVID symptom had been ravaging me. It wasn't physical and would not be doctored away. It was soul malnutrition, the need for something to gnaw on, for something warm and nutritious to go down into my nonphysical digestive tract, disseminate into my invisible bloodstream, and energize my spiritual arms, legs, hands, eyes, and feet. I had a core deficiency that could not be diagnosed in a vial of blood, seen on an X-ray, or medicated with steroids.

I am a pastor's kid. Because of that, or perhaps despite it, I knew and loved Jesus from a very early age. I found at about age twelve or thirteen that something in me was awake to a presence, a personality, that seemed to impress things on me whenever I would read the Bible. It excited me. I would wake up at 6:30 a.m. to read a passage or two, and I would feel him. There were moments in which I felt that if I turned around fast enough, I might see him standing in the corner, smiling, and for some reason, this was not creepy to me.

Over time and age and struggle, I lost most of that spiritual clairvoyance. I grew up and became an adult woman with responsibilities, more urgent goals, and new driving ambitions. And then suddenly, I got sick, and all my grown-up concerns and accomplishments were no longer sitting out like a sumptuous buffet to sustain and motivate me. Suddenly, I had all the time in the world to watch my potential go bad in the fridge.

I became hungry.

Although I had never strayed too far from weekly Bible studies at my church over the years, I was now on a more urgent mission to find sustenance, to hunt and eat and live. It was a life-or-death expedition. I remembered where to go and what paths to take through the brush. I stalked Scripture and Christian books like a predator, looking for a phrase, concept, or truth that I could impale, skewer, and cook over an open fire. And then I bit into it, juice running down my arms through prayer.

The writing of the prayers was what did it. My pen was like a fork, and it fed me as I dragged it across the page. So many of my prayers were really sermons to myself about who God is, who I am, and what to make of my current situation. I was both preacher and pray-er. Sometimes I was whine-er. Sometimes I was silent.

As I was flipping through my journal one morning, I had a very distinct impression for a book titled *Chronic Grace* because that was the theme running through each page of these private prayers: grace that endures alongside chronic difficulty. I began to feel the need to reach out and share my prayers with others who have stubborn problems of their own. As an actor, I know that sometimes it's best to have a script to follow, especially when it comes to talking with God about touchy subjects like why he hasn't delivered us yet or what his plans could possibly be. And thus came to be this devotional-memoir of sorts, part-story, part script.

And then I met some saints. As I was developing my prayers into more of a proper memoir, I realized it might be helpful to bring along some companions. I had heard of the faith ancestors in this book here and there, but I had never actually sat down to read what they wrote. I thought maybe I'd see if their stories had anything to say to mine. Wow. Did they ever.

The truth was, I didn't think my story was dramatic-enough memoir material. I needed help from people who had suffered through the Black Death and the Inquisition, or so I thought. It turns out these men and women had rather normal lives that were punctuated by extraordinary historical or spiritual events. Kind of like me. The difference was they responded in ways — and with theology — I hadn't yet fathomed.

At any rate, I hope you'll take what you need from whichever part of this book speaks to you the most — my story, the saints, the prayers — and leave the rest behind.

This kind of jungle expedition requires light packing.

# INTRODUCTION

This is not my first book. Well, all right, it is. But it was never meant to be. Let's call this my pre-first book.

My first book, coming out someday when I write it, is a brilliantly conceived, bitingly funny and sweeping spiritual memoir, the likes of which Anne Lamott would be proud. It is also a deeply profound, gorgeous manifesto that would make Annie Dillard and Frederick Buechner cry sad, sad tears of regret for their comparatively subpar writing lives. Additionally, my first book is transportive, in the way of Anne Morrow Lindbergh, who carries her reader to both the seaside and life-side at once.

Perhaps this nonsense is why I'm writing *this* book and not my first book.

In the Spring of 2020, I fell ill with what several in my medical team ultimately decided was COVID-19. I have a "medical team," you'll notice right off the bat, which never bodes well. People with MEDICAL TEAMS have an overflowing backpack of maladies.

Fever, malaise, cough, shortness of breath, crippling fatigue, racing heart, diarrhea, and brain fog were my symptoms, and they were symptoms that would live on and on, in varying degrees and frequency, for the following year of my life. The whole thing was made worse by the threat of cancer and its resulting surgery. But I'm getting ahead of myself.

Before my Backpack of Woe was thrust upon me, I was a generally healthy 39-year-old running mama of two, with a career performing on stage in regional theaters. I know you are clutching your pearls with surprise at how someone as non-dramatic as me could possibly want to perform.

My agenda for my illness was to "kick against the goads," as old Johnny Cash and (I think) Jesus said. This whole chronic illness thing was ridiculous. I wasn't having it.

To make matters worse, my diagnosis was never confirmed clinically. On April 11, 2020, I went on a jaunty three-mile run. On April 12, I was crashing. Multiple PCR swabs came back negative, as did antibody tests. My bewilderment at all of this was a thrashing, snarling animal in my abdomen, like a feral ninth COVID symptom. I had become an *unidentified flailing object.*

In 2 Corinthians 12, the Apostle Paul tells his readers that a "thorn in his flesh" was given to him so that he might not become conceited about the great revelations God had given him. You might recall that Paul, as a historic and religious personality, was a titan of intellect, leadership and charisma. This makes me, shall we say, *hesitant* to set myself and my thorn alongside him and his. His writings to and shepherding of the early church exploded the Christian phenomenon onto the world stage, and this has gone on to affect billions and billions of lives ever since. God had clearly given Paul some big-time insider information. He had real reasons to feel smugly self-contented, as he admits in Philippians 3. Maybe he too wanted to unseat Annie Dillard and Anne Lamott.

And then comes his thorn. A tormenter. A *messenger of Satan*.

Although Paul begs God to be rid of his thorn (whatever it was), Jesus tells him, "My grace is sufficient for you, for my power is made perfect in weakness." A short, simple reply, really. No explanation of how long the thorn will last or when it might ultimately resolve or how he might be using it to further advance the kingdom. Jesus skirts all of that and serves up his *grace* as a reasonable answer to Paul's every other question.

This answer seemed to satisfy Paul, but those of us with thorns know how easy it is to fixate on the thorn and dismiss the grace. We don't give grace a chance, really. What IS grace, after all? It's much more human, when you have a hangnail, to squirm at that tiny centimeter of irritation than to insist on appreciating your broad, strong back or clear lungs or brilliant brain that is present to register and pass judgment on the pain.

Is it even possible to consider that our thorns are actually less vital, less real, and less powerful than grace, which is the truly dominant force in the universe? Is even asking that question disrespectful to our pain? I think it's almost impossible to see correct proportions because our thorns are *not* hangnails. Most of our thorns feel fully assaultive, poking at our eyes so all the world looks red.

So, we have our lives before our thorn, the one we must grieve.

And we have our definitions of grace before our thorn, the ones we must modify.

I do know this: we all have a thorn or will at some point. Look at your life, your neighbor's, your co-worker's, your mom's, your dog's. One of my thorns has been a prolonged, unexplained illness. Maybe yours is also an illness. Or a perpetually difficult relationship or financial situation. A deeply irritating relationship with your child. A mental illness. A death you can't get over, don't even *want* to get over. Maybe you've begged God to take it away. Maybe part of it is even your fault, which doesn't make it any less of a grace magnet. I'm sure you had your thorn in mind even as you picked up this book because the title caught your eye.

*You* know why you're reading this.

Whatever our thorns may be, I'm beginning to ever-so-slowly accept the short, mysterious reply of Jesus to Paul. Because as chronic and inexplicable as my thorn is, there seems to be an equally chronic, equally unexplainable, and inscrutable dynamic keeping up alongside it.

That dynamic is grace.

This book is an invitation to join me for a while, to give grace a chance together.

Oh, and we'll have some company, too. You may have heard their names, maybe not. Ignatius, Augustine, Julian of Norwich, Teresa of Avila, and St. Francis all knew what it was like to have thorns. And in each of their own weird, wonderful brains, found ways to think about them and pray through them. They can teach us so much. Also, they're aliens, and I don't understand a lot of what they say.

So really, this memoir is crowded, and you'll have made a lot of friends by the time you finish. One of them will be sick, and the rest of them will be dead, but hopefully you will feel better.

## A NOTE ON THE PRAYERS

I pray in this book. A lot. Mostly, I pray how I would have liked to have prayed during key moments of my journey, incorporating what I've learned since then from our ancient friends. Sometimes the prayers here were almost identical to what I wrote in the moment. (Usually the desperate, faith-less ones.) I'll let you wonder about which is which.

Maybe you'll even pray the prayers with me? I thought I'd ask you to consider it. If you've got a thorn in your life, maybe they will help. Even the desperate, faith-less ones.

As you do this, you might find yourself wrestling with what a phrase means or implies. That's OK. Praying is having a conversation. Ask God about it. Negotiate with word-choice. Add and elaborate. Consider this your carte-blanche to co-author these prayers along with me. I provide a vulnerable little skeleton, and you build up the muscle and ligaments and apply the skin, so the prayer breathes and talks in your voice.

Ok, that's enough. Let's begin my pre-first book and see how things go.

# CHAPTER 1

# LIFE BEFORE ILLNESS: STRIVING, SABBATHS, AND HOW GOD PRAYED TO ME.

I could see my illness coming from a long way off. It was a tidal wave that started as a thin white line on the horizon and was growing ever larger, more purple, kicking up breezes. I saw it coming from a telescope of sorts, which is what a newspaper can be if you let it, and I guess this makes me lucky. Usually, we don't get any warning that a life-altering, dangerously unpredictable intruder is coming not only to assault us in broad daylight but also to take up residence in our basement. Or maybe that's not so lucky.

It was the week of Spring Break, March 13, 2020. We were visiting my grandparents' house in Paris, TX, a house that has been a feather nest of warmth and safety my entire life, filled with unchangeable, permanent things like

"HIS WORST FAULT IS THAT HE IS GIVEN TO PRAYER."
– WILLIAM SHAKESPEARE (THE MERRY WIVES OF WINDSOR ACT 1, SCENE 4)

Grandmama's Limoges collection on the side table in the living room, the milk glass vases set like jewels in the windows flanking the front door, and the tones of the Baldwin baby grand hammering their way into the sunroom when a toddler has found the treble keys. The foundation of the house plunges deep into the earth's crust. Even the furniture is part of my memory's Permanent Collection.

Upstairs, in the dormer windowed room that belonged to my mother as a child, I swiped open my phone and came across an article from the *New York Times* about two doctors who had contracted the mysterious illness in China we had all been hearing about. Both were young mothers. One survived, the other did not. This new virus sounded stealthy and heartless and arbitrarily violent. And then the words came to me, as easy as pie, before I had time to autocorrect myself. "I'm going to get it," I said aloud. It was a truth that I knew, an oracle.

Exactly one month later, I would be exhibiting symptoms. Exactly one year later, I would still have many of them. But at that moment, the prophecy felt distant and theoretical.

I went downstairs where preparations had begun to sing "Happy Birthday" to me. My mother had baked her famous chocolate cake and arranged two candles — a three and a nine — on top, where they sputtered smoke. The little paper napkins had Eiffel towers on them. Things looked festive, but with an ominous, weird glow, like I was seeing the dining room table and the faces of my family through a dark blue milk glass vase. Soon I would get a notification that my kids' spring break had been extended by an eternal week.

We had arrived in Paris the day before: my kids, Drew and Maddie, my sister Bonnie, and my parents, all rolling up the long blacktop driveway in our cars like a motorcade. Bonnie had abruptly been forced to leave the East Asian country where she had been a missionary for ten years because of this SARS-CoV-2 that was bleeding black onto that part of the globe. She left so fast she didn't have time to make travel arrangements for her dog, Finn, so he had been left behind and the plan for his care was still a dice rolling to rest. Bonnie was buzzy and tender, trying to be brave while so many of her nerves were drying out in the sunlight and wind. She was sitting shotgun as I drove us towards Paris, and I was trying to get us there fast because Paris comforts all things.

In the pictures I have of them that day, the kids are surrounded by bold, primary colors, as though painted by a kindergartener. Drew, who was twelve, wore a color-blocked rugby shirt in kelly green, limey-yellow, and cornflower blue. Maddie, who was ten, wore stripes of pink, yellow, blue, and green. They spent the afternoon in these multicolored shirts stacking multicolored blocks into towers and then knocking them down onto the multicolored ikat rug in the sunroom. The blocks had belonged to eighty-year-old Grandaddy in the 1930s and were stripped clean around the edges of what is probably toxic lead paint. They have been irresistible to four generations of our family because of their staggering potential: the green cylinders can become columns for a grand entryway, and the L-shaped red blocks can encase the blue half-moons to create an arched double-door. The flat red slats can help create multi-stories, the black triangle blocks can cap a chimney or be strung together to form a fortress wall, and the rectangular yellow blocks and shorter red blocks do the monotonous work of outlining walls — but they make the biggest clatter when it all crashes down. Up and down the towers went, increasing in both size and complexity and in a cacophony of demolition.

Before they pounced on the blocks, the kids watched Grandmama do a crossword puzzle. Diminutive at five feet zero inches and elegant in her black-and-white gingham, Grandmama sat with a pencil, Drew and Maddie on either side. The pencil's eraser was lavender, but she never had to use it.

"This row is '____-life,' and the clue is 'a cry to a busy-body,'" she said, almost to herself. "I would put in 'Get a life,' don't you think? So that would be a G-E-T-A."

The letters were scratched in.

Grandmama moved on without waiting for a response as though her trance might dissipate. "We've got an M here," she said, the tip of her pencil finding a top square. "Let's see what that is. 'Word with washing or slot.' Well, since it begins with an 'MA' and it's a long word, I would say 'machine,' wouldn't you?"

Drew got up in search of something, which he clarified was "a better pen," because he had intuited Grandmama was clearly incapable of making a mistake.

The next morning, I received an email from the Fort Worth Independent School District. "Like everyone right now, we know you are needing to make decisions about how best to protect your family in this current health crisis," it began. "After consulting with Tarrant County Public Health and following many conversations with community leaders and other superintendents about the impact of the Coronavirus, we will extend Fort Worth ISD's spring break for at least two weeks. Further details will follow today and through the weekend." There was more elaboration after that, more acknowledging of the burden this would place on families, but the first paragraph was the thing, the news, the all-I-needed-to-know.

I took a screenshot of the email and texted my husband, Gordon. He was back in Fort Worth, where we live, working at his office since we had just been away earlier in the week hiking in Palo Duro Canyon. Whatever it was I said to him has been lost to the sands of time, but it probably involved very few words. Perhaps only a single word. A single word with four letters.

And whatever it was I said to the children is also vague in my memory, but I remember coming into the sunroom where they were playing, my feet heavy and squeaking on the wooden parquet floors as I held up my phone like a wand. With a flourish, I broke the curse of school and schedule and inevitable vacation endings that had always defined and constrained the childhoods of Andrew James and Madeline Mae Rhodes. The world was new but tilting sideways. I'm sure the kids cheered, but all I remember was a wild sense of pillars falling away, like the green cylinders in the block towers. Life was now a pile of random colors strewn around our feet.

The first prayer I could ever recite was the one Grandaddy prayed around the dinner table whenever we would visit Paris. There he would be at the head of the table, larger than the house itself and all the oak trees that surrounded it. "Shall we bless it?" he would say. We held hands.

His great baritone voice had all the restrained strength of Ferdinand the Bull and blended so well with Grandmama's delicate soprano when they sang in the choir of Central Presbyterian. It

OUR FATHER,
WE THANK YOU FOR ALL OF OUR MANY BLESSINGS.
WE THANK YOU FOR THIS FOOD AND FOR THE HANDS THAT HAVE PREPARED IT. FORGIVE US OF OUR SINS, WE ASK IN CHRIST'S NAME.
– AMEN.

was rich and light, a dark chocolate mousse voice. God was inside that voice, too, crammed down into it and then rising up out of it, even as he prayed.

Prayer was more real within this communal act. It seemed the more of us who were gathered around the dining table to pray it, the stronger the frequency shooting up into heaven or wherever it was God was listening from that particular day. And if you had a voice like Grandaddy's, certain and deep, it almost seemed guaranteed the prayer would be heard. If I were God, I would want to listen to a voice like that. And if that voice said the same things over and over again, there would be no missing it, like deepening the groove around a sandcastle. The more you scooped, the better the moat and the more your prayers would hold water and protect you from intruders.

The weeks leading up to March 13, 2022, were cozy in our little Rhodes family cocoon. The Palo Duro trip was an effort towards the adventure and outdoorsy life Gordon feels a moral obligation to thrust upon our indoor children and his indoor wife. Drew had begun Boy Scouts, and Gordon, Eagle Scout Extraordinaire, would see to it that he loved hiking and camping before he had time to resist. Bringing the pug Eloise was a joint decision, and it was probably born of necessity since I am forever forgetting to make boarding arrangements for her until last-minute. On the long, straight, ceaselessly changing scenery of the road up to Amarillo and beyond, past the windfarms and silos, her whining lifted out of the backseat and up into outer space.

I had planned stops along the way to see a series of giant oddities that can be found in the backroads and byways of certain small Texas towns: the "World's Biggest Bowie Knife" in Bowie, the two-story shovel in Wichita Falls, and the house-sized pair of dice in Decatur. We stopped in Aurora to inspect the cemetery where an alien had allegedly crashed his spacecraft in 1987. The only grave marker is a pock-marked limestone boulder under a spreading oak tree, covered by the tokens pilgrims and enthusiasts have left behind (in order to what? Receive a blessing? Good luck?): a neon yellow softball balanced gingerly on top, a pen, a piece of candy in a pink wrapper, a tiny blue fan that plugs into an iPhone, about a hundred pennies, dimes and nickels, a plastic Viking-suggestive axe, a Styrofoam cup full of fake flowers, and a makeshift cross with a little green alien face on the place where Christ's head should be. Eloise sniffed around the boulder's mossy edges. Maddie and Drew stood and stared, scratching themselves and folding their arms across their chests.

The hikes of Palo Duro were stunning and successful by Rhodes' standards. No one broke any bones or broke down into tears. Even Eloise, with her soft padded torso and short snout, kept up the pace and never plopped down in overheated rebellion. We would bring out her water dish whenever we'd find an outcropping of red rock where she could rest her softness on the sand and drink. "That's a good, good girl, Eyeballs," we crooned.

The top of the canyon, where you start the hike, looks down over a valley that seems to be minding its own business despite the stark mesas that pop up out of it in rhythmic, jarring intervals. We started our descent through scrub brush and along steep embankments, winding into the river base. Later in the day, after getting back up to our car and eating hamburgers and ice cream, we followed another trail that spat us out into a scene straight from Pride Rock and *The Lion King*. Gordon held The Eyeballs aloft for an obligatory Simba impersonation.

In the back of our minds, we knew that things back home were changing and that the news coming out wasn't good. I had begun to ask the internet to tell me about "Covid symptoms." But out here in the wind and wide expanse of sky over brush and tree and trail, all that mattered was the next place to stop and pour water down our throats. I didn't know breathing deeply would soon seem like an unfamiliar practice from another life.

Soon, reality could no longer be avoided. School as a general concept and scheduled event was officially up in the air, but what that meant for Monday, March 16, was that school was certainly, definitely, unmistakably

NOT happening at all whatsoever that particular day. Or any day for the foreseeable future.

Over the weekend in Paris, some very smart and hyper-overachieving lady on the internet had designed an attractive "Covid-19 Daily Schedule" that was color-coded by type of activity: Wake Up, Morning Walk, Academic Time (whatever she thought that might actually mean), Creative Time (where she provided helpful suggestions like "Legos, Magnatiles, drawing, crafting, play music, cook, or bake, etc."). This was followed by Lunch, Chore-Time (which involved a lot of WIPING DOWN of things), Quiet Time (defined by "reading, puzzles, nap"), and then another Academic Time (in which "electronics are OK"), followed by Afternoon Fresh Air, Dinner, Free TV Time. Bedtime was listed at the bottom in a dark navy stripe, and it appeared twice: one Bedtime at 8 p.m. for all kids, and a second Bedtime at 9 p.m. for "all kids who follow the daily schedule and don't fight." Brilliant.

I pulled up the chart on our family computer in the kitchen to show the kids. How about we...live sort of like this? Drew, ever so very firstborn, hit PRINT and taped the schedule to the refrigerator. We were literally, exquisitely, on the same page.

My oversized daily planner was also sitting in the kitchen like the tablets of Moses awaiting instructions to be chiseled into it. "Meal Plan, Amazon Order, Run, Piano," I wrote. The *weekly* goals of my to-do list came next. It was Monday, and Monday was the day to determine your weekly goals in a color ink that differs from your daily goals. (This feels aligned with a deep moral truth.) These involved various items like "Decorate for Easter" and "Work Monologue."

Auditions were coming up soon for two Dallas theaters where I had not yet worked professionally: Theatre Three and Dallas Shakespeare. Now that the world was folding in on itself, the first electronic audition submissions were being requested. Would these plays actually happen?

What came before "Work Monologue" on my weekly goals list, however, was "Plan Academic Time." Hyper-overachieving lady said I had to have this as part of our daily schedule, and I was willing to obey anybody who had found the self-possession to stare down the school-less, rudderless wreck of the old dying world and open her Adobe Acrobat. This woman would be feared and obeyed. And, of course, in theory, I knew Drew and Maddie could not simply continue frozen permanently in mid-sixth and mid-fourth grades.

As a homeschooled child growing up, I could feel my mother's voice in my ears: *you can do this.* I clapped a hand over that invisible mouth. This was only going to be an extra couple of weeks, right?

In my journal on March 18, I wrote, "Day Three into the Coronavirus social-distancing break from the world. A strange, enforced Sabbath. Nobody knows what will happen next."

The kids were also writing in journals, as I had proclaimed this would be part of Academic Time. "Day three of coronavirus," wrote Maddie. "My life has changed by staying home every single day. I enjoy it because I'm a homebody."

The times we did get out of the house were to walk Eloise around Ward Parkway under the massive oak and magnolia trees. I felt an obligation to teach the kids about different types of flora and fauna: "This one here is a Live Oak. These pretty little shrubs are Hawthorns. This type of grass is Bermuda. See how it's dead? Only Saint Augustine can grow in the Texas heat."

Soon, the heavy pink crepe myrtle puffs became known as "bottom blossoms" for vaguely gross reasons. We collected hard pits of magnolia flowers and stuck them into pockets. Eloise began to lose weight.

"Never noticed how much church bells ring in the neighborhood," I journaled the next day.

The journal was becoming more of a daily touchpoint. And then, suddenly, it was a daily necessity.

For much of my life, journaling, not prayer, had always been my most personally sacred act, except for perhaps taking walks under trees. (Walking under trees is a highly profound business.) These two things, prayer, and journaling, were separate, or so I thought, but I never felt closer to reality than when I wrote about what I was seeing within my own private mental coliseum.

Surely there was no overlap of journaling and prayer when, as a third grader, I swooned over Philip Yarborough in my chicken-scratch, or later in college when I drooled over the guy I took to the Chi Omega mixer with the Louisianan accent and a shirt that said, "Hold on to me; Someday I may be valuable."

I'm not sure when I started praying inside journals with any regularity, but I do remember the year in high school English when Mrs. Hoerger began requiring spiritual life journaling as part of our weekly assignment. It was the start of some blending.

I had been in "real school" (I called it, as opposed to my dearly departed homeschool) for only a couple of years and was starting Freshman year at a new private Christian high school. "Where are my glasses?" Mrs. Hoerger demanded, pacing around to her desk and then up to the blackboard. Her inherent suspicion of high school boys convinced her they had hidden them.

She spoke with a Michigan accent, fast and stream-of-conscious, always dragging us behind her verbally. "Did you take them?" she yelled at pink-cheeked Steven. Bursts of laughter. The glasses were perched, had always been perched, on the top of her head. Somebody, probably a girl, but probably not me, finally had mercy and told her.

The journaling assignments were due once a week, and sometimes we could work on them in class. We could either journal about a particular Bible verse (a verse from the class Psalm was easy low-hanging fruit), or we could talk about a certain event in our lives and our feelings towards it, or we could write a fictional story. You couldn't just do one format all the time; all three approaches had to be used at some point.

I found myself drawn to the fiction entry, filling notebooks about an old couple named Avery and Hazel who adopted a little girl in the 1870s. I was essentially reimagining *Anne of Green Gables*, but it all felt terribly original. There was something about a train, and there was a riveting scene in which Hazel died in bed. I'd sneak out my journal during Spanish class, scribble ferociously, then hand it off to my friend ShaNee, who would devour my pages and praise my literary prowess when we joined up in Show Choir practice later in the day. Journaling had become a means of showing off and becoming famous with ShaNee. I'm hoping, though I can't remember for sure, that Hazel had *blue* eyes, just to confirm my belief that I was precociously ironic.

But I did begin to explore spiritual truths in those pages in spite of myself. There was something primordial about playing with one word or two words of the Psalms verse that suddenly seemed bigger and bolder in my field of vision, and watching my pen scrawl out things I didn't think I thought or suspected I understood. If you really looked at a verse, really let it strike you in a certain way, all kinds of surprising things could happen. Your pen could get away from you.

This wasn't prayer. At least, I didn't think it was. It wasn't a litany of requests or a recited script. It wasn't spoken aloud in an authoritative baritone. But it had the nature of communication about it because so much of it felt un-invented by me, like when you take dictation, or when you sit across from someone telling you an odd, engrossing fact about their own personal history that has nothing whatsoever to do with you.

There was a loss of control, but there was also agency. I could ask my journal a question, and then begin to wrestle that answer down like an alligator in a weird entanglement where my mind and maybe a greater Mind were conspiring together, interrupting and talking over each other like people caught up in a rush of enthusiasm. If prayer was talking with God, then maybe sometimes he would talk back. Maybe you talked together at once. Maybe he even talked first.

Maybe He *prayed to you* before you prayed to Him, and your prayers were really just answers to whatever it was He had said. We want God to answer our prayers so badly, but maybe He is asking the same thing of us: *Answer My prayers. Respond to a thing I have already said.*

The week before I got sick was much like the two weeks prior: full of walks and funny memes texted between friends, but all now with a new lurking stress over acquiring toilet paper. Surface-level, the kids were in good spirits. Gordon and I watched *Tiger King* with our mouths agape. Very little of it all felt *imminently* dangerous, but there was still a low hum of threat, like living inside of a movie set where you're vaguely aware you could be dragged into the dramatic action at any point without warning.

Another little habit had been added to our schedule: lighting "The Candle of Learning," which sat right in front of my day planner like a bowl of fire inside a pagan temple. The candle would be lit at about 9 a.m., a worksheet would be produced from the stack I had printed from the internet for Academic Time, and the kids would play-act being children in a pandemic who are forced to homeschool. The routine was steel, three feet deep.

On April 4, I was prepping for another audition, this time for film. I would be taping two scenes as a redneck mother with a son who is running from the law. Sally said "ain't" a lot and took the Lord's name in vain. From what I deduced from the script, there was no way she could look pretty or well-kept, and she couldn't possibly dress all that well. This would be a dreaded No-Makeup Audition.

I washed my face clean and pulled my hair back into a messy low ponytail and threw on a plaid shirt over a white wife-beater. The dark shadows that were always drawing themselves underneath my eyes made my irises a pale, icy blue. I cringed. I shrugged. And then I recorded.

Afterward, I rushed to the bathroom for my concealer and mascara, even though nobody but my family and The Eyeballs were around. I brushed out my hair and put in some earrings, edited the audition together and hit send. I was not going to be one of these pandemic moms who decayed down into visual, stinky, unkept nothingness, and I was going to get a lot more done than baking sourdough bread. I had big burly thugs guarding the perimeter of my productivity, and I paid them heftily.

A few months before Covid reached its arms around the globe, I read a book by John Mark Comer called *The Relentless Elimination of Hurry*. It had a bright orange cover that looked so very insistent sitting there on my nightstand like a glowing tangerine. I was struck, stunned by its citrus-bright wisdom, especially the part about the importance of embracing the Sabbath. Yes. Sabbath had been missing from my life, the settled trust that all the world did not depend on me and that I could take one day a week to prayerfully rest from my work and create negative space where God could get at least a foot in the door.

I began allowing myself more leniency on Sunday, cracking open a little wedge where sunlight could warm the parts of me that were frozen into poses of constant activity.

What continued to haunt me in a good but perplexing way was what John Mark Comer said about the rest of the week: it wasn't a ninety-mile-per-hour sprint. Apparently, Sabbath contained within it a "spirit of restfulness that goes with you throughout your week."[3] A spirit of restfulness following me into Monday, Tuesday and Wednesday? Well, I had found a way to embrace the Sunday Sabbath part, but it was the mid-week part I couldn't get a hold of, the habitual slowing down, the way-of-life surrender.

And now that Covid had bulldozed its way into my day planner, Sabbath seemed even farther outside my ability. Everywhere I looked, it was all Sabbath, all a swath of unstructured time that could quickly descend into chaos unless every last tick of the second hand was accounted for. We had to be vigilant in these times. We couldn't afford the luxury of being loosey-goosey, yet the need for pause was haunting. It stalked me every bit as much as the virus itself.

The Psalms of Mrs. Hoerger's class sometimes contained within them a mysterious word that has been explained to me in different ways throughout the years: *Selah*. From what I have gathered, it seems to indicate a point of surrender and reflection, or perhaps some kind of musical interlude notation, like a rest mark. *Selah* occurs seventy-four times in the Bible, mostly in the Psalms. Like the word "Hallelujah," translators have left the word much as it sounded to its original hearers — a *transliteration* instead of a *translation*— perhaps because there is no good English word that can slide in for a one-to-one exchange.

It seems plausible (to me, at least) that *Selah* could be two things at once: a musical rest notation, where the song, having reached some climactic moment, can cut to silence and leave all its power to settle on the hearts of the hearers, which naturally creates a moment of emphasis. A call to reflection. A little Sabbath in the middle of a song.

If I couldn't find a way to reconcile Sabbath living with pandemic living, perhaps I would have to create little Selahs along the way, where the cacophony of Covid life could be punctuated by micro silences, like the highway rest stops on the way to Palo Duro Canyon or the trail breaks to water The Eyeballs.

Maybe the strategy for this was prayer. If life is like a song — dramatic, flowing, jarring, beautiful, sad — then prayer can hit pause. Prayer isn't a thing that happens to you like the passive reception of melody upon eardrums. Praying is an act, a pushed button. I could Selah any time I wanted to. At least, that was my working theory.

Out came the journal with more frequency, my pen poised for focus. It was time to stop and talk. To God. Or hear Him talk to me? What could be said in the silence of Selah? And who should say it first?

Out came the Bible, Scriptures scrawled at the tops of pages with dates, His words in black ink with their unapologetic mystery and stark permanence, and then out came my words. Awkward, it was, to interact with these words, to absorb them first and then to respond with thoughts of my own.

Awkward it was.

Is.

Continues to be.

Scripture, rambling, prayer — in that order — like a little self-conscious formula.

My words were not written for communal consumption, and they were not pretty or sacred. Certainly, they were nothing Grandaddy would voice and cement into family lore. At their best, my wobbly sentences were a fierce commitment to stop, stand squarely in the present moment, and tell myself — and Him — the truth. This truth, I knew, was somewhere between my feelings and the parameters he had challenged me to set with the dang book of his, if we could just work out what those were and what they meant for me.

At their worst, my words were rote cliches, little spells I thought could be used to compel or control Him, or, even worse, mask the horror of my truly ugly thoughts. Maybe at their very best, my desperate words army-crawled up to the front line of heresy because at least one of us was being truthful.

God and me, we began to pray.

# CHAPTER 2

# LIMBO PRAYER: WHEN THE NORMAL IS NEW AND THE SAINTS ARE OLD.

And then I got sick.

It was a yellow, sunshiny Easter morning, April 12, 2020. The kids were charging through the dewy backyard to hunt down eggs. Maddie popped up with a pink one from behind the grill. Drew snatched the blue one from between a V in the tree branches—dimples, competition, counting. We wouldn't be going to church on Easter Sunday for the first time *in actual ever* due to the COVID shutdown. Gordon took a video of the kids on his iPhone. Eloise watched obsessively with her swimming, planetary eyes for an egg to roll free.

> "TAKE, LORD, AND RECEIVE ALL MY LIBERTY, MY MEMORY, MY UNDERSTANDING, AND MY ENTIRE WILL, ALL I HAVE AND CALL MY OWN. YOU HAVE GIVEN ALL TO ME. TO YOU, LORD, I RETURN IT."
>
> – IGNATIUS OF LOYOLA

For Easter lunch, I was serving up the plates — ham, scalloped potatoes, asparagus — and that's when a weakness started just above my shoulders, in my neck. As I scooped, it began to settle down, down, down, heavy over my arms and through my spine. It was gentle, gradual, and silent. I needed to sit.

I got up to take a family picture. I had ordered a ring light and tripod for my auditions and wanted to try it out. I positioned it opposite the fireplace and mantel, then rounded up the family from their various corners. Yes, we were dressing up. Yes, Eloise would be included. Everybody 'say cheese' on three.

I needed to sit down again.

A bit later someone had the idea to take a walk around the block. Soon Maddie was on roller skates and clutching my hand as we moved around Ward Parkway and its many blooming bottom blossoms and dead Bermuda grass, ambling steadily forward like a pastel micro-parade. I got home, slumped onto the couch. Then came a chill. My temperature was climbing, now 99. 3.

Later in the day, when the kitchen had been cleaned and the leftovers consumed on paper plates, I rallied for my usual solitary Sunday walk in Park Hill, the neighborhood adjacent to ours. The grand 1930s Tudor homes had shut their eyes under the eternal, continuous canopy of live oaks. I passed some friends walking their dog on the other side of the street. Waved. Began to notice the way my right arm was starting to bend at the elbow and press itself into my side as if trying to buttress my torso. I needed some propping.

*Propping?*

This was trouble.

After what felt like ten hours of walking, I fell through the back door and onto the couch.

Thud.

Me, the boulder, had rolled to a stop, and it was hard to get up much after that.

My thorn arrived on a beautiful day, on the brightest and best of holidays. I was surrounded by goodness, by gifts, by God himself, and then — I couldn't get out of bed. No one would know what to do after that for months and months and months.

When I was pregnant with Drew and in the ravages of the weeks-long morning, noon, and night sickness, my nausea miraculously lifted on Easter morning of 2007 after twenty weeks of misery. It was a blessed emancipation, a resurrection of wellness and relief, and the Easter metaphor *fit* and the narrative was *tidy*. Not this time. This time there was just a weird, incongruent dissonance, a clash of wrong chords.

Who is this shepherd who interrupts His own celebration of life to lead me into the shadow of death? And what can you really say to Him in a prayer journal?

As the weeks turned into months, these questions revealed a spikey, sad truth: I was, in fact, no saint.

Those Catholics, man.

I was not raised Catholic, and am not currently Catholic, and therefore have a vague suspicion of anybody with the word "Saint" before his or her first name. The iconography and veneration of mere mortals always seemed a little grotesque, but mostly it felt like a veiled threat. Standing before these people who spent their nights sleeping on hard cots in musty cells only to rise at midnight for prayers, who wore burlap tunics and went barefoot over stones that toughened their heels into even rougher stones, who devoted their waking hours to contemplation amidst the muddy rows of vegetables they were cultivating from indifferent soil, who turned from sex and love and family as if glancing away from their reflection in a still, clear pool — who was I compared to them? And their revelations, the appearances from Jesus himself, the healings, the stigmata — wasn't all this a little out of hand?

My childhood Evangelical environment in 1990s Texas reserved, at most, little if any space for the mystical. We even distanced ourselves from our Pentecostal brethren who were always "speaking in tongues" or being "slain in the Spirit." (Even raising your hands during a worship song could provoke slight discomfort among those around you.) These things were distractions to the main thing, which was Jesus as revealed in the Bible: central to every part of it, Old and New Testaments alike.

This meant that there was no obligation to venerate church fathers or any other ancient person. Jesus infused and informed the Psalms. Jesus reconciled the themes of Genesis. Jesus births a new people, the church, in the book of Acts, that goes on to tell other cities and countries about Jesus, so that those people, too, become part of Jesus' very body on earth. Jesus pulls all of history together like a drawstring and then cinches it at the end. Jesus is the absolute star of the show, and you might as well write Mary off as a minor character relegated to Christmastime.

And as for those grand cathedrals wrung in stained glass storied with the exploits of apostles and martyrs? Those little nooks where votives flicker over statues of Saint Whoever? Think instead: a giant, unadorned cross suspended above a concert venue.

And yet, for all its independence from organized denominational oversight, the Bible church can't help but pull from its quirkier, mystical ancestors. This is only a half-kept secret, like the family lore of eccentric great-aunts. But if a secret is unlocked, the lid often flies open like a Jack-in-the-box. It seems that in the emergencies of life, even a good Evangelical could be willing to dig around in the church attic for treasures.

The idea of having a "quiet time" is one thing. I can still see Carolyn, a teen just a few years older than me in high school, beautiful, with kind, clear eyes that made you feel like you might just be kind and beautiful, too, saying she had a "Quiet Time" every morning. A little bit of Scripture, a little bit of thinking about it, a little bit of talking to God about it. A time set aside. A ritual — if you want to risk using that bronze-green word — a ritual where suddenly joy can run all down your body, pool at your feet, and water dry ground.

Where did these prayer practices emerge? And why?

And wouldn't it make sense, in a time of suffering, to go back to those barefoot, burlap-covered people who had advanced degrees in suffering and yet had emerged glowing like pieces of the sun? Maybe we phone-addicted, comfort-reliant Christian babies need those odd, old ancestors to pick us up, hush us with soothing words we can't understand yet, and bounce us around on their hips.

And by "we," I mean "I."

So. I poked around a bit.

It turns out anyone can walk through a door that has never been locked.

After a cannonball shattered his leg in 1521, the red-headed Iñigo López de Oñaz y Loyola (who would later be known as St. Ignatius of Loyola) was bedridden for several weeks. His sister-in-law brought him religious texts to read to pass the time because there wasn't anything more entertaining in the castle, what with it being sixteenth-century Spain.

Iñigo's imagination was seized by what he read — the blues and purples of the gospel story, the rough sackcloth hanging from the bodies of saints, the fire of transfiguration. This rapture served to inform the *Spiritual Exercises* he would develop over a period of twenty-five years as the first Jesuit monk, which relies on the imagination to help rummage around your day and find God where he may be found.[4] Pain and pressure had created a watershed moment in the young Spaniard's life. It set him on a quest, and the quest became a book.

Ignatius was clear about the point of his little book: to reorder the heart's affections, which of course, implies, among other things, that the heart naturally orders its affections in the first place. We have affection for work and for our beloved children and for the sacred health of our bodies. We have the demands of our community and of our friends to care about. We have dreams and desires that dictate how we spend our time and where we spend our money. We have affections, and they line up behind each other in a particular order on a particular day because there is just no way to care about everything equally, all in the same moment.

What should top this list? According to Ignatius, God himself and, therefore, his will for my life, and, therefore, the salvation of my soul.[5] One, two, three, boom, boom, boom. Prayer, for Iñigo, then, was a path toward *priority*. Any exercise he developed was designed to put first things first and last things last and middle things middle. And if God is the First Thing, and we have agency to promote him in our hearts, there must be a few strategies for putting him there.

Over the course of decades, Iñigo crafted just such a strategy with an approach that relied heavily on imaginative prayer. If you have a strong imagination, he reasoned, you have a superpower: the power to revisit moments from your past or from the day you've just lived, the power to imagine events from Scripture as they might have happened under sun and sky, even the ability to carry on mental conversations with Jesus in the privacy of your heart. Of course, all of this requires a willingness to embrace creative courage, but the payoff is big-time: experiencing God and reality itself in deeper ways. (Admittedly, this imaginative readiness is easier for someone like me who uses my imagination in my vocation on stage.)

After all, it's easier to love God the most and put him first if you've experienced him deeply. At the end of an evening, when we've sunk into bed and are about to blur away into dreams, we can revisit our day, imagining the blues and purples of God's quiet attentiveness to us, perhaps in a moment of quiet, or in a moment of great joy. When was I closest to Him today? How did he love me well? When was I most connected to Him? What instances of warm sun and kind words flash up and seize me? When that velvet coffee hit the back of my throat this morning and exploded into joy – was that Him? *Was that You?*

*Oh my God, it was You.*

But when a bomb drops into our life, when the loving God we thought we knew seems to have betrayed us, and all our imaginative rummaging ends in futility — if we can't even find Him in the first place *and* don't know what to say to Him — all that is left is silence, and a series of events with the meaning drained out of them.

Some things in life must be practiced before everything detonates.

Maybe Iñigo realized this too before he realized anything else, his leg throbbing and swollen in its bloody dressing as he lay in his castle bed, the night refusing to break into the sun. All he knew was he needed a way to practice getting out of the dark.

What I knew, all I knew, for sure on April 12 was the strange heaviness of my white tennis shoes as I lifted my feet to walk, and how much odd effort it required to steady Maddie as she pitched back and forth on her roller skates. All I felt in that instant was her little grasping hand as she tried to stay upright and somehow keep her chicken legs from flailing in opposing directions. She was a wobbly, elegant reed.

Would we make it home?

I also knew something else: that it was time to act. To push the prayer button, whatever that might mean, even if it meant blinking like a cursor on a blank page.

Selah.

~~~

Oh Lord, where are you?

It hurts.

All my givens have been upended. The given of my health. The given of my career, of my family, of my fill-in-the-blank. And there are more givens that haven't been touched yet, and this makes me afraid. I realize all is in jeopardy, all is fair game.

You are called the Giver of all good gifts, and yet You are just so strange, a Withholder of relief. How can You be both these things at once? I thought *You* were a given.

I can't see You in the day I've just lived. I'm looking everywhere for evidence of Your presence, and all I see are white walls with the pictures removed.

Where is the God I thought I knew?

## LIMBO

Gordon was out jogging when my COVID-19 test results finally came in on April 22—ten days had passed of unrelenting fatigue, fever, and shortness of breath with no sign

> "SINCE, THEN, YOU HAVE BEEN RAISED WITH CHRIST, SET YOUR HEARTS ON THINGS ABOVE, WHERE CHRIST IS, SEATED AT THE RIGHT HAND OF GOD."
> – COLOSSIANS 3:1

of abating. These were the days when tests were not readily available at the corner drugstore, and a long list of criteria must be met to qualify, so I was well into my second week of symptoms before getting a swab. I was slumped in a chair on the back porch with big ridiculous tears coursing down my cheeks like I had just received an Ebola diagnosis.

"What's the matter?" he said.

"I DON'T HAVE COVID," I heaved between short, gasping breaths.

"Isn't that a GOOD thing?" he asked.

I wanted to punch his sweaty, stupid beard face.

The second negative COVID-19 test was not as upsetting. Odd. It came the very next day. Gordon had somehow arranged a second test AND a flu test, and the turnaround was lightning-fast. Still no COVID-19. No flu.

What now, I thought? My frustration stemmed from how much I CHERISH, no, INSIST UPON, neat, organized categories. The hyper-overachieving lady on the internet said we *had* to live by categories. Even the awful things in life can be named and put into groups, and this gives a sense of pitiful mastery.

I took a twelve-minute walk around Ward Parkway to poke yet again at the parameters of my energy. I ambled slowly, looking up into the soft green hands of newly sprouted red oak leaves. Had I told Drew and Maddie these were not just oaks, but *red* oaks? I couldn't remember. I breathed in as deeply as I could until the coughing came.

When I finally arrived home, my heart rate was up to 146, as though I had been jogging. I sank into a chair for an hour before I could get myself into the shower. Everything was slow and slowing down except for my heart, which pummeled even when I trudged down the hallway to go to the bathroom. My mind was slowing, too, like wax drying down a candle shaft.

In the afternoons, I would lie on the couch and stare at my phone, feeling all brain dexterity and cohesion of thought meld into a fuzzy smear as my temperature went up. A quiver would start between my shoulder blades and hold steady while wet cotton filled my brain. I scrolled Instagram and Facebook, watching the bright, colorful squares of posts flit up and away without comprehension, lumbering my way through each minute like a cavewoman, eyes blank, breaths shallow. This was my "turning to stone" portion of the day, and everyone in my house became familiar with it.

Eloise, The Eyeballs, propped herself on the side of the couch, begging to be brought up. I stared at her and mumbled an apology. Too tired, baby girl. She relented, allowing her front paws back down to the floor before taking a running leap, somehow managing to hoist her soft porkiness up onto the couch. Her weight on my torso mirrored the weight in my brain. I was melded into the couch as if by centrifugal force.

The early days of Drew's infancy were a blur of helpless, squawking hunger. My sole purpose was to sit in a velvety rocking chair and nurse, funneling down the milk over and over again, holding the baby and loving him desperately, but also feeling shiftless, like a mossy underground pipe. I swung between the extremes: profound joy at sustaining life and a profound sense of hollowness. At least I wasn't morning sick anymore.

I undertook to read the classics. As one does. Nothing is as far removed from diaper rash as literary grandeur, so Dante was a necessary bit of self-imposed whiplash. With Drew nursing on my right side, I propped up the *Divine Comedy* on my left arm. I bent over the ancient words determinedly, looking for a star over a troubled sea. Some have compared Dante to St. Ignatius in the way he uses the power of imagination to help readers connect with divine spiritual realities[6], and I was needing imagination and all its creative power more than ever. But all I found in Dante was more limbo.

Ignatius describes a limbo of sort himself in his *Exercises*, a natural daily waffling we do as human beings. He called the two extremes "Consolation" and "Desolation." You might call "Consolation" that feeling you get when a surge of delight rushes in at the thought of God, any *"interior joy which calls and attracts one toward heavenly things,"*[7] any feeling of increasing love, hope, or faith. Even on a laundry day or a day spent in Urgent Care can have flashes of consolation.

Desolation, on the other hand, is the opposite surge: of turmoil, agitation, *"an impulsive motion toward low and earthly things."*[8] With a little imaginative rummaging, a person could look back over a day and see his or her emotional wavelength undulating back and forth between the two extremes. You could travel back in your mind's eye and see God's presence and activity, yes, but you could also see yourself — and what things pushed you closer to God and what drew you further away. The more frequently God is the first thing in your life, the more you'll discover you were on the consolation side of that day's wavelength.

But what is the solution if life is more desolating than consoling? What if you're stuck on the wrong end of the waffle?

Iñigo, who had a military background before his religious fervor took hold, insisted on "vigorous changes," such as increased times of prayer, meditation, and rigorous self-examination.[9] Desolation didn't have to be the rule every day. A good soldier could fight for a better perspective and raise her heart above the nauseating limbo towards a steady, Fixed Star. There were steps you could take, disciplines you could commit to. Prayer. Meditation. Self-evaluation. All in an effort to focus the eyes of the heart on God.

Which, I mean. Fine. The problem becomes, even if the Fixed Star has already been established, why is the sea still so rough? Why am I plunged at the very bottom of the undulation, not even given the chance to break the surface of the waters for a gasping breath? Exercise is impossible for a suffocating person, and maybe this is why it's better to start exercising before you're thrown into the deep end.

The truth was, in April and into the summer of 2020, breathing itself required concentration. I was able to accomplish little more than taking a shower most days. My ring light was askew, abandoned in the living room. I had even stopped printing out pages for academic time and "The Candle of Learning" wasn't lit. This all seemed like a terrible waste of a woman, but the truth was I was too tired to get that worked up about it, and definitely too tired to take on any "vigorous changes" to beef up my spiritual musculature. I had no fight left in me.

Worse, nobody could tell me what, exactly, was wrong with my body, which was an emotional limbo added on top of my spiritual limbo. There are as many ways for a thorn to waste your life as there are hairs on your head, and if it's going to waste your life it should at least have the decency to come into the light and identify itself.

Oh well, whatever it was, Covid or cholera or croup, it was time to close my eyes. Again.

I knew, somewhere deep inside my brain as I languished, that there was something I was failing to see, a sharp, bright thing that was not blurry or indistinct. I couldn't make it out because I was a statue on a couch with cement for eyes that wouldn't squint into focus.

~

Oh Lord, I'm exhausted.

You invite me to look up out of my limbo and into the clarity of your face. What a dare that is.

What I also mean is, *how dare you*? You're either wildly cruel to have me here or unfathomably loving. You can't be neutral. Do I curse you or melt into you?

My thorn is bewildering, but your love, your presence, and your promises for my future are utterly shocking — if they're true. Could I really be raised with you into some new order of life above it all? What does that even mean?

Help me dwell on the puzzle and potential of grace today more than on the problem of problems. I don't understand either, but I know I don't want to be caught in between.

Are there micro-disciplines I can take today to keep my focus on You?

**DADDY**

After I received my negative COVID test results, I did what any rational human lady would do: I Googled my symptoms. They all aligned perfectly with COVID-19,

"...THE SPIRIT YOU RECEIVED BROUGHT ABOUT YOUR ADOPTION TO SONSHIP. AND BY HIM WE CRY, 'ABBA, FATHER.' THE SPIRIT HIMSELF TESTIFIES WITH OUR SPIRIT THAT WE ARE GOD'S CHILDREN."
– ROMANS 8:15-16

I knew, but these were the early days in the pandemic where test results were sacrosanct. It was difficult to hear the clashing in my brain, the almost audible head-on collision between objective data and what felt like common sense. But googling turned down the volume of this crash, and then swiftly made it clear to me that I had contracted Leukemia.

"You DON'T have Leukemia," my ER doctor neighbor Rich said later. "LOOK at you," he continued, waving his hand in front of my body. "You clearly have COVID." Ongoing fevers and malaise? Check. All kinds of respiratory and bowel issues? Plus, a host of other non-Leukemia-ish symptoms?

But maybe this was a coincidence. I needed a white blood count test to rule it out, right? I went home and Googled "white blood count test."

A few years earlier, when my dad was in his early 50s, he was suddenly diagnosed with Stage IV colon cancer. It was like falling down into a manhole in the middle of the street — daylight, sidewalks, and then swift falling, darkness. He had no family history, and his colonoscopy a few years earlier was completely clear. When Dad started looking and feeling like hollow-eyed Edward Scissorhands minus the steel fingers, his doctors ran a battery of tests for things like ulcers and viral infections. After several weeks of turning up with no answers, the doctors threw a Hail Mary and ordered another colonoscopy where, lo and behold, they found a lemon-sized tumor nestled into his gut.

Those were strange days. I knew things weren't good, but it was the one time in my life that I refused to Google anything. If I had, I would have learned Dad had only an 8% survival rate, a fact I learned only later, after he was in full remission. This was a delayed trauma, learning this fact. It sent something cold running up my spine where it implanted itself in several vertebrae.

I didn't see my dad much in the early weeks of my illness. I was quarantined away from the world at large and especially from those I loved, to keep them safe. Nobody knew how long this maybe-probably-Covid was contagious.

We zoomed with my parents and siblings once a week, and when their faces would appear in the little box, I gulped down un-cryable tears. Dad's face was so searching, so open and ready to take in the full brunt of me. Helplessly, we turned up the volume on our computers so words wouldn't be lost.

The Catholics call it the "Our Father," which I like better than "The Lord's Prayer." Yes, it was the prayer Jesus, our Lord, taught his disciples to pray, but if you take a look at the prayer itself, it's not addressed to a Lord or a king or a boss or a celebrity, but to a father. And it's not just my father, but it's addressed to *everyone's* father — he's *ours*. These two elements, the fatherness of God and the commonality we have with him and with everyone else, are the things Jesus thought we should intuit first about prayer. Guess they're important. Ignatius agreed.

In his specific Lord's Prayer exercise, little Iñigo gets detailed and a bit formulaic, which I can appreciate as an ardent list crosser-offer. First, he recommends sitting or kneeling accordingly *"as one feels better disposed or finds greater devotion,"* but he is clear that the person praying *"should keep the eyes closed or intent on one place, and not allow them to wander."*[10] With the physical posture of prayer established (seated, eyes closed), the mind can run wild and free and see all possible colors and shapes and associations that spring from the simple word that Ignatius wants us to ponder imaginatively for the next hour: "Father."

We are to "relish" the good things that come to mind with that heirloom word, and then heave all that richness onto God himself. Father God is all those things and more.

Father.

A lullaby begins, the one from prehistoric times circa 1985, sung in a gentle tenor over my head as he tucks me in:

> *Out of my window looking in the night*
> *I can see the barges' flickering light.*
> *Silently flows the river to the sea*
> *And the barges too go silently.*
> *Barges! Are there treasures in your hold?*
> *Do you fight with pirates brave and bold?*

~~~

You are the Savior, the Salvager of me. You've claimed me as your daughter. I choose to live in this reality today, even though I feel decidedly orphaned.

Ultimate death, ultimate apocalypse is not my future. The worst-case scenario has already been avoided.

You gladly respond when I say, "Daddy." Because you've given me the family name, the family spirit, I'm life-bound, peace-bound. I won't ever lose myself, my dignity, or my purpose. I say these things because they are true even if they don't feel true.

I fix my eyes on the upward spiral.

## BLAME

One of the only ways to get access to a COVID-19 test in the early days here in Fort Worth was to pinpoint when you were exposed. You could have all the classic symptoms, but if you didn't know where you might have picked it up, *sorry*.

I had a couple of theories, one of which sounded the most plausible, which I declared to my doctor with the confidence of an actor who fakes emotion for a living. My kids had been playing outside with the children of doctors on our street who had COVID, I told her. One doctor hadn't been tested. One had tested negative. But they were both fit runners who had been suddenly overtaken by pneumonia and crushing fatigue after ER shifts, and to me, the COVID theory seemed unassailable. The story had been enough to qualify me for a swab.

> "'MARTHA, MARTHA,' THE LORD ANSWERED,
> 'YOU ARE WORRIED AND UPSET ABOUT MANY THINGS,
> BUT ONLY ONE THING IS NEEDED. MARY HAS CHOSEN WHAT IS BETTER.'"
> – LUKE 10:39-42

But it ate at me. I kept revisiting my memory like a library shelf, looking for the spine of a lost book.

There was also the grocery store theory. This was before our state-mandated mask-wearing, and on a cool Friday evening I rushed over to Central Market to pick up supplies for our Dinner Club to make personal pizzas at home. Our group had stopped meeting in person and was still finding fun ways to share dinner once a month before we knew the pandemic was more than a short-term phenomenon. The store was crowded, and "social distancing" might not have been a term yet. About half the people there were wearing masks, and I was not one of them. I found dough, sauce, veggies, pepperoni, and perhaps a little touch of Sars-CoV-2.

Many people have asked where I might have picked up COVID. I see-saw between the theories, sheepishly admitting I probably wasn't as responsible as I should have been, scanning my brain yet again for memories that had perhaps been lost between the couch cushions.

Exactly how much of this thorn was my fault?


St. Ignatius was frequently given to intense bouts of guilt over the sins he had committed pre-conversion and was prone to asceticism of many kinds. One of his confessors, who I picture with eyes frozen mid-roll, apparently even demanded he stop confessing the same sins over and over again.[11] You can see him, can't you, skinny little Iñigo pacing around his cell, taken up into extremes by dark memories of hot fleshy interludes, petty unkindness and private greed, his imagination dragging him back again into the past.

Was he ever wracked by things left undone? How he imagined he *might* have behaved? Imagination is useful for prayer, and even more useful for shame-shoveling.

Back in the 1500s, people would confess their sins formally to a priest only about once per year. These were very detailed confessions, and the penitents would use books called "confessionals" that had long, detailed lists of sins from which to pick. One of Ignatius' confessions took a whole three days,[12] which indeed seems a little eye-roll worthy.

If there's one thing we Evangelicals love, it's the idea of God's unmerited favor — grace — freely given in Jesus, but those Catholics, man. I'm telling you. Pre-Martin-Luther, eternal salvation was always in the balance if you forgot a sin to confess; at least, that was my impression growing up. Sin got a bit of a demotion in 1517 (or did it?), but Iñigo hadn't yet gotten the memo.

One of his exercises was an imaginative recollection of sin you had committed. (Oh boy, oh boy.) He advises imagining yourself as a prisoner in chains or as a humiliated knight brought before the good king you had failed who had been so generous and loving. If you can't manage to stir up enough distress through your own imagination, Ignatius even instructs people to "pray for tears" and to try to tamp down any anticipatory feelings of absolution and joy, all the while trying to *foster an attitude of sorrow, suffering, and heartbreak.*[13]

Well. Could Ignatius be any more of a martyr? Perhaps he hadn't heard of self-care.

But wait, I can hear him saying, holding up one cold-chapped finger: these emotions aren't the actual point. These emotions, contrary to the contemporary opinion of most Diet Coke drinkers, are actually healthy and welcome as an *avenue*.

Ignatius, remember, was always aiming at that state of harmony we feel when we're putting God first: Consolation. Confession is not an invitation to wallow in shame, but to move through to consolation *by way of desolation*, which is sometimes the only avenue possible.

Yikes.

How contrary to the norm, which is to rush to the fountain of grace before truly feeling our thirst. And if we're talking about the new normal here, the typical response to the idea of "sin" and "guilt" is aversion: these ideas are too antiquated in a self-esteem age. We shouldn't feel shame and obsession because sin isn't a true reality. And yet, why are we so haunted by the need to justify ourselves, to live up to the standards we ourselves have set for our own behavior? Is there another word we can use in place of "sin"? Whatever we call it, whatever metaphor we use, it seems to be a real dynamic in motion, one we cannot brush off with Inigo and his penitent, chain-laden knight.

Shame and obsession, however, which are the opposite of sorrow and heartbreak, are nags. They hound me to come up to the counter and pay for the order I received, over and over again. I'm strangely eager to receive my punishment. And the funny thing about shame and obsession is, they proliferate. All of a sudden, I'm rushing around to pick up guilt like socks because then maybe I'll find a way to fold them and put them away at last. But there are too many I see and too many I'll never find and too many I'll wonder about later. At some point, you have to give up the rushing around.

Getting sick was always (maybe) my fault. It was just something to accept. If I had known there was a place in my imagination where I could sit down for a moment on the side of a canyon creek, look Jesus in the eye, and say *I'm sorry* and *I should have been more careful*, would I have done it? What would have been the look in his eyes?

45

~

Lord, today my spirit is *seated*. Mostly. Until I jump back up to find ways to justify myself.

But if you finished the work you came to do on my behalf, then I can be finished with it, too. Right?

I can punish myself or not, but the fact remains you are resting from your work. You've taken my shame, my guilt, my blame. The job is done, the glory secured, the guilt scattered to the wind.

•

Today, it is better to rest in your presence and know you better.

Still, I'm sad. Still, I only half-believe it. Still, I think I brought this on myself.

## MASTER

In the year before I got sick, 1 B.C. (Before Covid), I would run about three miles four times a week. This was not because I loved running but because I am terribly vain and wanted to remain in a certain-size jeans despite all the tortillas. St. Ignatius and I, we

"THE LORD ALMIGHTY IS WITH US;
THE GOD OF JACOB IS OUR FORTRESS.
COME AND SEE WHAT THE LORD HAS DONE,
THE DESOLATIONS HE HAS BROUGHT ON THE EARTH.
HE MAKES WARS CEASE
TO THE ENDS OF THE EARTH.
HE BREAKS THE BOW AND SHATTERS THE SPEAR;
HE BURNS THE SHIELD WITH FIRE.
HE SAYS, "BE STILL, AND KNOW THAT I AM GOD;
I WILL BE EXALTED AMONG THE NATIONS,
I WILL BE EXALTED IN THE EARTH."
– PSALM 46: 7-10

couldn't have been friends because I have never once fasted in my entire life. On the other hand, I am quite good at physical discipline, and accidentally became a pretty good runner in the end, lengthening my miles and even going up HILLS, even waving at people as I breezed past them. (How obnoxious.)

If you had told me that year that only six months later, I would struggle to walk down the hall without my heart racing into overdrive, I wouldn't have believed you. That particular symptom took a couple of weeks to present itself, but then suddenly, I couldn't wipe down a counter without feeling like I was sprinting up my ascent to Park Hill Boulevard. And the very idea of going up my stairs seemed impossible, so I didn't darken the doors of my children's bedrooms for weeks on end. The bedtime routine soon involved summoning Maddie and Drew from their rooms via the Alexa app so they could come downstairs to the couch, my eternal home, and kiss me goodnight. On special occasions, I would crawl up the stairs one at a time.

Gordon was with me the afternoon I took the fateful trip to the bathroom and doubled over in exhaustion. I couldn't catch my breath; my chest was pounding, and my whole body was revving like a car in park with the gas pedal pressed firmly to the mat. Hot tears fell freely and fully. I began to sob in the slow-motion way of someone who doesn't have the energy to sob. Gordon held me and I held on to him, willing my heart to calm back down, fighting to regain composure with the deepest breaths my lungs allowed me to take.

One morning during the second week of my illness, I tried to be helpful and change Maddie's pillowcase. It didn't take much tucking and finagling before I was gasping for breath like I had been pushing a hippo in a wheelbarrow. I doubled over and focused on drawing air in and then out. The cough was getting worse, too.

It was then I decided maybe we should purchase a pulse oximeter to make sure my blood was, in fact, oxygenated. My ER doctor neighbor Rich recommended it for all his COVID patients to guard against the silent "happy hypoxia" doctors were beginning to see — people obliviously suffocating at home and then tanking fast once they finally ended up in the hospital. I had just read about a man in my city who was exactly my age and also had a ten-year-old daughter named Madeline, who also started symptoms on Easter Sunday. He was dead by Friday.

A pulse oximeter clips onto the end of your finger and reads your pulse rate and oxygen saturation through your fingernail. I poured some ammonia onto a cotton ball and removed my eggplant-colored polish from my pointer finger so the reading would be accurate. I waited for the strident beep. My oxygen was at 97 percent. Relief! If I hit 93 percent, Rich said I should go to the ER.

The next day, I rubbed away the remaining nail polish on each one of my fingers with macabre focus. I heard they would do that in the hospital anyway, so I figured I would be a good sport and streamline a few things. I investigated my closet where my gym bag was sitting. Should we pack a go-bag like we had when I was pregnant?

"We need to decide what our protocol is for a midnight ER run," I said to Gordon.

We needed a plan. Would it be scarier for the kids to wake up in an empty house with texts on their devices from us, or would it be worse for them to wake up with my in-laws or neighbors in the house trying to downplay things while nervously checking THEIR phones?

It was all a chess game of emotion management. If this pawn moves, that queen falls. If that happens, this is how we hedge. I was in full-out trauma neutralization mode.

And I was calm like a cucumber still buried in the dirt.


In the second week of his *Spiritual Exercises*, St. Ignatius prescribes a time of reflective imagination on the idea of Jesus as King. Back in 16th-century Spain, the idea of the sovereign, monarchial rule was a comfortable idea, one involving all sorts of mortal punishments for the rebel and a whole lot of rewards for the loyalist. A king demanded something of you and you needed something from him. And perhaps Iñigo himself was particularly enthralled with the idea of crowned heads, having served as a loyal knight to a royal relative of his[14] and becoming a very skilled fencer in the process.[15] If we are so loyal to our human leaders, he reasoned, how "*much more worthy of our consideration it is to gaze upon Christ our Lord, the eternal King, and all the world assembled before him.*"[16] Prayer, then, should be used as a way to ponder this enormous gulf between King Creator and created, to realign hearts and heads with the nature of the truly gaping spiritual hierarchy.

If you were one of his hardcore students, St. Ignatius would ask you to ponder this twice a day for a week during the *Exercises*. What would spring to mind, exactly? How would this king coalesce in your imagination? A man with a white robe and a golden crown? Would there be words exchanged?

There are too many royal cliches crowding the mind these days — sapphire rings and Megan and Harry and paper Burger King crowns and playing cards and fairy tales. Is there a more helpful image for this time and this place that communicates the ultimate rule? Bringing a cliche metaphor to the mind's eye to bear during prayer can get...cheesy. Real fast. But the principle is fascinating: finding a concrete metaphor for God's ultimate rule that realigns my heart with reality. And thinking about it, seeing it, conjuring it with color and smell and association and all the power of the imagination. To dwell in metaphors is not just a writer's pastime.

Maybe my metaphor could be a spice rack. Yes, God is an Organizer of a Pantry, with every glass bottle in alphabetical order, from Cumin to Sage. Nothing out of place. Everything in perfect view for making a nourishing, deeply satisfying meal for a table of friends. All is at His fingertips, pulled out perfectly in time. I see his fingers roving over the cans and boxes of rice. His eyes flit up to where the canisters of pasta sit. He's decided to pull something off the shelf now. It must be necessary.

Well, we suburban moms with our lower-case pantries and coasters, we know something about sovereignty too, and it usually involves the fiefdom that sits around our kitchen tables. And for bodies out of control, we can find solutions.

The worst thing about being out of control, out of sovereignty, is that the flailing that follows erases any last remnants of control you might have managed to keep in the first place. Control is a commodity we only appreciate when it's under threat because we experience it as a given, a birthright, a normal state of being. We control our schedules, our diets, and our spending; if we're especially talented and maniacal, we feel in control of certain people. I love to control people's perception of my social media image, my mothering ability, and of my intelligence. Even as I type this, I'm exercising control, so you see only what I need you to see in order to get a point across. Mastery, competence, and control — these are default settings.

In the spring and summer of 2020, I was sovereign over a besieged city, and I thought my crown was straight.

Details helped. The detail of the nail polish, of the gym bag, of the persnickety penciling down of my fevers and pulse ox numbers. I took on a matter-of-fact posture. My words were curated, to the point. I had a weird cheerfulness about me, a grim contentment of having something very specific to tackle and overcome, i.e., taking in enough air, and coming up with contingency plans.

Just because I couldn't breathe very well didn't mean we all had to panic, and the not-panicking and the breathing in and out lent the days a certain simplicity that I could appreciate. Where anxiety should have reigned supreme, a calm industriousness had spread out and covered over everything like the neon green potato vines that were piling on top of themselves in my neglected flower beds. My fear didn't feel like fear. My fear felt like a flight check.

~~~

Lord, there is just so much grand language about you. You rule the nations. You bring an end to war. You shatter spears. But mine is not some ancient, epic context.

I think I am more competent at running my life than you are. There. I said it. When can I be master? I'm trying to ask reverently.

I know, intellectually, that no amount of hand wringing will change my situation. Neither will quiet diligence. According to you, I am already secure. Shielded. Safe.

I haven't emotionally practiced this truth.

## WHIPLASH

St. Ignatius died in 1556 at the age of sixty-four, after a prolonged illness involving mysterious pains in the abdomen. He was thought to have

"BUT MY EYES ARE FIXED ON YOU, O SOVEREIGN LORD; IN YOU I TAKE REFUGE — DO NOT GIVE ME OVER TO DEATH."

– PSALM 141:8

been dying six years prior in 1550[17], however, of the same malady, so he had apparently suffered for years before finally succumbing. The man knew about chronic illness in ways we, in the palliative care age, cannot fathom. His career as the great monk began and ended in a prolonged sick bed. Would this day be his last? Would he languish here through the spring or summer, or...?

Iñigo was putting the finishing touches on his *Exercises* up until the end. There he must have been lying, in a fetal position, turned to stone, perhaps with a pug nearby, breathing through the ache, with nothing but a white wall before his face. Within my own imagination I imagine his imagination, wild with color and texture, materializing golden pillars topped with fire, the halls of heaven blazing. He could see anything he wanted to see — the dusty trails leading up to Nazareth, the mossy boulders that prop up Golgotha, the sunburnt creases at the corners of Jesus' eyes. For all of his wild suggestions for imagined scenarios and creative self-evaluation, in the end, when the pain was great and the end was taunting him, could Iñigo retreat within himself to the garden he had cultivated?

The mind can be the one remaining retreat when you're trapped in a bed with no good view, even in a brain-fog haze of Covid, depression, and fever. And even when there is a window overlooking a valley, and there is the ability to run and leap and breathe deeply, the imagination is still a place to meet God and to meet yourself. It's the place to practice God's presence before, and during, and after, thorns.

I wish I had known this earlier. I wish I had been able to focus my imagination prayerfully on God. To intentionally picture him at work, say, at the beginning of things, scooping up great handfuls of dripping red clay, the raw material for a human body. To imagine the gentleness with which he ran forefingers down a lumpy ridge and up another, smoothing things out, making things functional. To see the corner of his mouth raise ever so indiscriminately – a smile? A restrained satisfaction of an artisan, maybe. The beginning of his tenderness towards me.

On May 4th, I went to my GP for a spirometry test to see if ASTHMA could explain anything. The nurse took some blood because giving blood had become a new hobby of mine and I was very good at it, having received multiple compliments on the chub of my veins. The woman in charge of this process was 36 years old and had just had her first grandbaby, which was a distracting enough concept for me to ponder while trying to avoid watching the needle and the vials.

It wasn't asthma, turned out. Or mono. Or a bacterial infection. I was given a universal virus swab, which also came back negative. There were spots in my lungs, but they were explained as evidence of a past infection.

We did discover I have a rare genetic deficiency of A1-antitrypsin, which makes it difficult for my lungs to heal after infection, but this couldn't explain the fever, fatigue, or racing heart. The whole exploratory exercise had become a mad game of pinball, where the little silver ball was me pinging from one possible theory to the next, snapping in one direction and then another in search of answers, but mostly in search of relief. One doctor would pose a theory that pinged me into a state of relentless Google research. Another would pooh-pooh the idea and send me rolling down and away. My mind was "blown and tossed by the wind," as the old apostle says.

And I just wasn't getting better. I was relentlessly sick, and it was becoming clear I was going to have to cobble together my own motley team of specialists, but I wasn't sure where to begin and I certainly had no experience being the CEO of my own health. In the months that followed the onset of my illness, a few Long-Covid Care Centers would begin popping up in various cities around the country, but not soon enough for me.

It was a strange zip code. My life had never required this kind of oversight. The truth is, I wasn't even really sure how health insurance worked or who decides which doctor's advice trumps another's. The whole experience turned me infantile, into a little girl who doesn't know the meanings of words or the logical next steps. The whole thing was also violent and absolutely compulsory, like being signed up by someone else to fight in a war I didn't believe in.

Little girls shouldn't have to fight in war. Maybe I'd become a Warrior Woman soon if a miracle happened.

After several tests came back negative or inconclusive with my general practitioner, I signed up for a new COVID antibody test that was available at one of the local Urgent Care places. A large, bearded nurse in a hazmat suit escorted me from the car to the exam room where he took my vital signs, which set off a chain-reaction.

Suddenly, the doctor was in the room looking me over, saying things about heart rate and blood pressure and how he needed to take more blood and do a CT scan. I began to understand, though I could not see his masked mouth or goggled-and-shielded eyes, that he was worried I was about to have a stroke. My big male nurse friend was suddenly sticking EKG stickers all over my abdomen and starting an IV, just in case I had to be rushed in for emergency surgery.

My shortness of breath had now added another playmate to the sandbox — what would become a long struggle with a racing heart (tachycardia) — but for all the doctors knew, I had a blood clot and was excavating my plot at Greenwood Cemetery. Not thirty minutes before this, I was sitting in my kitchen eating leftover pizza from our local favorite place, I'Fratelli's. I had gone from eating lunch to being about to die within the hour.

The lady who conducted my CT scan was swathed in what looked like a yellow trash bag. She wore a car windshield on her face. With efficient movements of hands and feet, she helped me onto the machine as I struggled to breathe and told me I had to hold my breath for five seconds at a time, which proved almost impossible.

I collapsed back onto the raised bed in my triage room, where *Star Trek* was droning on the TV in the upper left-hand corner of the room. The trash bag lady brought me a warm blanket while we waited for the results. I was so tired, languid, ready for sleep, but also alert like a reptile.

Results would have been lovely.

What I soon learned was that the antibody test was negative. As was the "universal viral swab." Once again, no mono. No flu. My CT revealed I did not have a blood clot after all.

The ER doctor told me, in summary, "You need to see a cardiologist. Something is going on." And so, feverish, exhausted, short of breath and with a doggedly racing heart and "something going on," I went home and ate dinner at the same table where I had eaten I'Fratelli's four hours earlier.

Gordon, equally traumatized and dazed, sat across from me with his tired beard face. He had sat in the parking lot for over four hours alone. Covid protocols had banned visitors and with no bathroom available to him, he had been forced to pee in an empty water bottle that had been rolling around the floorboards of our SUV.

Such extremes in a day. A quiet meal, a turbulent flurry of tests, a fitful waiting, a frantic lead-up to...nothing. All was shrouded in darkness; all was covered over with ambiguity. I was left with a profound distrust of the soft, quiet moments because they seemed to exist only as a prelude to disastrous extremes. It was like lying in a dead-quiet room with a snake hiding somewhere nearby, biding his time.

Imagination, used for ill, runs bloody tracks over your back. It can be used for better things.

～

Lord, how do I operate in this new category of *normal*? What a terrible, terrible word. This is how things are now.

I'm absolutely chafing in the seat of this roller-coaster. Give me bad news any day (within reason), but uncertainty? The relentless up and down, backward and forwards? It's all so very power-sucking.

I look to you for stability.

I see you standing there. I force the image to materialize into sharper angles: You are still. You're sitting now, on a rock, maybe, jaw relaxed, breathing steady. You're holding something delicate in your hands, something like a dandelion pouf, and it does not collapse into a million airborne particles. It stays intact, exquisite.

I breathe. I watch it in your hands.

# CHAPTER 3

# KICKING, SCREAMING, READING: A TIRED REBEL PRAYS A BOOK.

My good friend Schuyler texted me one day, asking if she could come baptize me in her many essential oils and homeopathic remedies. She didn't use the word "baptize," but I think it's what we both were hoping for — a rebirth into health via blessed liquids. The day was hot. We both wore masks on my back porch, and her short hair was under a red baseball cap. She was one of the first friends brave enough to sit in my presence, and I sort of hated myself for loving it because of the risk she was taking.

> "MANY AND GREAT ARE MY WEAKNESSES AND ILLS, MANY AND GREAT,
> BUT YOUR MEDICINE IS MIGHTIER."
> – AUGUSTINE OF HIPPO

What if I gave COVID to her? The doctors *had* said that if COVID was to blame for my symptoms, I hadn't been contagious for a while, yet it's a hard thing to believe when you're actively running a fever. So, we sat on the porch, masks obscuring every expression.

One by one, Schuyler pulled short brown vials out of her brown paper sack and gingerly placed them on the table between us, like jewels. She showed me which essential oils to mix with which: where to apply them, when to apply them, how to diffuse them into the air, and how to ingest them via capsules. She gave me a mason jar of her homemade elderberry syrup and told me how to take it, even how to garnish ice cream with it. She showed me how to fill a diffuser with water and told me how many drops of oils to add before pushing the little button to make it work.

There were oils that could be rubbed on the soles of my feet, oils that could be rubbed on my temples, oils that could be added to a spray bottle filled with water and sprayed across countertops, and oils that, when combined, enhanced the effects of the individual oils themselves. I had instructions for oregano, frankincense, eucalyptus, clove, lemon, lavender, melaleuca, and peppermint. She typed up all her instructions and handed me the sheet so I wouldn't forget anything and told me to text her with questions. I reviewed everything grimly. I was determined to follow my marching orders with the devotion of, well, a monk.

My friends were all completely out of sorts about my whole situation. They simply did not understand why doctors couldn't seem to get a handle on things and they refused to abide it. I think if there was a magic pill somewhere remote, like in Bolivia, they would have put me on the first plane out and they would have come, too, with snacks in purses.

Dear ones like this affirm a very deep-seated emotion of mine that is quite common among genteel southern women, and especially of the Christian ilk: utter rebellion. We refuse to be defined by our problems. We kick our little pedicured feet against the door and shall not accept defeat. We get up in the mornings and make our beds, quietly propelled by a thousand micro-explosions of insurrection.

*Why do you hide yourself in times of trouble, God?* We cry this out with the Psalmist, that faceless friend of ours who can say such things aloud.

I myself am restless, and I want God to be restless on my behalf.

Like me, like my friends, like Mrs. Hoerger, my 9th grade English teacher, a man named Augustine also loved the Psalms for doing his dirty work.

Saint Augustine (yes, let's call him Saint right off the bat, for kicks) was born in 354 A.D. in North Africa, which seems impossibly long ago and far away, yet he continues to influence all of Western Philosophy and Other Capitalized Things. Even though he wasn't a pope, I picture him wearing a miter on his head, (one of those very tall hats, the white ones with the gold embellishing it up to a tippy-top point, like he is wearing a steeple). He was probably of Berber descent, so his skin was olive, his beard dark, eyes black. He had the Jesus look going.

Augustine's most famous work is probably the *Confessions*, but he wrote an even longer book of commentary on the Psalms, a book so big it could prop open the sandy door of the Great Pyramid. I've heard the Psalms referred to as "the Bible's Prayer Book" in various times or places, so if anyone is interested in learning how to pray, the Psalms would be a great place to start. Augustine chiefly saw the Psalms as a way to understand the unity between Jesus and his people, and therefore the Psalms were also a way for his people to connect more closely with him.[18] (Ironically, he, too, sees Jesus as the star of the whole Bible, much as an Evangelical Texan.)

The Psalms are so raw, so emotional, and the fact of their existence shows God knows and affirms our real human emotions, that he wasn't too squeamish to include them in his official book even though sometimes they could sound a little bit on the disrespectful side. Then God went a step further to become a human himself and yell out the Psalms with his very own middle-Eastern-man lips, cracked and bloody as they were, and with a weak and ragged voice, "My God, My God, why have you forsaken me?" (Psalm 22).

But before Augustine found the Psalms or the God who was behind, before and within them, he, too, was a rebel — minus the pedicured feet. Augustine's mother, Monica, prayed for him constantly and tearfully to forsake his lustful, devil-may-care life and become a Christian. One can picture her in a shaft of light, knees on hard stone, tears about to spill over and out, begging the unseen person just beyond that shaft of light for help, as countless mothers have done for countless sons for countless ages. I like to imagine she picked up a Psalm or two herself and threw them back up into the sky. *How long, Oh Lord? Why do you stand far off?*

There's a difference between being honest with God and rebelling against him, but it can sometimes be hard to see this difference. Maybe you're a person who can do a little of both at the same time. Maybe you've discovered, like me, that you consider yourself a darling rebel, righteously rebelling against *bad* things, things that *need* rebelling.

Because if you accept your thorn, you've actually decided to become a martyr, to give up and float down current with the dead minnows and sludge, with all the sad and useless debris. Worse, this means you've lost faith in God's ability to correct the situation, and this kind of unbelief is clearly off-limits. So, we must *rebel against our inner rebellion* against God, even if our stiff upper lips make it impossible for us to be honest with him. At any given point, we could be rebelling against rebellion, rebelling against our thorn, straight-up rebelling against God, or doing some combination of all three at once. In any case, we're fighting, and what's so wrong with doing everything possible to survive?

I had decided: nothing was wrong with it.

I would fight. I would scream. I would kick and I would punch and I would *try*.

~

Lord, don't stand off to the side! Stop hiding! Come out into the open and own what you're allowing to happen to me.

It's not lost on me: a thorn is small and tactile, like a splinter off a cross. My instinct is to rebel against crosses, not to ask them questions and certainly never to embrace them.

But then comes reality. Tired and unsuccessful, I finally must welcome reality as it is because you come with reality, not with illusion.

My thorn is real, too. I hold it in my hands and look into your eyes.

## DENIAL

Sometimes what you need is a makeover.

The last show I did before Covid shut the theater industry down was *Beauty and The Beast*. I got paid to dance around as a plate for six weeks and I loved every

"AS A FATHER SHOWS COMPASSION TO HIS CHILDREN, SO THE LORD SHOWS COMPASSION TO THOSE WHO FEAR HIM. FOR HE KNOWS OUR FRAME; HE REMEMBERS THAT WE ARE DUST."
– PSALM 103:13-14

single minute of it, even though I had to drive forty minutes into Dallas at the crack of dawn every day. I also got to play the Enchantress at the top of the show who is disguised as an old hag and curses the prince for his cruelty, then reveals herself to be a blonde in a great dress. Schools poured pitchers of children into the rows morning after morning, the auditorium growing louder and buzzier with a wonky electronic pulse that carbonated my blood. I'd wait in the wings and shift my weight. When the iconic opening stanzas of the show boomed into the darkness, little shrieks rose up from the crowd. I calmly took my place center stage to confront the prince, levitate the prop rose, and transform into something beautiful and threatening. Then I'd dance around as a plate in Act II. It was magic.

The double bonus was that even if I yelled at my own children that afternoon or ignored them that night, I didn't have to be that Julie in the morning. When the alarm went off, I had another Julie I could call upon, which was Entertainer and Delighter of the Children of Dallas. It's nice to have the option to shift around to whichever identity feels most doable on a given day. I look inward and ask, "What resources seem available?" And then go with the version of myself that meets the least resistance and matches whatever strength I've determined I have.

By the time May of 2020 rolled around, my son Drew was tired of my being sick — well, *looking* sick – so he bought me a palette of Maybelline eyeshadow with his own hard-earned money from washing dishes and taking out the trash. The palette was auspiciously named, "The Blushed Nudes." He wanted me to be pretty again. My cheeks were hollow, my face was dry like onion skin, and my under eyes were deep and mushroomy, almost bruised.

Drew asked Gordon to take him to Walgreens so he could make the selection himself, then he wrapped the palette up in a gift bag and gave it to me as a Mother's Day present. He sat on my bed, holding out the gift bag. I felt his weight on the mattress next to me, this boy becoming a man faster and faster like a rock gathering steam down a hill. His dimples were relentless.

After that, I put on *The Blushed Nudes* almost every day. I also started dressing in normal clothes, complete with earrings and perfume. It felt weird to lie around on a couch wearing bracelets, but that's what I did, and I'm not going to tell you I didn't enjoy the tragic Scarlett O-Hara aura it bestowed upon me.

One day we took the kids on a picnic at the beautiful green lawn of the Kimball, our city's fancy world-class art museum. It took me ten minutes to walk ever so slowly from the car, up a short series of limestone steps, and across a walkway to the lawn. I couldn't catch my breath, my heart was racing, and I was feverish — my sad, new normalcy— but I hadn't attempted an outing like this since getting sick. It was a maiden voyage into realms beyond my house.

For such an occasion, I wore a teal fluttery top, cute white cutoff jean shorts, and a delicate gold star necklace, and my hair was up in a thoughtfully executed — not haphazard — ponytail. Schuyler's essential oils were alive and flowering, smelling me up like a Wise Man. We spread the blanket out on the grass, ate our sandwiches, and the kids ran in zig-zags through the perfectly aligned oak trees that cut a straight aisle through the grass. I lay down on the blanket and tried to read my book.

From a distance, we looked like a regular family trying to break up the quarantine monotony. Getting up and hobbling back to the car was another ordeal, but I made it, and the whole field trip felt like a shaky success. It was almost *basically ordinary*.

I'd like to say I did all of this for my children, so they felt safe and secure in the knowledge that mom is fine, she's going to be Ok, she's essentially normal. It would be easy to say I did this for my husband, so he would remember I'm still a woman who remained a bit of the girl he married. Those are partial truths.

KICKING, SCREAMING, READING: A TIRED REBEL PRAYS A BOOK.

But when I looked in the mirror and saw beauty instead of illness, I felt the same rush I experience when I'm in costume, ready to go onstage as a completely different person in a show. It's like a performance about to happen, and I'm enchanted by the Enchantress herself, of being someone new in front of strangers who don't know or care about the actor beneath the character. It felt like a brush with freedom. It felt like the denial I deserved.

When he was eighteen years old and studying rhetoric in school, Augustine (minus the "Saint" — he was no saint then), came across a book that set his heart on fire. It wasn't the Bible. It was a lost work by Cicero called *Hortensius*, and suddenly, by reading it, "*every vain hope became empty*" to him, and he "*longed for the immortality of wisdom*."[19] Augustine credits God for this wake-up call, for using Cicero to woo his heart away from the charms and numbing agents of his life. Maybe God could be found, after all, and maybe he wasn't so bad, and if God was able to talk to him through Cicero, maybe Augustine should just go ahead and read the book God himself had written.

And then a species of denial set in, one that would delay Augustine's conversion for another nine years. What happened, exactly, when he cracked that Bible open? I'm not sure, but for someone so eager for wisdom, it was ironic that the simplicity of the text (compared to Cicero) turned him away.

Wisdom couldn't be so pedestrian. God couldn't be so accessible. Augustine found himself unable to "*bow my head to climb its steps*."[20] What kind of self-concept did Augustine have that made it so hard to learn? What magic mirror couldn't he set aside in order to look at his true reflection on those pages?

Unlike Augustine, I had no other available selves ready to carry me forward. My mirrors had been shattered and I stood before the shards. All I had were cosmetics, well-made beds and bracelet stacks, layers on layers upon layers. They helped, for a while.

~

Help, again. Still needing help this morning, too.

It's easiest in the mornings to feel You comfort me. But when my thorn starts to call attention to itself, when I'm too focused on my failing abilities and faltering roles, the switch flips hard, and I am once again living for old self-conceptions.

Low-grade anxiety and irritability come with the costumes.

Instead of leaning harder into ultimate reality, which is living, breathing You, I pull back inside. Instead of looking for You outside of me, in creation, in others, in your book, I fold back into myself and then cover myself with pretty, superficial, or distracting embellishments.

You know who I am. You know I'm dust.

Help me to know it, too, but in a way that's not too sad.

## ANXIETY

It turned out that Augustine's pride was no match for his first-ever Quiet Time.

A friend had been telling him about a monk named Anthony.

"HUMBLE YOURSELVES, THEREFORE, UNDER GOD'S MIGHTY HAND, THAT HE MAY LIFT YOU UP IN DUE TIME. CAST ALL YOUR ANXIETY ON HIM BECAUSE HE CARES FOR YOU."
– 1 PETER 5:6-7

One day, Anthony's spirit had been cleaved in half when he heard something God had said in his book, something about selling all he had and giving it to the poor and following Jesus. The words had shot down through Anthony's heart and bowels and skin and bone so thoroughly; he had sold his house, given away all his money, kissed his one and only family member, a sister, goodbye forever, and become a hermit in the Egyptian desert where he fought demons and studied more of the book — this same book Augustine had been avoiding and scorning for the past decade. Here was a fellow African, a fellow member of normal, educated society, felled by mere pages and words.

Augustine began pacing around his courtyard, sweating through his toga or his loin cloth or whatever, the biceps of his soul trembling against the pressure of an unseen, muscle-bound man who seemed bent on breaking him. Was this the same entity that had so thoroughly obliterated Anthony's paradigms? And then, in a moment of weird incongruence, Augustine heard a child singing. It was a real embodied child in a room just within earshot, who was perhaps playing a game or singing whatever fourth-century nursery rhyme was popular at the time: "*Pick up and read, pick up and read.*"[21]

Taking it as a command, Augustine ran for God's book himself, flipped it open haphazardly, and immediately Romans 13 was before him. He picked it up. He read.

If you're a theater actor, your life is spent searching out auditions, prepping for auditions, auditioning, and then wringing your hands waiting to hear if your audition has gotten you the role. Every now and then, a couple times a year if you're lucky, these auditions give birth to real, live opportunities to perform in front of actual people and get paid for doing it. And when they close, memorabilia of each show is collected like precious family heirlooms. You hang their souvenirs on your walls, you keep the playbills in letter boxes from The Container Store, you stash your script on the shelf with the others like it's a Gutenberg Bible.

The pandemic shut down all these processes. There were no auditions to search out; there were no shows to perform and document; there were no new friends to be made. Not only was my body in full shut-down mode, but so was my industry.

If I'm honest, this parallel track comforted me in a dark, miserly way: at least I wasn't missing out. But then I got a call from the producer at one of my favorite theaters asking me to audition for a role in an audio play they were preparing to attempt. Suddenly, theaters had gotten creative. They would now be trying radio shows and Zoom plays.

I was blinded by a shaft of light. Here it was, an abrupt opportunity to reclaim at least part of myself that had been cut off. But how sick was too sick?

The role would require a German accent and classical singing. Lying on the sunroom couch, bolstered by the pug, I started watching YouTube videos of German people talking about the weather, noting all their "Ws" sounded like "Vs". I practiced on Drew and Maddie and Gordon whenever they'd wander into the room just minding their own business.

"Vee need to velcome zee vonderful Vitches and Vizards!" I'd wheeze (veez).

The day I taped my audition, I was running a fever. Naturally. I couldn't quite catch my breath. Predictably. I sat on a chair, pushed RECORD on my phone's camera, and sang *Summertime* from *Porgy and Bess*, which is hard enough for a healthy me. I knew it wasn't what it would have been the year before. It was effortful, laborious. I knew I probably looked so very tired singing it, even though I was wearing a vibrant emerald-green jumpsuit.

I emailed the producer the link to my audition with a full disclosure, "I've been battling COVID symptoms for several months now, but I'm assured by my doctors that I am not contagious anymore. And I'm doing MUCH better than I was!" Which was true, technically, but also not true enough for that exclamation-point.

I didn't get the role. The show would later be hailed by *The New York Times* as a pioneer in creative regional theater-making in the midst of crisis, and, naturally, I couldn't bring myself to download and listen to it. I had *tried*, after all, so let us leave it at that.

I had tried to push through, tried to reach up and out of my broken body, tried to grab the life preserver bobbing on the water's surface. I had made a valiant effort, and now we would seal the door closed and pretend it never happened. It was easier to blame my body than my talent or lack thereof, in the end, but what if both talent and body were permanently diminished?

Oh my God.

What if, what if, what if.

Augustine, with his scroll blazing open, received the words of God's book into his chest like buckshot: "*Not in riots and drunken parties, not in eroticism and indecencies, not in strife and rivalry, but put on the Lord Jesus Christ and make no provision for the flesh in its lusts*" (Romans 13:13-14). Ever enslaved by sexual urges, the rebel Augustine heard the words as if spoken for the very first time. They were to him and for him, a voice almost spoken aloud.

And then, a weird release. *"I neither wished nor needed to read further,"* he would write later. *"At once, with the last words of this sentence, it was as if a light of relief from all anxiety flooded into my heart."*[22]

How strange. The opposite of anxiety is not peace. Not at first. The opposite of anxiety is humility. By some supernatural act of surrender, Augustine had finally stopped stiff-arming the person behind the words, the person who was speaking the words to him in real-time, through a text, and he stumbled upon a total, blessed rest. He had *picked up and read*, and that humble act alone was enough. Whatever else he did in his life after that, Augustine did it differently, and all his writings afterward spill out Scripture like buckets sloshing.

What alchemy enabled such a submission and such a relief from mere words in a book? What mighty, gentle Author?

⁓

Oh, Lord, you are strong enough to take this thorn away. You could do it instantly. You could allow all my plans and hopes to come to fruition totally unencumbered. But you're not right now, and I'm offended.

But who am I? Who am I to say that my life is wrongly ordained, that you are making mistakes right and left?

Your book says you love me. I duck down underneath that truth.

Who am I to cup things inside little palms?

## WORD

Nothing will make you feel quite as mortal as visiting your local cardiologist. There's a royal aura, a supremacy. This person holds the keys to the center of yourself, to that pulsing reminder that you are alive. Even a neurosurgeon, whose organ of specialty *controls*

"IN THE BEGINNING WAS THE WORD, AND THE WORD WAS WITH GOD, AND THE WORD WAS GOD. HE WAS WITH GOD IN THE BEGINNING. THROUGH HIM ALL THINGS WERE MADE, AND WITHOUT HIM NOTHING WAS MADE THAT HAS BEEN MADE."
– JOHN 1:1-3

the heart, doesn't seem as important. We don't feel our brains transmitting life throughout our bodies every second of every day, but our heartbeat reminds us that when its rhythm stops someday, we must also leave right along with it.

I was daunted by the walk from the parking lot into the medical building, but I made it with slow, deliberate steps even as my heart accelerated. I was wearing a navy linen sundress and hoop earrings, which was the dressiest I had been since getting sick, except for maybe the Kimball picnic with the ponytail. To look at me, I was a normal suburban mom who was just oddly taking her time.

Dr. T put the stethoscope up to my chest, then moved it around to my back. "Listen to it go in there!" he said, as though my heart was The Eyeballs sprinting to her dinner bowl. He took an EKG, then sent me down the hall to a dark room for an echocardiogram with a young man whom I would learn had just become a father. I lay on my side facing him, hospital gown open to the front, as he discreetly moved the sonogram wand down my bare sternum and under my breasts, taking pictures and measurements.

I am not that good at many things in life, but making small talk during awkward medical procedures happens to be one of my specialties. How bizarre that my heart was just an everyday, measurable muscle that a total stranger could assess while chatting about new babies! And yet there was a sort of priestly energy about him as he reached in with his computer to solemnly make contact with my ticking-like-a-time-bomb Mission Control.

After this, in another room, a different guy stuck about twenty electrodes onto my chest, abdomen, and back, which were attached via long cables to a little black box that could be worn like a not-so-cute crossbody purse. For the next twenty-four hours, I was to wear it and record any noticeable symptoms at the specific times they struck so Dr. T could match up my live experience with actual data. I was obsessed with this task. I put myself in situations that might make my heart race just to prove it tended to behave badly — specifically folding Gordon's undershirts, which for me was like running full-tilt uphill. My resting heart rate was now in the 90s, so that was helpful to confirm as well.

I received a call a few days later from Dr. T. When I saw his number on my phone, a thrill of fire shot through my throat. I was about to be given a master key—a clue, at least.

Thankfully, he said, no myocarditis was present per the echocardiogram, but the Holter monitor had shown tachycardia and some arrhythmia. Yes, yes, I thought. This is good; this is validating, this makes sense, and this is leading to the ah-ha moment.

"This is inflammation, probably due to a virus," he said, and then he fell silent, as though this was totally new information to be absorbed — as if I hadn't already been aware of this way back in the parking lot in my blue linen dress.

So much for illumination and revelation. Just when a little crack of light was visible in a dark doorway, the whole thing slammed shut. Even the High Priest of Doctors, who operates in the inner sanctum, could not provide a new oracle.

Back in the second century, before Augustine or Ignatius had begun writing about God, an Egyptian named Origen came up with a new concept: *thea anagnosis*, a Greek phrase meaning "divine reading." Origen was born just 150 years after Christ had walked the same dusty Roman roads, so his relationship to that chronology is parallel to ours with, say, the Civil War. We feel a certain proximity to that history. There are still streets named after people from that history.

Yet even so swiftly after Christ's physical presence was gone from view, people in those first few centuries afterward were beginning to use God's book as a way to reconnect with him again, to search the Scriptures for a personal message from him.[23] Not just general truths about God, but personal truths, things that were specific to them, given for that particular day or situation.

Later on, in the 6th century, after the Desert Fathers and Mothers like Augustine's hermit-muse Anthony had integrated *thea anagnosis* into their daily rhythms, an Italian named Benedict would formalize it for all of the monastic movement moving forward — calling it, in Latin, *lectio divina*. The intent was less to understand a concept of the words of the Bible (although correct interpretation according to context was important) but to have a real encounter with The Word himself.[24] It's a strange concept, this idea that reading something written in a past time could somehow connect you, in real-time, to the person who originally wrote it.

It would be like, suddenly, while reading a letter from my now-deceased grandmother penned twenty years ago, I hear her speaking to me again, speaking the words afresh as if they had never been spoken before, and the words are especially prescient to my frame of mind that day, the "thing I needed to hear." Maybe she isn't actually ... dead, after all?

No wonder this discovery was such a watershed. This was specificity, and we human beings can't get enough of specificity. If you're writing me a letter, I want it to come to my specific address. The letter must use the specific language we use because we are friends, all the little jokes and pet names. You must address me by my specific name and sign off using yours.

Specificity means we are known to one another, and specificity also means I exist apart from you, which is essential for intimacy. This mystical communion between two specific people was now somehow possible between a person and God, as Augustine had discovered that fateful day, sweating through his toga.

But I look for specificity elsewhere too. In fact, I look for specificity first in about five other people before I will approach God himself. I want a specific doctor to pinpoint a specificity in my disease that can be tackled with specific medicine, a specific physical therapy routine, and all within a specific timeframe. I am face-to-face with these people, with these doctors and nurses, and they're embodied and real as far as we can tell, and we are conversing in real time, not separated by a high stack of centuries, and yet our encounters yield *no good particulars.*

When there is no true Word, we are formless and void.

~

Oh Lord, I'm putting my faith in all the wrong things. I keep hanging my hat on people, on answers, on fixes. I can't even rely on my own personal ability or potential or character or wisdom or power.

My body is weak.
My heart is tired.
My mind is fuzzy.
My perception is flawed.
My intentions are often selfish.
My love is limited.
My perspective is narrow.

Make something of me today. Talk to me. Tell me a joke — anything to let me know I'm real, that we're friends, and that You are enough.

**FORGIVE**

Back in the summer of 2020, when COVID was starting to gain traction in the U.S., but we hadn't had the awful fall and winter surges that would suddenly mean everyone knew someone who had been sick or had died, a group of people started to

"PUT ON THEN, AS GOD'S CHOSEN ONES, HOLY AND BELOVED, COMPASSIONATE HEARTS, KINDNESS, HUMILITY, MEEKNESS, AND PATIENCE, BEARING WITH ONE ANOTHER AND, IF ONE HAS A COMPLAINT AGAINST ANOTHER, FORGIVING EACH OTHER; AS THE LORD HAS FORGIVEN YOU, SO YOU ALSO MUST FORGIVE."
– COLOSSIANS 3:12-13

collect themselves online. They called themselves the COVID-19 Long Haulers. They were people who had gotten sick with COVID-19 and just hadn't recovered yet, some of them already five months into their thorns.

The symptoms ranged wildly in severity and in variety, but there were broad, common themes: fatigue, heart/breathing issues, fevers, brain fog, joint issues, and rashes. I joined a group called *Long Haul COVID Fighters* and *Survivor Corps*, both on Facebook, and instantly found what I had been looking for over so many long weeks: validation.

Even more distressing than the ways their bodies were constantly failing, the group found gaslighting from doctors to be the worst of all. These were the days before there was much-documented research confirming the existence of Long Covid. The basic understanding was that if you caught COVID-19, you either recovered in two weeks or you died. Any patient who presented in a fashion outside of these parameters was just being dramatic.

I had friends whose doctors stopped returning their phone calls. Anxiety meds were prescribed for "psychosomatic" symptoms. People were sent home from ERs with little instruction or sympathy.

And there were a good many of us with all the same Long-Haul symptoms that had never tested positive for COVID or its antibodies in the first place. We now know that the testing can miss infection if you're out of a certain window of time and that many COVID-sick people did not make enough antibodies to register, especially on the early tests that were not as sensitive. But back then, we were constantly faced with scrutiny, always on the receiving end of the raised eyebrow.

Thankfully, my doctor acknowledged my symptoms enough to write me referrals to specialists. Although she never returned the email in which I outlined the problems with testing and sent links for articles supporting the high likelihood of me having COVID-19, at least she didn't fire me as a patient. At least I hadn't been driven to call suicide hotlines like several of my Long-Haul Facebook friends had.

Saying "at least" is the basic grammar of self-preservation.

I've heard doubt and suspicion is also a common experience for many people with autoimmune problems or chronic fatigue, where sneaky disease evades testing and symptoms don't flare at just the right time to get a diagnosis. With quiet professionalism, doctors gently ask if the patient "has been depressed lately." Not that there's anything wrong with trying to address mental health, but so often, a certain *tone* runs underneath the question like a sewer leak, implying the symptoms *themselves* are really just in your head. Or worse, that you somehow prefer to be sick and maybe even see it as a legitimate way to craft an identity in the world.

If our thorns are public, they automatically make us into Ambassadors of Goodwill to the outsiders, to the Muggles, to the great masses of people who just do not understand or worse, who *think* they do.

I, for one, didn't ask to be this sort of diplomat.

Well into his career as a bishop, Augustine wrote a letter. It was to a very wealthy and socially prominent Roman woman named Anicia Faltonia Proba, who had asked him for instructions about prayer. How should she pray? What should she pray for?

For all his writings and sermons, Augustine hadn't talked much about prayer[25]. He was always talking about things God had said in his book and less about the words we might say in response. So it's no surprise that Augustine would pick the prayer Jesus prayed in the Bible off the shelf, dust it off, and hold it to the light for Anicia to observe it by way of instruction.

*"For whatever other words we may say…if we pray rightly, and as becomes our wants, we say nothing but what is already contained in the Lord>s Prayer."*[26]

Now there's a claim: good prayer is always some iteration of the Lord's Prayer. Ignatius would later raise a toast to this idea.

There were things shimmering off the sides of this Prayer if you turned it this way and that way to let the sun hit it. Implications. Possibilities. The prayer had a broad enough framework that could allow you to make God's words your own, letting the seed of them go down and sprout up something new from the rich soil of your circumstances.

You could take the truth of Scripture and pray them back, like a tennis volley, except with a unique spin of your own. The words of Jesus' Official Prayer should not be confused with magic words to use as shorthand for a core of truth that could take on self-serving interests, but they could provide a way into a more personal experience of prayer.

Very unfortunately, "Forgive us our debts as we forgive our debtors" is part of this prayer every bit as much as the comforting warmth of "Our Father" is part of it. Augustine clarified that for Anicia, while praying along the grooves of forgiveness, *"we remind ourselves both what we should ask, and what we should do in order that we may be worthy to receive what we ask."*[27]

Praying for mercy? Include a prayer for being merciful. Praying for absolution? Include a commitment to absolve others — even the gas lighters, the white coats, the well-meaning hurters.

And this is the problem when we let God's book draw a circle around our prayers. We bump up against the edges of our own tight and wounded hearts – our own scars, jaded bias, and the love we're holding hostage. Humility before a book has its costs.

~~~

Oh Lord, the prayer, your prayer, in your book, says to forgive. It also says I'm forgiven. Let the first flow from the second.

Give me extra armfuls of mercy for those who are not on the inside of my thorn today. Let me look at them with your eyes and hold my heart open. Let me see that they are also misunderstood, that they also carry quiet burdens. To quote Frederick Buechner, forgive me "Every face [I] cannot look upon with joy."

## HUNGRY

*"Pray for a happy life,"* wrote Augustine in the same letter to Anicia. This prayer was apparently not in conflict with the Lord's Prayer at all, and this is a concept I can get behind. A happy life — isn't this basically the gist of our natural, Tuesday afternoon-slump prayers, the ones we pray when we are not even praying when we are talking out loud half to ourselves?

> "GIVE US THIS DAY OUR DAILY BREAD."
> – MATTHEW 6:11

Why does life have to be so hard? Why can't happiness be normative? Let your kingdom come, let your will be done, and let me be happy on earth as I'll be in heaven.

My Infectious Disease doctor, Dr. H, kept his cell phone in the shirt pocket of his blue scrubs. Periodically, during our appointment, the phone would alert him of a call or a text via the sudden growl of a motorcycle engine, the worst possible ringtone. He seemed to be very popular as he scooted around the exam room floor on a rolling office chair, receiving one explosive text after another.

I had a little post-it note with a laundry list of possible diseases to ask him about because I am helpful in that way, and had become an internet doctor by that point in my research. Lupus? Fibromyalgia? A rare fungal infection? He agreed to run all the pertinent tests and threw in about twenty-five of his own, including one for HIV.

When I returned to his office for the follow-up, I had just gotten off the phone with my pulmonologist, who had the results from my lung capacity test. He said my lungs had been "air trapping" and were "*suggestive* of asthma, possibly caused by a viral infection", which to me was just a wimpy way to refuse me a COVID diagnosis. But at least it was some bit of proof that I hadn't been making these symptoms up through some ridiculously elaborate ploy for attention. An inhaler was prescribed.

I jumped in the car and drove to Dr. H's office, where I sat very briefly in the warm window of his waiting room before his nurse brought me back and took my vitals. "Are you nervous?" she asked, noting my elevated blood pressure.

"Well," said Dr. H, atop his rolling chair, "I have good news and bad news. The good news is nothing is showing up in these tests. The bad news is that nothing is showing up in these tests." He chuckled in the way of someone who tells a certain joke multiple times a week.

So, the fevers, malaise, racing heart, diarrhea, shortness of breath, and cough — were not evidence of a rare cryptococcus infection after all? Dr. H would suggest that perhaps I *could* be suffering from Fibromyalgia or Lupus, which didn't always show up on the tests we ran. There was no indication a test for Lyme was warranted. He ultimately put Chronic

Fatigue Syndrome down on my chart, probably with a tiny penciled-in question mark. Although I do not hold a medical degree, I am 90 percent sure you cannot contract asthma AND Fibromyalgia/Lupus/CFS together all on the same exact day.

Anicia Proba was a rich woman. Educated. Her influence was widespread. She had no illness we know of; she wasn't visiting doctors rolling about on office chairs with motorcycle ring tones.

Now why would Augustine feel like she needed to pray for happiness? For the fourth-century, she had it pretty good, all things being equal, minus air conditioning and ibuprofen. There was one problem, however, one ongoing thorn that trumped many others, especially in that cultural moment: Anicia was a widow.

Later in her life, after the hulking letter from Augustine was delivered in the mail, more thorns would prick their way through: she would be forced to flee Rome during its sacking and then endure imprisonment in Africa. I imagine her carrying the bishop's letter with her for years, in a fold of her robe, close to her body.

As we might expect from someone who had spent his youth pursuing standard, sexy forms of happiness, Augustine surmised there was more to the idea of happiness than we might think. Simply, real happiness is the ultimate consolation of having God himself, and God proves all lesser desires flimsy substitutes. God was always meant to be the first thing. But before we can be consoled by God himself, we must be desolate in everything else. We need to feel our lack before we'll think to ask for more of God. (It turns out Ignatius didn't invent the idea of consolation or desolation after all.)

*"The Christian soul ought to feel itself desolate, and continue in prayer, and learn to fix the eye of faith on the word of the divine sacred Scriptures,"* Augustine admonished Anicia, then quoting Psalm 63: *"O God, you are my God, earnestly I seek you; my soul thirsts for you, my body longs for you, in a dry and weary land where there is no water."*

The principle is simple: it's good to welcome healthy unhappiness sometimes. Holy discontent is like a healthy appetite that can be satiated with God, who scoops spoonfuls of satisfaction into our mouths from his book as we engage it in prayer.

This ability to feel desolate, to empty out to fill up, is easier if you're a widow, says Augustine plainly. A woman like that, like you, Anicia, understands more keenly that you are a pilgrim in the world, better able to leverage your thorn towards drawing close to God. You are already hungry; you feel your lack.

This is an advantage. This is a *leverage* mechanism. The poor in spirit, those who hunger and thirst for righteousness — theirs is the Kingdom of Heaven. They shall be filled.

I suspect someone could leverage long-term illness like that, too, if you didn't have too much else going on. It seems that suffering can either be creatively honed into a pulley system for constructing inner stability, or it can be a wrecking ball. Too much for one person, could be not enough for another, and it wasn't clear to me which direction I might go. Only God knows what our limits are.

No one told me when I graduated from college that no PhDs exist who specialize in MY own personal human body. No one told me that my own human body would be capable of going so wrong, so fast. No one told me I could still get sick even if I had been eating right, exercising, and not abusing alcohol or drugs. And the worst part, no one told me how isolating it is to be mysteriously sick. It's an island where people buzz overhead in little prop planes, dropping supplies and well wishes, but no one comes to stay.

And over and above all of this is a God saying that if all of this was made right and whole and reversed, the happiness of that still wouldn't compare with the happiness of knowing him. That the blessed relief of having all this corrected would still leave a hunger more profound than the sweetest feast of all wrongs being made right without Him.

Could God's book be a shortcut to relief, even before relief itself? Was God's book and praying through his book a shortcut to his very self, and, therefore, to an alien, thorn-defying happiness?

～

Give me this day my daily bread. My daily dose of You.

You have me at a standstill. I'm stalled out, and it's lonely here.

What is ultimately needed for me to flourish in this day? I just have to do it *today*, after all—one step at a time, one meal at a time. Let your presence be the bread that nourishes me. Be my company.

Let me practice thankfulness, like a difficult song that is good to learn.

Let me continue to practice honesty with you.

Let me be happy.

## THIRSTY

About ten days into my sudden symptoms, I found myself violently compelled to write about them. This was after my two negative COVID swabs and when my symptoms were at the very height of their powers, which meant I could only focus in short, desperate spurts. I'd lie on my bed with my laptop, shaking, and let my fingers fly.

"O GOD, YOU ARE MY GOD, EARNESTLY I SEEK YOU; MY SOUL THIRSTS FOR YOU, MY BODY LONGS FOR YOU, IN A DRY AND WEARY LAND WHERE THERE IS NO WATER. I HAVE SEEN YOU IN THE SANCTUARY AND BEHELD YOUR POWER AND YOUR GLORY. BECAUSE YOUR LOVE IS BETTER THAN LIFE, MY LIPS WILL GLORIFY YOU."
– PSALM 63:1

I'm not sure if what I wrote was all that coherent, but I think it was perhaps the slightest bit funny, and when I sent it to my editors at the blog to which I contribute, they agreed to run it. They even ran a series of blogs from me about (maybe) living with COVID-19, which was very generous of them. My editor was herself a COVID long-hauler, so she was sympathetic to my plight and eager for another truth-teller and advocate in the public space.

People were generally very nice to me in the comments section. Mostly, they were people who also had dealt with this unexplained, life-upending illness and all the thorns that come twisted together with it. People told me specifics, typed out in run-on sentences for the world to see.

One lady, a previously healthy seventy-year-old named Jeannette, practically re-told my story back to me about her progression through COVID symptoms and limbo-producing test results. Another man,

Mark, wrote about his battle with migraines. A girl named Stacy had gone through a similar experience with (maybe) COVID two months before I had when testing *really* wasn't available.

Every time I got a notification that someone had commented on my post, I cringed. *This is the one,* I'd always think, *that blasts and denigrates my experience.* But it never came. They were all affirmations, all similar accounts.

Reading them set my chin quivering. I wasn't a lone astronaut floating above the world of normal people after all. I had co-aliens. When another human being would blast themselves into the orbit of public discourse with me and make her story vulnerable to attack, I would think *God bless you. Thank you for joining me here, you brave, brave sister!*

I also got discreet messages from people who didn't want their illness or chronic pain, or doctor battles broadcasted over the interwebs — college friends, friends-of-friends, strangers, who felt the need to stay quiet. There is great dignity in this as well, and I save seats for them next to mine on the front row. We are sisters and brothers in a sometimes-functional family.

During all these real-time interactions, I was also reading about the chronic plights of writers who were also ostensibly typing on their beds with shaky hummingbird hands. One of them was Sarah Ramey, whose book *The Lady's Handbook for Her Mysterious Illness,* gave me many hours of entertainment, when I had the strength to read it. I silently thanked her for telling the really unflattering parts. I needed her vials of blood, her test tubes.

What makes her — and me — so compelled to share our fragility and to consume the fragility of others? My impetus comes from theater, where the story's power is in the full exposure of human beings as they are: essentially needy and fundamentally incomplete. We entertainment consumers like the good, the bad, and the ugly. We like to see fully drawn, complicated human beings up there under the spotlight.

Therefore, I have a low tolerance for not being understood or for being an unknown quantity, even if that quantity is deficient. *Especially* if that quantity is deficient. I need *to be seen*, by people.

There's a compulsion to seek validation wherever it can be procured, and I'm consumed with peddling the wares of my story so I can be rich again in normalcy. I want to feel like I'm one of many. I need others to see me as a regular gal and not some enigma with an unfamiliar problem.

And then comes the danger, which is a striving that can slide from healthy vulnerability into desperate thirst. Sometimes I can't tell when the conversion has happened, but vulnerability and desperation are as different in form from one another as water is from ice. Vulnerability, flowing and available, refreshes others. Desperation, hard and cold, self-serves. What a balance to strike, this razor edge between being helpful or self-indulgent. It's hard to see it clearly.

Meanwhile, as I was typing away, my friend Sarah was telling me about a group of ladies who met once a week on Zoom. Zoom was the only portal to the outside world in 2020, as we all know, and Bible Study was no different. Not that this was a Bible Study.

It was more of a spiritual formation group that was meeting to talk about *Desiring God's Will: Aligning Our Hearts with the Heart of God* by David G. Benner, which sounded a bit austere to me. It had been months since I had participated in any kind of small group or Bible Study, and it had been months since we had even darkened the doors of the church — though we would watch the Sunday services on YouTube every week, improvising communion wafers with Cheez-Itz. I was starting to feel my connection to God-through-others beginning to grow dim, the way the circle of light grows smaller the farther you progress away from it in a tunnel. For all the connection and commiseration, I had found through Sarah Ramey's book and in the blog to my fellow sickies, I needed a new and perhaps healthier way to bear my pink underbelly where other ladies with half-baked ideas about God could hear my half-baked ideas about God, and maybe we could find a common breadcrumb trail. I signed up with Sarah and logged in.

The discussion was led by a wise and longtime Spiritual Director named Betsy. I soon came to believe Betsy would be a great porch-sitting species of a friend, even though she was probably in her late seventies and on supplemental oxygen. Covid would almost certainly be a death sentence for her, I thought, grimly, when I first saw her intelligent face in the Zoom box.

Having had so much of my life upended, I had quite a few tiny questions for Betsy and the others about the nature of GOD'S WILL. It was becoming obvious that His will and mine were severely at odds. Clearly, God and I had a bit of a disagreement about how well my body should be functioning and about a career on pause.

Did God "will" for me to get sick? Does God lure us into dreaming and planning just to gaslight us at the last minute with unforeseen disappointment and tragedy? Maybe God was gaslighting us worse than doubtful doctors.

I wondered if these things were true about God's will. I also wondered what was true about *my* will. What was it that I really wanted, after all?

Was there something at the heart of all this worrying over my body and my performing and my future? Was it that I basically wanted four or five distinct things, or was it that I just wanted one ultimate, dazzling thing from which my other desires emanated like sunbeams? I wondered if it might be possible to follow the sunbeams up to the real source of heat and light, and find what Augustine told Anicia was the "one true and happy life."

David G. Benner writes, "Despite what you may have heard, Christian spirituality is not about the crucifixion of desire. Rather it is about the distillation and focusing of desire. It is about discovering the freedom of desiring nothing more than God and enjoying with detachment every other blessing and gift...Once we have drunk deeply of that love, nothing else will satisfy our heart."[28]

So said David G. Benner. He said other things too in the book, which we Zoom ladies discussed for weeks, mostly about how really, deep down, our desires and God's desires *are* aligned. We do want the same things, this God and us; it's just that we humans let certain other things cloud over the first thing, or even mistakenly substitute smaller things for the main thing, swapping the sun for the sunbeams.

And the main thing is Him. We want Him, mainly, and He mainly wants us. From a distance of centuries, I can see Augustine rising to his feet, gathering up his linen robes into his belt, and dancing a jig.

I tried to understand how wanting to be healed of illness was really, somehow, wanting God. Or how wanting to have a successful career was, at its heart, wanting God. These were good and exasperating questions to ask. Frustration and doubt were ever close at hand, but after a few weeks of practice, the asking soon felt like a discovery in and of itself, like having a map for finding something lost.

If the Widow Anicia Proba ever found her way to wanting God alone, it's impossible to say. My guess is she was already halfway there by writing Augustine that letter in the first place. Wanting to know how to pray even more than wanting to know how to find a new husband or how to deal with grief shows at least this: her spiritual throat was parched.

I, too, was beginning to discover my own desolation, the dry, empty tracks coursing from mouth to stomach, and yet the pull towards others, the necessity of their eyeballs upon me, of their smiles baptizing me, of their words giving benediction to me, was an easy gulp of salt water when the search for God felt muddled. I knew *they* could see me, *they* could hear me, *they* could relate to me. They were talking to me with mouths and lips and voices and even in attentive silences — not in a mere book. Not in old verses.

~~~

O God, you are my God. Not just vast creation's God — *my* God.

Your presence with me is cool water, the only lasting validity. You also see how strongly I want *other* things. It's taken a while, but I finally respect this predicament I'm in. I want and want and want and want.

Help me to channel this neediness in your direction. I seek you today out of respect for my heart and its design.

And then: let me serve others with my story instead of trying to short-circuit my growth by grasping at what they can't provide.

## PLACES

If a makeover doesn't help, then maybe a new place will fix things. This became a new working theory. After all, when a stage manager calls "Places," the actors know it's time to leave the small room backstage for the big room with everybody else.

"IN THE SAME WAY, THE SPIRIT HELPS US IN OUR WEAKNESS. WE DO NOT KNOW WHAT WE OUGHT TO PRAY FOR, BUT THE SPIRIT HIMSELF INTERCEDES FOR US THROUGH WORDLESS GROANS."
– ROMANS 8:26-27

Summer was upon us, and everything had been canceled — camps, Drew's much-anticipated trip to New York City with his 6th-grade theater class, and all organized sports and activities. My kids had been home from school for approximately forever, which was actually since the Eternal Spring Break of 2020 that would ultimately last a withering thirty-five weeks. Their wild, chestnut hair was getting ragged around the edges; their limbs were beginning to lengthen again in that way, particular to summer.

The one last hope for a getaway was a cabin in Colorado some acquaintances of ours were lending us for a week in August. We would have cool evenings, blue skies, and clear air in our future, even if it still meant I'd be on a couch most of the time. Being sick is one thing; allowing your family to be sick by association is another, and I just wasn't *having it*.

One afternoon, Gordon came into the sunroom where I was lying in a vegetative state with The Eyeballs curled in the nook of my abdomen. When I raised my head to look at his face, I could tell he didn't know quite how to tell me something, but soon enough, his sweet and sad beard face had made it clear: the cabin had been yanked away. He had mentioned my illness to the owner of the Colorado house and the offer had been reneged. It was a "safety thing."

An elderly woman was going to be among the next group of occupants to use the house after us, and the risk of exposure was too great. It didn't matter that I was now *months* from my onset of symptoms.

Well, it made me mad. I cried hot tears of shame for causing my kids' already shrinking world to shrink up even further, and I also cried for sheer rage at my unflinchingly sick body, and for what felt like outright discrimination against a special-needs person. After bemoaning my situation to some close friends, one of them came back with a wonderful offer: We could use her sister's cabin in Pagosa Springs instead.

Gordon, the kids, and I made the drive in two days. I had prepped for the trip with an herbal supplement that was supposed to get my lungs ready for higher altitudes. I brought my thermometers, inhalers, and my pulse oximeter. I wasn't sure how the Colorado air would interact with my "asthma-suggestive" lungs, but the whole thing was a risk worth taking a thousand times over. Drew and Maddie darted through the house like dragonflies, inspecting every room, and squealing at the view of stark mountains from the back deck. *Look! Look!*

Eventually, the delight of finding myself aloft in what felt like a giant treehouse sputtered out. I shut down. The couch, from which you cannot see Pagosa Peak rising up from its piney proscenium, sucked me in. There's not much difference between a couch in Texas and a couch in Colorado, it turns out.

One afternoon, Gordon took the kids for a hike. He texted me pictures of Maddie and Drew at various stopping points along the trail and in front of a public park they stumbled upon. Their faces were sweaty and shiny, happiness leaking from pores.

Their summer was beginning to resemble summer. I closed my eyes, wishing I was there, shaking with fever, wishing they had their mother with them and wishing for a lot of things, really.

When they returned, I set my mind on another place. Maddie would be turning ten at the end of July, and for almost a year, I had been planning an entire surprise overhaul of the upstairs configuration. Like her mother, she too needed some new scenery, a new window for seeing new trees.

The plan was to move Maddie into the larger playroom that had an attached bathroom, and it was going to be fit for the fluffiest little most darling angel princess. I hired my friend Courtney to help design the project, and we had most things picked out by the time I got sick in April. She came by a couple of times to survey the territory upstairs.

I'd answer the door, see her mask, and remember to put mine on as well. I hauled myself to the top landing with her a couple of times to appear helpful and engaged, which sent me gasping for air and coughing. She didn't seem to mind. I let her go up there alone, mostly, and she didn't mind that either. She was helping me finish the *plan*, which was the *goal*, and it was a relief to turn my attention elsewhere.

Being sick, at least initially, brings a flurry of care and concern. This is like an emergency rope thrown down into a snake pit. But after a while, my sickness was making me even sicker of things being about me all the time, every day. Every text from friends was written in Concerned Serif Font and blue heart emojis, asking about my health, and checking up on the latest doctor reports.

I'd get Facebook messages from acquaintances letting me know they were praying for me and asking if I had read the latest article in *The Guardian* about Long Covid. My parents and in-laws were constantly helping and fussing and worrying aloud, which, is of course, what they get paid to do, for God's sake, and which I could not survive without. I realize so many, *many* scores of sick people are isolated and never get such an embarrassment of loving, fretful people, and I can't imagine how they survive the indifference.

But then the weeks go by. Then the months. The days stack on top of each other like Lincoln Logs rising to a full nine feet, yet fewer people seem to be aware I'm still on the wrong side of the wall. People assume you must be better by now, and some days it's just easier to pretend.

I started to dread the question, "How are you?" because it confirmed to me my enduring label as a *chronic invalid,* and I didn't want to uphold that reputation among the general populace. That's not how I want to be known or remembered, especially by my children. I need people to peer through the window and see me in the living room, not the sick room.

When is moving day?

For all his harping on praying in accordance with Scripture, Augustine had something else to tell Anicia about prayer: sometimes you just can't find the right verse. Sometimes there's just not a Psalm that will be able to adequately voice your volcanic feelings. Sometimes you don't know how your emotions fit neatly into a line of The Lord's Prayer. Sometimes you have to let God's spirit within you groan, expressing *"longings for that great blessing, as yet unknown, for which we patiently wait."*[29]

The great, unknown blessing *is* there. We can sense it, but it's just out of the reach of the words and language we use and the categories we possess. We can't name the blessing we're after, but we can feel it, the glory and the bliss of it, the joy-hot union with our first thing God that is at the foundation of it and all other desires for glory, bliss, and union.

These feelings can be prayed by way of groans and sighs and sobs because there are no human words available to describe the glory to be revealed. Or maybe there are words, but we are still babies learning to babble them, to whimper and cry in a language yet unspeakable.

Even now, we can begin to learn them. Who knows, maybe these words are an incarnate language of sight and smell and touch and taste and breath and hearing, a multi-dimensional language that expresses more organically all we might want to communicate both to God and to others and to ourselves. If the Word invented words and had them written down in His book and speaks through the words in fresh ways by his Spirit, why shouldn't these Bible words be only the beginning of God's linguistic creativity? Why shouldn't there be even more words and whole languages that we have yet to learn?

In suffering, we open the primer. We start with syllables, the ma-ma and the da-da sounds, and they come out as groans. Childlike. Indecipherable. But they are deep, full-body upheavals that stretch us forward against the wind towards another place. A place prepared for us.

~~~

Oh Lord.

...

...

...

I know this is not my permanent home or my permanent language. I get a new dwelling soon, one that will fit my true nature, one that doesn't reflect my shallow surface but my utter essence. You are getting it ready for me even now as I struggle here, in this chair, in this house, in this body, with these insufficient words to describe all I feel and all I want.

And yet in you, I am re-homed, re-named — even now, if partially. Help me to wait in anticipation of my total renovation.

## POWER

For all his extensive scholarly commentary on the Psalms, Augustine never formally translated the word "Selah,"[30] that obscure word from Mrs. Hoerger's class that seems to represent some sort of pause or point of emphasis between the Psalm writers' prayers. Augustine sort of half-suggested Selah could mean "so be it,"[31] almost like how we say "Amen" at the end of our mealtime blessings. One thing Augustine was clear on,

"WHY DO YOU SAY, O JACOB, AND SPEAK, O ISRAEL, 'MY WAY IS HIDDEN FROM THE LORD, AND MY RIGHT IS DISREGARDED BY MY GOD?'

HAVE YOU NOT KNOWN? HAVE YOU NOT HEARD? THE LORD IS THE EVERLASTING GOD, THE CREATOR OF THE ENDS OF THE EARTH. HE DOES NOT FAINT OR GROW WEARY; HIS UNDERSTANDING IS UNSEARCHABLE. HE GIVES POWER TO THE FAINT, AND TO HIM WHO HAS NO MIGHT HE INCREASES STRENGTH."
– ISAIAH 40:27-29

however, was the need to pause and pray frequently in order to *"cherish uninterrupted desire"*[32] for God, to *Selah all through the day.* Interrupting your day to un-interrupt your attention to God was just good sense if you wanted a happy life.

"You're not crazy. This is not all in your head," Katie said to me on our first-ever Zoom call. I loved her from that exact moment on.

Here was a health professional offering to be a co-signer on the mortgage of my health, committing to take the burden of my healing onto her shoulders. Here was a woman promising to explore every possibility, strategy, and test to figure out what was wrong with me and to systematically eliminate not just the disease, but the *non-wellness*. She was all in, and she was confident in her ability. She even suggested I might feel better *than I ever had in my life* by the time we were through. And the crowd went wild!

Functional Medicine is a relatively new-ish discipline in the health and wellness field, but it's gaining respect among more traditional medical doctors and perhaps might hold the key to the recovery of many Long Haulers. The strategy is relatively common-sensical, though difficult: Take a 30,000-foot view of a person's situation, starting with medical history going all the way back to in-utero (was your mother a smoker? Were you delivered by caesarean?), then examine every life stressor of the patient, past and present; take the patient's complete family history of disease; assess the patient's current and past housing environments; explore all compromising gut health factors and nutritional profile.

All of this creates a holistic portrait of the patient, like one of those detailed 3D printouts engineers use to design a building. I could have existed as a mini bobble-head on Katie's desk, she knew me that well and saw me that dimensionally. And what she was designing was a plan for Total Thorn Elimination.

I was so ready to have a new basket into which I could roll every single last one of my eggs. It wasn't just the promise of answers and health, but the promise of having someone *else* be in charge of getting answers and health. I was willing to do anything and everything I was told simply because it was someone *besides myself* giving the orders. I had been piloting this plane without a license for way too long, and I was exhausted worrying that I would crash the whole thing by taking the wrong supplement or trying some obscure home remedy. Much love to Schuyler, but the oils just weren't cutting it.

There was also a sense in which, as time was passing, I had been missing key windows where a treatment or intervention would mean the difference between a year-long battle and a life-long war. I needed to be relieved of duty.

Suddenly, within a week, Katie had become the functional deity I had been looking for the whole duration of my thorn: all-knowing, all-comprehending, all-loving. She was Someone (with a capital S) who clearly wanted what was best for me, and what was best for me obviously equaled my physical well-being. She held this truth to be self-evident; she could see that I was endowed with this certain unalienable right.

By the time Katie had crafted a figurative 360-degree model of Julie Rhodes, she had some theories of why I had fallen off the COVID cliff. First, I had a "leaky gut," she said, which made me a simmering ball of inflammation from the outset. When this inflammation was exacerbated by a virus like COVID, the fire couldn't easily be quenched, putting my whole body perpetually in fighting mode. This was a plausible explanation for the ongoing fevers, fatigue, diarrhea and breathing issues.

This whole situation, in theory, was then also made worse by my genetic A1-antitrypsin deficiency. My general practitioner, Dr. G, had ordered the test for it as a Hail Mary and had struck what we Texas oil people call *black gold*. Antitrypsin, which cleans up the collateral damage of inflammation, can't do a great job operating at only 60 percent, which is what my mutated genes produce. This means my angry, angry white blood cells had been throwing a lot of fine china against the walls to smash the virus, and there wasn't enough staff to clean up the mess. The mess itself then causes damage, particularly to the lungs and liver, and the pile of broken shards just grows higher and wider as the immune system keeps throwing plates even after the virus is history.

In short: I had been positioned at the edge of a precipice with no guardrail. I had an insidious, invisible pre-existing condition and didn't know it until I was in freefall. There would be more discoveries later involving tick-borne bacterium, but we had enough to go on at the time.

Step number one, according to Katie, was to "focus on the foundations of wellness," which includes a diet that addresses things like adrenal function and inflammatory issues. Healing my "leaky gut" was a big part of this diet equation, as the digestive track can be a major source of inflammation in anyone's body. Apparently, irritating foods had made my gut porous and therefore prone to "leak" particles into my bloodstream, triggering an immune reaction. (I'm just the darlingest thing.)

Primarily, these are foods containing gluten, dairy, corn, soy, peanuts, sugar, and alcohol. Perhaps I should repeat myself. I said *gluten, dairy, corn, soy, peanuts, sugar, and alcohol,* which means all food everywhere that you might ever want to eat. It all had to go. All processed foods, all bread, cereals, and pastas (well, the palatable kind), tortillas (gasp!), peanut butter, corn chips, popcorn, cheese, milk, ice cream, desserts, syrups, beer, and wine.

Oh, and did I mention COFFEE? NO? WELL, LET ME MENTION COFFEE AS WELL.

I completely overhauled my diet. I was committed to utter adherence. I meal-prepped, drank spinach shakes, simultaneously planned pasta dinners for my family, and BOILED MILLET for myself.

I also learned how to make buckwheat and chia bread and explored the many uses of coconut creamer. I accustomed myself to eating almond-buttered rice cakes with no-sugar-added raisins. I would quickly learn the best traffic routes around the aisles of Sprouts and Whole Foods, and which restaurants were certified gluten-free in Fort Worth (not many). I would soon learn how to make sour cream out of cashews and toast out of rice cakes and soy sauce out of amino acids and fish sauce. (Without knowing amino acids also, in fact, have soy. Oy.) I also began to live a cheese-less life, which surely has its origin in the occult.

Flashback to Tavern on the Green in New York City, 1992. Grandmama and Grandaddy and I were seated, just the three of us, in front of vast, cold windows that looked out onto a courtyard. Snow frosted the trees lightly, the way it does in the most delicately styled window displays at the NYC Macy's.

Grandmama, elegant and ever proper, was teaching 11-year-old me how to eat a yeast roll like a civilized human female. "You pinch off one bite at a time and spread a little taste of butter on it — you don't *slather* the whole thing with butter — and then you eat it, like this," she said, taking a birdlike bite. She directed my attention to the small bread plate and the butter knife, just there to my left. A whole set-up just for the roll!

Bread and butter, my forever soul food, ever worthy of esteem and honor and specific chinaware. Give me sourdough for sopping up creamy soups, brioche for grilled cheese, everything bagels for rich lox and capers. Add to this pasta and mozzarella — al dente whirls of spaghetti heavy with wine-kissed marinara — and also tortillas, steam still choo-chooing from swollen griddle blisters, melting the Monterey jack. If I were a minstrel, these are the odes I would play on my lute.

When Katie told me giving up gluten and dairy would bolster the healing process, a new sort of weird and wiggly something felt unwell inside, and this was clearly the writhing of my deepest soul. What would I eat with my eggs in the morning, if not a piece of buttered multigrain toast? How would I make my weekly spaghetti without Skinner pasta?

How would I do lunch without Colby jack on my sandwiches? *How would I make sandwiches without bread?* And dear Lord, WHAT ABOUT PIZZA?

Now at every meal, my very plate reminded me of things I had lost. There was no respite from my illness, no forgetting it; not even in a bowl of ice cream or in the simplicity of a perfectly — and politely — buttered croissant. I figured out ways to modify my meals so my family's wouldn't have to be drastically altered, but my every breakfast, lunch and dinner now required a new layer of thought and preparation that demanded energy and an adventurous spirit I simply didn't have, and every pot and bowl now looked somewhat sinister without the usual suspects being stirred, boiled or mixed inside of them. (*Millet* boiling in a pot looks practically *primeval.*)

"This is an investment," I told myself, "In my health." This could even be life or death. But everything I said in these moments sounded hollow, like growls echoing off the walls of an empty stomach.

Yet there was a dark pleasure in it. I've read that eating disorders, at their core, come from a deep need to control chaos. If too many things in life suck away your agency, you turn to the one thing you *can* master and that is your very own body itself — what goes in it, what goes out of it, what *doesn't* go in or out.

A strict diet or exercise regimen can serve as the same mechanism. Monitoring every morsel when I can't moderate what the rest of my body might be doing leaves me feeling like I finally have the upper hand. It's a little check on my body to say, "You think you're getting away with this? Look who is really running the show!"

It is probably no coincidence that right about this time, my prayer journals sputtered out and rolled to a stop in the gravel.

I'll pay almost any price to get well, any price at all, except I will not concede one more coin of power. I must retain some currency for myself, a bit of control, a little capital of some kind.

If we are committed to engaging God's book in our prayers frequently as we Selah through our days, there arises a similar temptation. This looks like me trying to steal agency back from God by using His words against him, by trying to find the right phrases from favorite verses that might be used to pigeonhole him, like shorthand magic words used in "name it and claim it" prosperity gospel. These little mantras turn our Selahs into seances to conjure the response we're wanting from God. Augustine would never abide this.

We pray, he says, "*not as means by which we expect that God is to be either informed or moved to compliance,*" adding, "*When, therefore, we say: Hallowed be Your name, we admonish ourselves to desire that His name... may be also among men esteemed holy... which is an advantage not to God, but to men.*"[33]

In other words, you'll be better off praying Scripture on its own terms. It's to your advantage to take your eyes off the things you're trying to control. It's better to use God's book as a way to connect with him and his vision of reality than it is to use it as a spell book for your own ends. God will not be manipulated by my crafty, restless heart. His words aren't coins of currency that you trade in for a good or service.

But if his book is telling me anything, it's that God will be moved to mercy. He will be moved to strengthen. He will be moved to feed the hungry.

~

Lord of the Flies, of the chaos that surrounds me: be nearby. Be closer than the mayhem. Be my steady current of strength. My way is not hidden from you. You made every atom of my body. Your vitality persists day and night. You are intimately aware of what it takes to keep me going. I wait for true power, and this comes by ceding control to you alone.

Hallowed be *your* name, *your* plans, *your* timing.

## FOLLOW

At the end of September, I arranged for a photographer to take some new headshots of me. In the acting world, headshots are your calling card — your first impression with directors or producers — and they are even

"TURNING HIS HEAD, PETER NOTICED THE DISCIPLE JESUS LOVED FOLLOWING RIGHT BEHIND. WHEN PETER NOTICED HIM, HE ASKED JESUS, 'MASTER, WHAT'S GOING TO HAPPEN TO HIM?' JESUS SAID, 'IF I WANT HIM TO LIVE UNTIL I COME AGAIN, WHAT IS THAT TO YOU? YOU — FOLLOW ME.'"
– JOHN 21: 20-23

sometimes the key to landing a role. I wanted some new shots to supplement what I already had, shots that would communicate a few different sides of my character and personality.

I wanted a studious, intelligent-looking picture of me wearing glasses; a "tough girl" shot of me in my leather jacket with red lipstick and a no-nonsense glare; a "natural mom" look to show my sweet, maternal side. Behold my versatility! Hire me and make me forget I'm sick! What was particularly unfortunate about the photo shoot that day was that I still felt awful with COVID symptoms, *and* I had a brand-new spanking bruise blossoming out along the bottom of my neck.

This purple pansy was from a biopsy.

And thus began, in September of 2020, what we call "raising the stakes" in actor language.

Eight years before, a CT scan revealed I had four suspicious nodules on my thyroid. They didn't look friendly. My endocrinologist, Dr. L, biopsied them and was surprised to find them "very benign," according to the lab report. He said to come back each year for sonograms to monitor their growth or lack thereof.

Of course, my yearly appointment just happened to fall during my COVISH illness. And of course, in the midst of my COVISH illness, the nodules had grown enough to warrant another biopsy. The nurse had slathered my throat with white numbing cream that felt cold at first and then felt like nothing at all, and then a needle the length of an ice pick came out.

Preliminary results indicated a 5-15 percent chance of thyroid cancer. We had gone from "very benign" in 2013 to "maybe cancer" in 2020.

Dr. L would be sending my biopsy samples off to another lab for genetic sequencing. "This will give us a much more accurate idea of the likelihood of these being cancerous," he told me, as though this was a comforting thing to say. We would have to wait another three weeks.

The next day, I pulled up to the curb of my photographer's studio and breathlessly hauled armfuls of wardrobe options into the studio. The clouds beyond the Dallas skyline were heavy and purple, like my bruise — imminent and rain-ish. I knew a few things then, just a very few: one, that I had to work some makeup magic to patch over my biopsy; two, that I was possibly about to be diagnosed with cancer, and three, that I had a fever. And that I couldn't breathe very well. I guess that was four things.

Brian, playful and languid, snapped one picture after another with his woodpecker fingers, feeding me imaginary scenarios. "You've just been told you got passed over the job by a man when you are more qualified!" he yelled, trying to draw out a scowl. "Your teenage son is hurting, and you want to talk to him, but you don't know how!" he offered, goading me for pathos. "You just found out you have cancer!"

No. He didn't say that. But he should have if he wanted to get a real *look* out of me. The thought was niggling there just under the surface, ready to pounce and make its reality manifest, and I was barely swiping it away.

If I could just keep this ugly thing back up against the wall of my brain, if I could just ... focus on something less dreadful than the idea of battling cancer AND COVID at the same time. That version of me — that rattled, beleaguered person — was one I did NOT want to advertise. These were headshots, not mugshots.

The week before my biopsy and photoshoot, I auditioned for a small student film being shot in Dallas. I soon received a message back: I'd been cast! They weren't offering me the role for which I had auditioned, but the part of the oblivious sister who doesn't see the murderous pyro-tendencies of her nephew. I must have a profound talent for appearing oblivious, and I was prepared to fully own this because I had an actual, bona fide offer to be an actor in the middle of a pandemic! It was miraculous and jolting, like fishing for trout and nabbing a whale.

I made my way to the shoot. It was October 4, several days after my mugshots with Brian. Nobody from Dr. L's office had called yet with my results, and it wouldn't help to lie around and wallow. My neck bruise was less purple pansy now and more of a vague shadow. I got lost on my drive, looking for an old farmhouse in a remote area down country roads and through clusters of trees.

When I finally arrived, everyone was gracious. They even had a special meal accommodation for the Paleo-Whole-Thirty-Keto-all-combined diet Katie had prescribed for me, Fascist that she is. The other actors were all lovely and personable. Best of all, I didn't forget my lines in the porch scene. I was Meryl Streep!

Several hours passed. Film sets are like stationary road trips: nobody can leave, the scenery keeps changing, and there are snacks. Between the porch scene and the dinner scene, however, I was starting to get nervous.

My temperature was ratcheting up. The wet cotton in my brain was expanding out to the edges of my skull. Everything began to have a distant quality to it, like when you're halfway listening to a conversation before nodding off to sleep. I marshaled my focus.

We had to improv a scene at the dinner table. Repeatedly, between takes, I would scoop small amounts of mashed potatoes onto my plate to replenish what I had just eaten in the take before. There came a point where I fell silent as I tried to remember how to scoop, how to hold a fork, and how to nod and smile. I had lost my handle on the immediacy of what we were doing, as though I had left myself sitting there at the table and was watching my body misfire from the other side of the room.

By the time the director said CUT for the last time, I was trembling. I got in my car and took my temperature — 100.3 — and I still had a forty-minute drive home ahead of me. Still, I had done it. I had worked for the first time while sick and it had not been a *complete* disaster. It felt like I had gotten away with something, stolen something from behind a counter. But then I opened Instagram.

I came across posts from a friend of mine who is also an actor and had been stringing together a series of jobs one after another, even mid-pandemic. She looked beautiful in her many posts, and she seemed to be unfurling every feather of talent she had for the projects at hand and was truly hitting her creative stride. She wasn't sick.

She wasn't leaving her body to gin up a fever or worrying if her brain would fuzz over. She wasn't touching up concealer on a biopsy bruise and waiting for the phone to ring. She was living into her calling with full vibrancy, with no encumbrance.

I felt a little sting in my sternum, which puffed up into a huge welt of habanero jealousy. All my gains from the day had been lost.

There's a line in a play I did once that reads, "Through all the world there goes one long cry from the heart of the artist: Give me leave to do my utmost!"[34]

Doesn't seem like too much to ask.

In the biography he wrote about his longtime friend Augustine, Bishop Possidius recounts a story from Augustine's last days. Augustine was sick in bed with a fever that would ultimately end his life. I can see him there, curled up in his bed, shaking up temperatures and turning away food, his brain gauzing over while he tried to concentrate on the view from his window. One day, a man came begging for prayer on behalf of his sick relative. Can you imagine the audacity? The way Augustine must have struggled to raise his head off the pillow to look at the man in his doorway?

Predictably, Augustine said to him, in effect, "Don't you think if I had the power to pray for healing, that I would have prayed for myself?" I like to imagine his steeple-white pope-y hat over in the corner, still high and unwilted on its perch, a reminder that if this bedridden Saint didn't have the answers, nobody did.

But the visitor insisted, telling Augustine God had instructed him in a vision to visit the good bishop and have him lay hands on him in prayer. Well, this was a different story. Almost without hesitation, it seems, Augustine complied. Who was he to argue with God? He reached out, forearms trembling, and prayed. The relative was healed, but Augustine himself would never recover.

What an odd request of God to have made, to insist Augustine participate in a work of healing, but specifically *not* for himself. It almost seems like a slap in the face — unless you've gotten to know the God who wrote a book.

I wonder what questions must have passed unbidden through Augustine's mind in those last days about why things happen to certain people and not to others – *Master, what's going to happen to him? To me?*

What we do know is that Augustine spent his final two weeks on earth pressing in closer to his enigmatic God by praying the Psalms.[35] They were specifically the penitential prayers of David, and Augustine prayed and read them, weeping "freely and constantly." Was it sin that troubled Augustine in his last, dying days — the sin of comparison? Or was his distress clean, a blessed relinquishment of lesser things as he began the transition into the utter presence of God himself?

Whether or not his tears came from a place of strength or weakness, they didn't seem to keep Augustine from following the way marked out for him up until the end. He asked for a few Psalms to be copied by hand and pinned to his wall so he could read them as he lay in bed, staring at a wallpaper of God's book fluttering in the breeze from an open window. Perhaps he could hear that child again somewhere far away, singing with a lilting voice that shook the galaxy, "Pick up and read, pick up and read."

Eventually, Augustine asked that no visitors come to see him except when his meals were brought or when the doctors would examine him so that *"he had all that time free for prayer."*[36] As his life ebbed away, he gave more and more of it to God, tithing only a small percentage to other concerns, moving ever closer to the physician whose "medicine is mightier" than any weakness or illness or sin. When he had no words of his own, he used the ones he was given in a book, and then he slipped away to that final state where words must surely still exist, but only to draw us closer to the Word behind, before, and beyond them all.

On October 14, ten days after shooting the scene with the mashed potatoes, I too would be given yet another chance to press into mystery.

~~

I don't get it, Lord. I don't see it. Why me, why this, why now? Why do other people seem to glide seamlessly through life while I'm slogging through marshland?

But you don't tell all your secrets. You only tell a few, and you've only begun to disclose the biggest three of all: how much you love me, how much you've given for me, how much is in store for me. Bless me as I contemplate what is *not* mysterious today.

Bless me as I follow you through shadow.

# CHAPTER 4

# FEAR AND BLEEDING: WILL EVERYTHING GET WORSE AND DOES JULIAN EVEN CARE?

A couple years before Mrs. Hoerger introduced me to journaling through the Psalms, I had a History teacher named Mrs. Center who introduced me to chatting with Jesus. She wore the bluest eyeshadow, like a theme park mermaid. Her salt-and-pepper hair had been in the same coif since probably 1963. Her name was fitting since Jesus seemed to be at the very center of her being and was maybe even permanently residing somewhere inside the mass of her beehive. Like Mrs. Hoerger, she had a deep mistrust of teenage boys and most definitely would

"GOD, OF THY GOODNESS, GIVE ME THYSELF: FOR THOU ART ENOUGH TO ME."
– JULIAN OF NORWICH

have scolded thirteen-year-old Jesus himself if he were in her 7th-grade class with me. But she loved him. I could tell.

It was my first year of school outside my own house, and I was blinking against the bright sunlight of the wider world beyond — even though it was just a small Christian school housed in a Pentecostal church in my hometown of Irving, TX. Those Pentecostals, man. They were a little scary.

At Chapel every Wednesday morning, they would throw their hands into the air, eyes closed, swaying like fronds of seaweed anchored in a receding tide. Sometimes they started whispering in languages I didn't recognize, that maybe weren't languages anyone would recognize. I didn't know them as "Pentecostals" back then, only "Charismatics," but it's entirely possible they were "Assemblies of God." Maybe there's a difference, I don't know. There seems to be some definitional murk in this arena.

I do know they were unafraid of interacting with the Spirit of Jesus. They felt He was, well, *there*, so why wouldn't your whole face and body and lips and breath and even language itself be shot through with otherworldly electricity? God's presence should make a difference, and these people were open to the possibilities.

I didn't remain on the outside of this for long. Sometimes in our weekly Wednesday morning Chapel services, there would be what felt like a lightening of my shoulders, as though someone had taken off my backpack. There was an ability to draw breath deeper and fuller into my body, a weightless pastry feeling, a smile. I could raise my hands and breathe in what felt like silk, and I could leave that room and walk to my next class in simplicity, with nothing else on my mind other than the action of leaving the room and walking to my next class. Simplicity, lightness, breath. These were fruits of that Spirit.

Mrs. Center taught us about American History, but what I remember from her class was what she told us one day about her morning routine.

"I sit up in bed," she said, "And I say, 'Morning, Jesus.'"

She was suggesting we try it. The moment your eyes open and your dreams start draining off like drops down a windshield, you sit up. Then you look around, get your bearings. Take a deep breath. And say, "Morning, Jesus." It isn't even really a prayer because He is, well, *there*.

"Praying," as a term, had a quality of distance, of talking through tin can phones stretched from one tree to another. But with Jesus, He was just there — always there — so you didn't really need to pray to him or ask him anything or explain yourself. You really didn't even need to acknowledge His presence at all if you didn't want to, but you might as well if you wanted to live in the realm of What Is. It was just nice to say hello.

It was a bright fall morning — October 14, 2020. My kids were at school (finally, school had reopened!) and I had just gotten dressed to visit a friend of mine whom I hadn't seen in months. Various doctors had assured me that, whatever was wrong with me, I was definitely not still contagious six months later. Thus began cautious forays into public and distanced visits with friends.

The truth was, I felt beautiful, like an ailing Eva Peron. I was wearing *statement earrings* and my Chanel Chance Eau Tendre like a very proper, brave human lady who continued to find little subversive ways to resist her oppressor.

My phone rang. When I saw it was my endocrinologist's office, an organ or two fell out of my torso and onto the floor. I had been waiting for three unending weeks.

The voice of Dr. L's nurse, F, was on the line. A toddler was making some sort of noise in the background — a whine? A cry? It appeared F was calling me from her house. Dr. L was currently in the hospital with a severe case of COVID-19, so I assumed he was now either short-staffed or F was quarantining at home herself. She didn't explain.

"Hi, Mrs. Rhodes," she began, in a kind, professional voice that was tinged with bright fluster. "The genetic profile of your thyroid came back. Your biopsy is now showing a 70 percent chance of cancer. So, I need to talk with you about a surgeon."

Her toddler continued declaring his truth somewhere in the background. Random thoughts came to me then, like what kind of day was this woman having? Here she was, managing a baby, fielding questions for her dangerously ill boss, calling darling, innocent ladies to inform them of cancer, so. Probably a bad one.

After her napalm dropped, I only heard about every other word, like "radiation" and "ASAP."

"I'm still running almost daily fevers," I informed F in a shaky voice, cutting in. Couldn't we wait until I was over a few more of my pandemic symptoms before we removed a major organ?

"We advise you not to wait longer than three or four weeks," she said. "I'm setting you up with a surgeon's office — Dr. D — so please let us know once you've had your consultation and gotten a surgery date." She said some more words in the English language about a medication I would have to take for the rest of my life called "Synthroid," but I could only write them down robotically like a voice dictation app. No actual comprehension of meaning was occurring between my ears.

When I hung up with F, it hit me clearly and darkly: "Maybe Cancer" takes precedence over "Maybe COVID." We didn't know how taking a thyroid out in the midst of a COVID long-haul experience would affect me; we just knew we couldn't let cancer grow. We didn't know if it was dangerous to operate on an already inflamed immune system, but we knew that cancer was even more dangerous to an already inflamed immune system. The ante had been upped unfairly and without my permission.

The mysterious idea of talking to Jesus personally and in real-time did not originate in an obscure Pentecostal private school in circa 1993. It really didn't originate with Julian of Norwich either, but she was one of the earliest, most famous people to have had such interaction.

Little is known about her, other than what we find in her *Revelations of Divine Love*. Just as Dante was the first to write in the vernacular Italian of his time, Julian was the first woman to write in English, which means it could be said the first feminist literature of the English-speaking world was one woman's conversations with Jesus.

Her supernatural encounters with Him spanned the course of about fifteen years from the time she was about thirty years old. Prayer, for Julian, was an encounter with a person that was always persistently *there*; more than that, who was actually *within* her and available to her constantly and without interruption.

We do know this: Julian was an anchoress. Similar to a nun, an anchoress was a revered woman in medieval society who would live shut up in a small enclosure that was attached to the local cathedral. In her tiny house, she would spend the remainder of her earthly life praying for her community. She was not allowed to marry or travel, or even to attend church services themselves. A woman like this had time to pray and time to write about her prayers.

The imagination of Amy Frykholm pictures the ceremony inducting Julian into the anchoress life like a proper funeral[37], a funeral which she herself attended before being escorted to her room and locked inside — what amounted to an oxygenated, candlelit grave. Members of the community would be her support through the years, bringing her clothing and food, and supplies. Visitors would sit on the porch of her enclosure, perhaps, and she would talk to them through a curtain that hung in a small window, offering counsel, advice, and yes, prayer. She was an ever-lit lamp at God's kitchen table that illuminated the faces of all the people who were counting on him.

It's speculated Julian didn't become an anchoress until after she had her first encounters with Jesus.[38] These began two weeks after Easter on May 8, 1373, when she fell dangerously ill and began seeing visions on what she thought was her death bed. Over the next fifteen years, Jesus would keep appearing to her in what she called "shewings" where He explained the content and nature of her original visions. Lest anyone chalk them up to the feverish ravings of a dying cerebral cortex, the visions and their subsequent revelations proffered profound theological wisdom that has influenced Christian thinking for 700 years.

Well, and maybe Julian was a little nuts, too.

Case and point: the hazelnut.

One day, Jesus showed Julian a small hazelnut that can easily fit inside a palm, a "little thing," as she called it. Almost as if leaning over her shoulder, He told her simply, "*It is all that is made.*"[39]

Julian understood three things just then, three truths Jesus was impressing, and those were that God made everything, God keeps everything, and God loves everything. Everything. No matter how small.

And everything — all the worlds spinning at blinding rates through the cosmos, all the ducks flapping hard against headwinds, all the beetles and undersea mountain ranges and bacterium and all the people in Africa and in Asia and in Europe and on every random island, plus all the alien life forms, if they exist — all this amounts to nothing more than the size of a hazelnut in God's hand. Which he keeps and loves.

Julian draws out her delicate conclusion like the style of honeysuckle:

*"This is the cause why we be not all in ease of heart and soul: that we seek here rest in those things that be so little, wherein is no rest, and know not our God that is Almighty, All-wise, All-good. For he is the Very Rest."*[40]

Very Rest.

Simplicity. Lightness. Breath.

She was not a woman of bigness. She had not been raised in spirit-filled chapel services where people lifted their hands, swayed like seaweed, fell down in ecstasies, or spoke in tongues. This was a woman who was most likely shepherded by Franciscan friars[41], whose job was to be devout, to work quietly at her loom or in her garden, to bear children. And certainly, never to teach about spiritual truth, much less write it down.

To top it off, this was a woman who was writing in a commoner dialect, the language you cursed in when you stubbed your toe or used to gossip in the town square. [42] There was nothing large or demonstrative about Julian, though there was something of courageous audacity about her. She herself was in every way a "little thing," yet had found a very big, enveloping person.

There is a temptation we face as we pray, and that is to believe we are praying to a force more than to a Face. We know it is unrealistic to expect actual conversations with actual Jesus, but because we are left without a face to put with a name, as it were, we are left sighing our prayers up to the ceiling, hoping that by osmosis they will gel with whatever vague energy field comprises God or the universe or whatever. Even our Bibles can be used more to try to dial into a frequency instead of connecting to a friend. Similarly, our imaginations, even trained by Ignatian exercises, can fall short if we believe they are only being used for abstract impressions and not leading us to a true, personal encounter.

Oh, it's all so very risky. So fraught with the danger of woo-woo thinking and self-deceiving projections of our own mental states upon God when really what we need is a Xanax and a nap or a sandwich. But just because it feels uncontrollable and perilous does not mean it is not the way forward. More than its inherent danger is its inherent mystery. It's all so very mysterious when prayer begins crossing over from incantation to conversation.

But life is also mysterious. So much of our lives and circumstances dwells in the darkness, behind corners and under tables. We don't understand WHY THIS or WHY THAT and we ask WILL THIS or WILL THAT, and it all consumes and pecks at us without end. Mystery is the oxygen we must always unwillingly breathe.

We start asking how much worse could this get? If I have cancer, what will radiation do to my body? What if the cancer has spread and chemo is required? What if the virus and the cancer will be too much for my body to handle when all treatments have been tried and all interventions exhausted? "What if" thrums rhythmically like a pendulum, swinging from extreme to extreme.

Maybe praying to Jesus directly, as if He's really present and He really hears me, is the only remedy; to engage mystery with even greater mystery. The solution is not less mystery, but more.

〜

Oh Lord, I don't understand how You can be here with me now. I feel silly and a bit batty and kind of woo-woo. But here we are.

I don't understand my own life either, but You know my way — my trajectory — even if it's hidden from me. I can entrust the blurry, mysterious to You because it belongs to You already. It's not something I own that becomes Yours once I have turned it over; it's something that's Yours from the start which You offer to carry so I can be light on my feet.

The mass of mystery weighs too much for human shoulders. It's *Your* property.

## GRACE

On New Year's Eve of 2019, Gordon and I were celebrating at a dear friend's house. This was once upon a time before masks, social distancing, or COVID vaccines, before terms like "herd immunity," "variants," or "antibodies" were regularly strewn across conversations and social media feeds. It was just a regular New Year's Party, complete with retro 1920s flair — fringy skirts, peacock feathers, and bowties.

> "BUT GROW IN THE GRACE AND KNOWLEDGE OF OUR LORD AND SAVIOR JESUS CHRIST."
> – 2 PETER 3:18

We played our traditional dollar bill game and ate a potluck supper. Someone turned on the karaoke machine and I sang *Taylor, The Latte Boy* because this is unfortunately what one does when one is a thespian. We ate slices of the chocolate pecan pie I had brought — Grandmama's decadent recipe.

The year leading up to that night had held its own intense dramas, the biggest of which was losing one of my best friends to the manipulation of an abusive husband. Ultimately, she had cut herself off from me

— from most people who loved her — to stay with a man who had done unspeakable things to her and her children. Despite every effort, every tear shed, every plea leveled, and every dollar spent to rescue her from the situation, I had lost her.

She changed her cell number and stopped responding to my emails. Even though I could see she was clearly a victim in her own right, I felt harshly betrayed. I had been gutted and hung on a hook to bleed by someone who used to buy little toys for my dog and held my hand when I cried tender tears for secret things.

The word for that year was "Grace." It kept popping up all over the place, in sermons, in Scripture, and in the themes of the plays in which I was performing. I couldn't escape it. It was as if someone had told me *not to notice the color blue* — it became all I could see for miles, the only vibrant pop in a black-and-white world. Grace, grace, grace.

Grace for myself in how I had handled things with my lost friend — and was still handling them. Grace for my friend and the unspeakable horrors she had endured; grace for how the horrors had bent her away from me and away from reason. Grace that embraces all of us, all of the time.

Grace began to have an almost physical quality, substantial enough to cast a shadow. It was sweet and crunchy in the mouth, like brown sugar. But what was grace, exactly?

In the book she wrote, in the first English sentences penned by female fingers, Julian describes "the highest prayer," which she says simply is "The Goodness of God."[43]

I see her sitting there on her little stool, clad in white linen, having just eaten an orange or something else whole and pure and perfect. Her delicate head is wrapped in a tinsel halo and her feet are clad in Birkenstocks. I lean away from this two-dimensional iconoclast and mutter to myself, *well OF COURSE a great prayer would be for an experience of God's goodness.* Isn't that what all prayers are, in some form or fashion? Do something good for me, God! Or at least show me that you wish me well, that you're predisposed to have my best interests at heart!

But then I re-read her sentence and realize she is saying the highest prayer is not praying FOR the goodness of God, but that *the Goodness of God itself is the best prayer one can pray.*

By now, little Julian is standing. She tosses her orange peels out the window, jarring me with more inscrutable statements:

*"God's goodness already envelops, surrounds and encloses us,"* she continues, *"much like the body is dressed in clothes and the flesh is dressed in skin and the bones are dressed in flesh."*[44] We are in the dead center of God's goodness already.

So, what does it mean, I ask her, that this goodness can become a prayer within me? The best of all prayers, in fact?

Because the truth is I usually come to prayer to receive something, perhaps something I deserve, or at least something I would categorize as a "good thing." I rarely come to God to uncover something already in existence that I currently possess. Prayer is mostly a request-and-receive mechanism, never a stay-and-enjoy mechanism. Julian seems to imply it can be both, but that the best prayers are those that flow from an experience of God's goodness as it is, or perhaps even that reveling in God's goodness itself for a while is the best definition of true prayer.

But how? What is the clearest expression of God's goodness I can latch onto, allow to well up, and then relish?

Julian sits back down on the stool of hers, hands in lap. She slips her unpedicured feet out of her sandals and rubs her left heel.

The clearest expression of God's goodness is His presence itself, she says finally, and it is His presence in which we are forever enclosed though we may not be aware of it.

There's a contradictory longing here, she continues, a seeking for a person we already possess, a reaching for the arms that already embrace us.

*"And thus I saw him and sought him; and I had him and I wanted him,"*[45] laughs Julian for emphasis, waving away a fly at the window. The lovely irony shouldn't be missed: even the seeking and the wanting is, in a way, its own satisfaction.

Bible-y terms like "the Goodness" of God and "The Grace" of God are so ubiquitous in Christian vernacular that it might seem like they are interchangeable, like tires being thrown on and off a racecar by a pit crew. Perhaps they are a bit interchangeable in some ways, though grace carries the extra connotation of *undeservedness*. It's Goodness-despite-me. We might feel inclined to deserve God's goodness, but never His grace.

Is God's presence, therefore, something we feel we deserve to experience, a given? Or is His presence so extraordinarily good precisely because it is totally independent of my worthiness on a particular day? Why do I deserve to have the presence of Jesus himself available to me the moment my eyes flutter open in the morning? Why should He be waiting for my attention in that way, and was that something Mrs. Center had deserved, too?

Is this kind of intimate availability something I'm automatically entitled to access — me with the frazzled sighs and impatient grumbling and ungrateful eyerolls? Me with the little-to-no faith and a chip on her shoulder?

Experiencing Jesus is the pinnacle encounter with grace, the highest good we could ever ask or attain in spite of ourselves, the most audacious privilege ever given to audaciously distracted mankind. It is the *grace that the soul seeketh, and ever shall [seek] till we know verily that he hath us all in himself beclosed,*[46] says Julian.

Jesus *is* God's goodness. And because we don't deserve Him, Jesus *is* God's grace.

The highest prayer, therefore, isn't for a good event or a good development or for a good item. The highest prayer is an encounter with Good Jesus: to enjoy Him afresh, and then to want Him anew. And then to have Him again. And then to want even more of Him, to feel ourselves ever more fully in the center of His hand.

We, the hazelnut, can pray in this way.


On New Year's Eve of 2019, I surveyed my remaining group of friends, laughing, eating, and listening. My thorn that evening was the loss of my friend, and it pricked. Hard. That evening, I couldn't imagine the months of health issues that were in store for me, the coming loss of my body, which had also been a loyal companion to me all my life.

I looked up at the mantel above the fireplace, still festive with Christmas decor, and saw the word PEACE spelled out by the letters of five stocking holders. A low note, a subwoofer vibration sounded just then, deep and resonant. It hit my stomach, my heart. This was my word for this coming year, for 2020. I knew it, and it was unsettling.

If "grace" was the word for a year of awful woundedness, what would "peace" bring? Awful turmoil? And yet, Peace was making its introduction like a friend with something weighty to put into my hands.

~~

Just being with You is the best prayer, Lord.

I dwell with you today. You are grace incarnate.

And you, Grace, hold the door open for peace.

You have already accomplished my life for me: my future glory, my present belovedness. You have achieved for me ultimate health, ultimate wholeness. I trust the work you have done on my behalf, and I trust that it will play out comprehensively someday, finally and forever.

I allow you, Grace, to work peace into my heart today.

## SERVANTS

My ten-year-old Maddie's soccer team was moving up and down the field on a cool October evening. We had plopped ourselves into collapsible chairs to watch the unofficial scrimmage with our

"THE LORD HAS MADE EVERYTHING FOR HIS PURPOSE."
– PROVERBS 16:4

favorite rival team. My parents were there, too, along with their newly adopted Cavachon, Annabelle, who began attracting toddlers. The field was enormous — not our team's standard size — and the girls were showing signs of just-trying-to-hang-in-there. It was a lot of ground to cover, back and forth, back and forth.

My parents had come to watch Maddie play, but they were also there for another reason: to help us tell the kids that I might have cancer and was about to have surgery. This was not something I was sure Gordon and I could do on our own. My dad, who had defied the odds with his lemon-gut tumor the decade before, could offer an encouraging perspective. My mom, fount of wisdom that she is, could step in with measured, comforting words. I wasn't sure how the kids would react.

The whole thing felt like a Bomb Squad mission. In my mind I could see them — Maddie and Drew standing there, offset and alone together on a dusty Middle Eastern-esque roadway — ignorant, casual; we adults standing along the periphery of the desolate scene, trying to remain quiet and bide our time. When the moment was right (how would we know it?), we would advance, covered head-to-toe in protective gear, wearing gloves and carrying tools. Our mission would require swift and delicate moves: both to cut the cord of their security and yet keep them from exploding with anxiety.

Other factors complicated our mission. For one thing, Maddie had been dealing with mysterious nausea for the past year, which we ultimately determined was probably a physical manifestation of anxiety. And who could blame her. She had been shut up at home from school, from friends, from activities, all while watching her mother take bucketful after bucketful of supplements each morning and be laid out on the couch every afternoon.

The second unfair stressor for both was the ambiguity that had also been stressing me. I "probably" had COVID, and now I was about to tell her I "probably" had Cancer? The word *probably* is just plain mean. It inflicts all the pain of "definitely" but adds another layer of shame for feeling the pain prematurely, perhaps unnecessarily.

The time became right somehow, just as dusk was falling on our back porch. We were home from the soccer game and from dinner, and the kids were jumping on the trampoline while we watched. "Hey kids, y'all come here for a minute," I called, feeling a charge of odd giddiness. Was I losing my mind?

They came, they sat, and somebody told them the situation using words I don't remember. I think my dad must have led us in a short family prayer employing the language of elementary school students. What I do remember was how Maddie and Drew shuffled their feet and squirmed in their chairs, like something was itchy under their skin. "Can we go back to the trampoline?" one of them asked.

"Um. Ok," I said.

I wasn't going to make them bathe in the tension if they didn't want to.

"If you have any questions about any of this, you know...we will tell you anything we can," one of us said. And they were off the porch fast, gone to process the concepts of thyroids and of cancer and of surgery in between each deep and stretchy landing on the trampoline's surface. Thwomp, thwomp, thwomp.

I was hurt. I would have appreciated at least a *mild* outburst if you want to know the truth. Here I had been so fearful of so many things for so many weeks, and tonight especially the *fear of their fear* had such a solemn weight to it; it felt like the moment of clipping the bomb's proverbial red cord, and then, nothing.

From a mother's perspective, it was at first hurtful and then ominous. Did this mean my kids would blow up suddenly, later? A delayed detonation when we would be least prepared?

I was bound to be afraid either way. If Maddie and Drew had cried and carried on about their mother maybe having cancer — fear. If they were stoic and wanted back on the trampoline — fear. I'm afraid of my future, but I am also afraid of my fear, and of the fear my fear creates in those I love. Back and forth, back and forth, I run from this fear and that, trying to remember the rules of the game.

By now, I've made myself a little palate on the floor of Julian's enclosure. The golden autumn light creates a shaft of dust motes between this elfish, sort-of-nun, and me. She's interested in what I might ask next, I can tell, but she's not going to be in any hurry to answer. There's some bit of dirt under her fingernails.

What about praying through thorns, I ask? The ones that drag on with no end in sight? If the highest prayer is experiencing the grace of Jesus' presence, is there no need to pray for lesser things?

She nods even as I'm speaking, anticipating the question, opening her folded hands before opening her mouth. There are six things to know, she says: three things to know about how Jesus answers our prayers and three things to know about ourselves.

Regarding the relief of thorns, Julian begins: *"For I am sure, by our Lord's meaning, that either we abide a better time, or more grace, or a better gift."*[47] I take this to mean: Jesus hears our prayers, even the most-predictable-save-me-from-trials ones, and he wants us to know that there is a *purpose* for the current pain, either that somewhere down the road is a "better time" for relief, or that we need a deeper experience of endurance that is even more valuable than relief itself but which will certainly precede it, or that we are about to be given an even greater gift than relief itself — if that can be imagined.

In any case, He hears us. He knows. And He intends to over-answer our prayers.

In fact, we are asking too little when we ask only for mere relief. We're not asking for *enough* relief, *enough* wholeness. Jesus is ordering everything on the menu, from soup to nuts, appetizers to desserts.

Julian can tell I'm skeptical. I'm ever suspicious of the "everything happens for a reason" crowd, especially those people who use this phrase on me. Isn't it more comforting to believe that sometimes things just ... happen? That accidents and illnesses are inevitable? Why does everything have to happen for a reason, and even if it does, isn't God big enough to not make the process so painful?

But there is more for Julian to say, including three things to understand about us. She can see I'm a little worried about what's coming, so she allows a wry expression, almost a grin: You need to understand and believe down to your toes, Julie, first, the profound reality of *"our noble and excellent making,"* she says; second, your *"precious and dearworthy again-buying;"* and third, that *"all thing that he hath made beneath us, he hath made to serve us, and for our love keepeth it."*[48]

I take this to mean, almost against my will, that everything happens for a reason because everything was made for a reason. You were made excellently and nobly, with dignity and purpose, and then you were preciously reclaimed by Jesus himself — "again bought." Nothing else has been reclaimed, not yet anyway, not ants, dogs, trees, or planets. Just people, the highest order of life, which every lesser order exists to serve even as we are their caretakers. Our servants are the maples that catch fire in November, the velvet sheen of a pug's coat, the orange carrots sliding up out of dirt. These are servants — or, maybe "helpers" is a better term for the modern ear — designed to support and comfort and instruct us in some profound or menial way. And we are, in turn, to serve them as caretakers.

If *all* things are helpers, then, so too are the viruses. The bacteria. The cancers.

Well, a person can sometimes have too many helpers, I tell Julian.

But then I pause. I consider her face, the craggy lines at her eyes, her bare feet on the stone floor.

When Julian was about six years old, the plague had arrived in her town of Norwich. Within a year, more than three-quarters of the population was dead.[49] In 1392, when she was about nineteen, Julian watched the plague re-ravage everything again. It is speculated that she herself could have lost a husband and a child or two during that wave.[50] Her enclosure as an anchoress didn't happen until midlife, which was probably unusual for someone who hadn't had a family.

At any rate, she describes having suicidal feelings sometime before her revelations by saying, *"I had great longing and desire of God's gift to be delivered of this world and of this life."*[51] To die would be a gift and she wanted to be next in line.

Julian had both lived through two pandemics and died through them, too, over and over as friends and family succumbed. She was just one girl amidst a helpless population that had no hope of vaccines, masks, or emergency rooms. No CDC. No sanitation. No gloves. No antibiotics.

When would the next wave strike again? Will I be next, she must have wondered. Oh please, let me be next.

Suddenly, quarantining in an enclosure doesn't seem like such a bad idea to me, but that's not why Julian the Anchoress is here. She is here, not to run from a bacterium or from further griefs but to commune with mystery, to wait quietly in a world in which these things are allowed. Despite all the horror she had endured, Julian has not come here to ask if God is good or if he has a plan. These questions never seem to enter her mind, and if they do, they did not make it into her one little book. The only question she seems obsessed with asking is how to draw nearer to reality, to Jesus, to Grace, through all things good and awful.

She leans forward towards me with great gentleness, like a mother, and only then do I realize she is speaking again. Jesus sees *"our frailty and our failings, our afflictions and...all our woe,"* she whispers. He keeps us *"as tenderly and as sweetly...as he doeth when we are in most solace and comfort."* Our thorns he will someday turn *"all to his worship and our joy, without end. For his love suffereth us never to lose time."*[52]

He sees. He comforts. He will turn all to endless joy. He wastes no time and no tears.

All things are servants.

~~~

Lord, it is so exhausting, running from fear to fear, and yet it is also so hard to stop running from the wolves, and from the wolves who chase the wolves chasing me. Being still, being quiet, feels like it might be suicidal like I'm inviting the attack.

But nothing can assault *You*. Nothing can come up past Your knee, and I am in Your arms. Your steady presence, Your eternal goodness, and Your forever love are safe.

Let me trust Your reasons and Your timing and Your tools.

## WATERS

Dr. D was a big, vaguely eastern-European specimen with long flowing locks of curly black hair. A bib of gold necklaces fancified his blue scrubs. A black mask covered what I assumed to be a chiseled face, based on his picture from the website. I texted all my friends with snapshots of said picture and they (and I) immediately began referring to him as Dr. Fabio. I had mixed feelings about being operated on by a man who could grace the cover of a romance novel. Shouldn't surgeons be a little more unattractive?

"BUT NOW, THIS IS WHAT THE LORD SAYS—
HE WHO CREATED YOU, JACOB,
HE WHO FORMED YOU, ISRAEL:
'DO NOT FEAR, FOR I HAVE REDEEMED YOU;
I HAVE SUMMONED YOU BY NAME; YOU ARE MINE.
WHEN YOU PASS THROUGH THE WATERS,
I WILL BE WITH YOU.'"
– ISAIAH 43:1-4

The exam room was smallish. Dr. D towered over me to inspect my thyroid and the dimensions of my larynx and throat musculature. A long scope was fed up through my left nostril and swallowed down almost to my stomach, which would have been less horrible if Dr. D had looked more Gollum-esque. I told Dr. D my story of ongoing fevers and exhaustion post- probably-Covid — my dilemma — and he agreed to wait a total of six weeks to see if I improved before taking out the thyroid.

Another fear was niggling, too. It had been distant and kept to the periphery, but now that I was in an actual surgeon's office and meeting the man who would slice open my throat with a scalpel, the fear took center stage for its big number.

"Anybody who tells you that the risk of vocal cord damage is zero is lying to you," Dr. D had said.

The inferior laryngeal nerve (RLN) runs right next to the thyroid and straight into the larynx, providing all the necessary innervation for the muscles of the voice box. If the nerve is cut or agitated or damaged, one or both sides of the larynx become paralyzed, either temporarily or permanently, in which case you either lose your ability to produce sound altogether or your voice becomes quiet, weak, and lacks range of pitch.

"Even if we bother that nerve a little, you will still have an OK voice," he reassured me, trying to be comforting. I wanted to punch his stupid Fabio-face.

AN "OK" VOICE?

He went on to explain that the size and location of the thyroid nodules did not seem to impact vocal cord outcomes. He had seen women with huge goiters emerge with their voices still intact, and women with tiny little nodules come out of surgery whispering forever. I had two roughly 1.5 cm growths on the right side of my thyroid. There was no way to predict my outcome, but he assured me that he would use a nerve-monitoring device that would sound an alarm if he got too close. The plan was to take my entire thyroid out altogether. And really, the odds were very much in my favor.

This was exactly 100 percent unhelpful to my quivery, shivery heart. I had already defied the so-called odds in some upside-down ways: getting sick in the first place with something that nobody could definitively diagnose, and now probably having fluke cancer for which I had no family history. I was the Bad Luck Lady, and if there was even a smallish chance of vocal cord damage, my chances seemed inevitably 100 percent.

I can tell Julian wants to back up a bit. By now dusk is settling down hard and the shaft of light streaking in is dying like a failing flashlight. I've pushed her far and fast about praying through unfixable things and she wants to talk more about prayer in a general way. A candle is suddenly lit, then two, then three.

Ok, fine. Prayer in general. Go.

Once again, there are three things to know, she says, holding up three fingers.

One: Jesus is the Ground of our prayer.

Two: Prayer should be used to align our will with God's.

Three: the ultimate purpose of prayer is to unite us to Jesus himself.

Oh, it's that simple, I say.

But Julian is adamant I sit here and take it.

Number One: Jesus had told her, *"I am the Ground"* of all your prayers. He is *"the Ground on whom our prayer springeth."*[53] I notice a little pot on her windowsill just then, only because she's bringing it into her lap now, and I perceive a small green shoot of something beginning to emerge. The green is the prayer, and the dirt is Jesus. The impulse to pray, to open ourselves to God in the first place, is a divine quickening.

*"God is nearer to us than our own Soul: for he is [the] Ground in whom our Soul standeth,"*[54] she continues. All spiritual stirrings, growth, and flourishing come up out of God, working deep within the molecules of our invisible self. Prayer is a gift, in a sense, not a natural impulse we gin up and propagate.

What difference does this make, I ask? But then I see the little sprout, the way it's arching up toward the ceiling. It wasn't planted to die. It was planted on purpose. Our prayerful attention to God will have its full effect because God himself is the originator of it, and nothing he does fails. If you're reaching out to God, he's already been reaching for you. You will connect with him because God doesn't start an organic process he won't see through to blooming.

On December 1st, the day before surgery, I recorded a little voice memo of me singing one of my favorite songs from all of Broadway: "They Were You" from *The Fantastiks*. Someday years from now, I could push play for my grandkids and show them that there was a time long ago when I could have sung them lullabies.

I wondered if theater people in the Dallas/Fort Worth industry would notice if I stopped coming to auditions. I wondered how it would feel to watch a cast of *Les Misérables* sing *One Day More* from the mezzanine. I wondered if I would feel like a stranger to myself, unable to interact with the world in the arena of service where I had been at home for so long. Who would I be then?

But there were other risks with surgery.

Because my endocrinologist and dentist had both observed I now seemed to be bruising and bleeding easily, Dr. D was having me evaluated by an Immunologist and a Hematologist. That plus the other COVISH symptoms bothered him.

Dr. S, the Immunologist, was the first specimen of this sort I had ever seen. After visits with the Infectious Disease doc, Cardiologist, and Pulmonologist, I had become familiar with the magazine selection of every waiting room within the hospital district of mid-Fort Worth and braced myself for a new collection of waiting room chairs and collages of what was meant to be inspirational wall art. Had I been a Sick Person Boy Scout, I would have had quite a grid of merit badges emblazoned across my chest, one for every specialist and the specialist's particular office regalia. Well, Dr. S didn't have any good waiting room magazines. Or posters. She did have a movie playing that starred that short and beautiful *Game of Thrones* actress Emilia-something.

After doing an exam and breathing evaluation, Dr. S said she would test me for all the usual suspects again — autoimmune diseases, HIV — plus a host of other immune deficiencies and allergies. I could sense she was just covering her bases out of due diligence.

Dr. S, who was a lady about my age and of Indian descent, sat comfortably atop her rolling chair, casual. She didn't seem the type to have a niche ringtone. She struck me as more of a texter who keeps her phone on silent. Like me. With the directness of a friend who isn't afraid to tell you things plainly, she leaned in. "I believe you had Covid, and that you are just very gradually recovering."

SHE THINKS I HAD COVID! I rejoiced via texts to my friends in my car afterward. Validation was sweet and sure, even if it was late and useless.

My next stop was Dr. M.

The very word *HEMATOLOGIST* sounded dire, vaguely conjuring leeches.

Dr. M's waiting room was perhaps the most difficult room in which to wait for anything at all. Nary a magazine or movie in sight. Nary an inspirational poster. I clucked my tongue like a restaurant critic. It seemed the more specialized you were as a physician, the less charming your waiting room.

A fake fireplace was shoved up against the far wall and had an uncentered tryptic of painted panels above it. Could the fireplace be scooted ever so slightly to the right? I dug my fingernails into my palms and sighed the sigh of a person who knows what the standards are.

Mercifully, a large, curly-haired nurse soon led me back to a lab area where Dr. M's team did a few rather medieval procedures on me, one of which was a bleeding test to see how long it took for my blood to coagulate. With brows furrowed, the nurse punched a tiny razor blade into my forearm and watched the clock, methodically dabbing my blood onto a piece of white paper until it finally congealed and stopped. We both stared down at the centimeter line of bright red, that, had it only been made bigger and broader, could drain away my life. This all seemed, shall we say, rather *old school*.

What was *really* old school, it turned out, was Dr. M herself, who could not have been one day younger than eighty-five years old. "We will test you for some rare genetic disorders," she declared from the seat next to me in the exam room, as though we were both waiting for a bus. "But your blood count and clotting appear within the normal range, at least today." This held a veiled implication of more tiny razor blades in my future.

At my follow-up appointments with both Dr. S and Dr. M, the verdict seemed to be a resounding *shrug of the shoulders*. The two doctors could have been standing side by side in a mini chorus line, center stage, wearing their white bedazzled lab coats, singing in unison with jazz hands splayed open:

*We don't know why you have your symptoms!*

*But you appear healthy enough for surgery!*

*We are signing off for Dr. D!*

Blackout. Curtain. Scattered applause.

The last two barriers to surgery were down. Now the whole thing was imminent. A total of four specialists were now saying, at the very least, that surgery wouldn't be a problem, and at the very most, that surgery was crucial. This was *happening*. There was no escaping.

I couldn't possibly disqualify myself any longer, as much as I had tried — not with COVID, not with a shadowy bleeding disorder, not with my vocal and career concerns, not with anything. There was no other loophole to explore or delay to milk. I could only look ahead to the inevitable, towards the parted sea and the shoreline beyond. And this is the complication of thorns, that they do not lift in time for you to deal with other, newer thorns. They compel you to move forward, to take steps through the mire in a straight-ahead line, to bear down upon whatever new land awaits on the other side of the waters.

The plant had been returned to its spot in the window. Jesus is the Ground of my prayer, I repeat, and Julian nods. My prayer is a response to his quickening within me. My prayer will reach him because he has given it life in the first place.

Number Two, says Julian, moving on. You need to understand, Julie, that our intention when we pray should be that *"our will be turned unto the will of our Lord, enjoying."*[55] Oh here we go again, I'm thinking, talking about God's Will with a capital W.

Julian nods, smiling broadly like I'm about to trip backward into a pool of shiny chocolate. Jesus wants colleagues, she is saying, colleagues who understand there is great beauty afoot in the world and who are willing to enter it willingly and participate fully. *"For he beholdeth us in love and would make us partners of his good deed, and therefore he stirreth us to prayer for that which it liketh him to do."*[56]

Good prayer always lifts us up and out of our own personal agendas and connects us to the greater narrative, His Will, which can be an *enjoyable* experience. Such a pleasant relief, really, to join up with a bigger context. And then to find ourselves *beheld in love*, a precious, seen part of that great and beautiful whole.

Even praying to *want* to want God's will is a gorgeous example of the prayer being answered in real-time, Julian observes. *"For I am sure,"* she continues, *"that no man asketh mercy and grace with true meaning, but if mercy and grace be first given to him."*[57] This is a bit comforting to me because I am still very suspicious of the pain that seems necessary to access that greater beauty. I'm not entirely sure this is good news.

Now Julian is standing, towering over me despite her small stature, and I see that she has saved the best for last.

Number Three, she says, and she's not holding up her third finger, but opening her arms wide as though she's about to break through Finish Line tape. Number Three: the ultimate purpose of prayer is to unite us to Jesus himself. *"But when our courteous Lord of his grace sheweth himself to our soul, we have that [which] we desire...And this is an high unperceivable prayer, as to my sight: for all the cause wherefor we pray, it is oned into the sight and beholding of him to whom we pray."*[58]

Our greatest desire is to be *"oned"* with Jesus, and all prayers are streams that feed into that river. All of life, all of prayer, she is saying, is a *"coming into him...until we shall die in longing, for love. And then shall we all come into our Lord, our Self clearly knowing, and God fully having."*[59]

Prayer, then, is not merely a foretaste of heaven, of the final and bliss-drenched union with the object of all our longing, but an actual experience of eternal life in the here and now. It's bringing a bit of the actual future into the actual present. We will be fully united with Jesus someday, but in a sense, we don't have to wait. The union can begin today, even through walls of water, even while stumbling towards foreign shores.

Even while all we are is under threat.

~~~

God of straight-lines-through-trouble, be near. You *are* near. Let *me* draw near to *You*.

You clear the path for my journey, even the paths through fire and water, and shadow. You lead me through these things, not around these things. Why is that?

Lord, You made me first, and then You redeemed me. I'm Yours twice. If you went to the trouble of inventing my personhood — my personality, heart, soul, abilities, essence — and then buying it all back for glory and permanence, will You really let this thorn wash me away here and now? Will You really leave me to drown?

## BULLHEADED

We have what the State Farm commercials might call a "she shed" in our backyard, except it's not nearly as wry and adorable as it sounds. It was home to a small nation of spiders for the many years it served

"REJOICE ALWAYS, PRAY CONTINUALLY, GIVE THANKS IN ALL CIRCUMSTANCES; FOR THIS IS GOD'S WILL FOR YOU IN CHRIST JESUS."
– 1 THESSALONIANS 5:16-18

as a dumping ground for suitcases, rugs, Christmas lights, bikes, hoses, pillows, cots, old ceiling fans, and costumes. For most of that time, we called it the "guest house," but only Kathy Bates from *Misery* would host a guest out there. In addition to the arachnids, a family of raccoons lived underneath the guest house. The mother and her three babies held aggressive little rodent squabbles that you could hear from our back porch at night.

We began officially calling our guest house the "she shed" when, in the fall of 2020, right before my surgery and possible cancer battle, while in the middle of Covid-symptom-whack-a-mole and extreme dietary upheavals and supplement regimens, I converted it into a studio for auditions. Out came the old couch my infant babies had stained with their spit-up; out came the old headboard from the first bed Gordon and I had bought for our first apartment; out came the side tables that matched said bed but now had coffee rings and scratches; out came the boogie boards and Little Tykes golf clubs and real, grown-up golf clubs and boxes of books.

We held an ill-fated garage sale on a chilly Saturday morning that no one attended. We sat in fold-out chairs, masks on, freezing and alone amongst the detritus of our lives. We ended up paying a junk hauling service $400 to pick everything up and take it away, which meant we were still in the hole about $360 after the paltry sales we had made that morning.

I threw myself into cleaning the empty space that was left behind. Despite my fever and diminished lung capacity, the extreme diet and supplements were beginning to improve my energy, and the beta-blockers were keeping my heart in check. I managed to mop the whole floor and dust the slats of the windows' big plantation shutters.

At the last minute, I had Gordon pull a rug back from the garage sale, the red one I had bought when Maddie was a baby. Down it went to anchor the space. Then I set up my backdrop for taping and covered the windows behind it with the classiest possible aluminum foil to shut out the light. I would soon find a dark blue chair for the corner and a cool floor lamp to arch over it, along with a woven ottoman on which to prop my feet.

This vignette was now a *nook* for *studying lines*. I bought big box lights to illuminate the backdrop. I brought in my dusty ring light that had been languishing for months in the living room. After about a week of setting up, shopping and decorating, huffing, and puffing and dragging myself around like the corpse from *Weekend with Bernie*, I was officially open for business. I couldn't begin to guess what Spider Nation's foreign policy was on all of this.

So much had been changing in the theater world during the pandemic. What shows were being produced were all auditioning online now, as were Film/TV projects. I was trying to adapt.

If I was honest, the whole she shed endeavor *should* have felt like measuring the width and breadth in cubits for an ark that wouldn't be used for decades, if at all. So much loomed in front of me — and was looming within me — that to put effort into my career at a time like this was just more futile denial. Yet there was an engine in my core, like a boiler room in the hull of a steam liner (Titanic?), chugging out all kinds of power forward.

I joined a couple of online actor databases where I could make myself available for a wider pool of projects beyond the local Dallas/Fort Worth theater scene. I would be able to upload my headshots, give my measurements (have mercy), and list all my credits to date. I could peruse projects shooting in Dallas and Austin and apply to whatever looked good. I didn't care about pay when it came to the TV/Film world, in which I was basically still a first grader, having given the past decade to live theater. I just wanted experience and was even prepared to be a good sport about *student films.*

I auditioned for a cute team at the University of Texas who were making a rom-com. I auditioned for a proof-of-concept thriller that was like a dark twist on *Multiplicity* with Michael Keaton. One day, I found an online play being produced in New York City in which the main character's name was Julie. This was literally why I applied, *because my name is Julie,* and it turns out the producers also believed I had a certain Julie quality.

I submitted an initial Zoom audition, which was followed by a two-hour Zoom callback. This involved me re-enacting a scene where my character is sexually assaulted in an elevator. This all transpired on Halloween evening, so I figured if people heard screaming coming from the inside of the spidery she-shed, they wouldn't worry too much about it. My temperature spiked over one hundred when I was finished, and I was shaking.

Was I just being bullheaded? Wasn't I just doing all I knew to do to "be faithful" to my calling as an actor, as an artist with stories to embody for the relief of others and for myself? Yes. Yes, and sort of.

There was also a sneaky whiff of something like this: if I could book a string of projects, one after the other, then God would see I was simply too busy and important to be sick. Maybe God could be shown a proof-of-concept *life* and realize my proposal was much more aesthetically pleasing and eternally productive than the course we were presently taking. He should be made to look my potential in the face before he washed it away with the tide.


But Julian, I say, and my courage is building from a place of confident frustration, I don't usually *feel* like praying. I'm too tired. Too sad and sore. These are high and lofty ideals for prayer — to align with God's will, to unify with Jesus — but most days I just feel like moaning and fixing things myself.

I don't feel His presence. I can't see Him or touch Him or taste Him or smell Him. If He's the Ground of my prayer, shouldn't He be doing a better job, frankly, of keeping me engaged?

Oh, she just loves me, I can tell. She's placing a little clay cup into my hands and is telling me to drink, and I sip at the cup sporadically and shift my legs so my right foot will wake up. Her eyes are soft and bright, like an otter's.

"*Pray inwardly,*" she begins, "*Though thee thinketh it savour thee not: for it is profitable, though thou feel not, though thou see nought; yea, though thou think thou canst not. For in dryness and in barrenness, in sickness and in feebleness, then is thy prayer well-pleasant to [Jesus], though thee thinketh it savour thee nought but little.*"60

Prayer is profitable even in sickness and feebleness.

Now she's handing me one of her oranges and I'm taking the first perfect bite of a wedge, spurting juice across the room.

"I get the metaphor," I say. "I can't always savor my prayer time like I savor this orange or this cup of cold water."

Exactly, she replies, but notes this doesn't have to be problematic, for *"God accepteth the goodwill and the travail of His servant, howsoever we feel."*

But Julian, I say, I thought the highest prayer was a personal experience of Jesus. If I can't feel any progress towards that intimacy, what's the point? I thought prayer was supposed to bring some measure of peace.

She hands me another orange wedge. The wedge is like small slice of sun which would have been vibrant in the daylight. Here in the dark meld of shadows, its glory is tempered by the warmth of candle glow. Evening has descended without me noticing.

Sometimes prayer does bring peace. But sometimes prayer is labor, a certain dogged persistence. *"It pleaseth Him that we work,"* Julian continues, *"Both in our prayers and in good living, by His help and His grace, reasonably with discretion keeping our powers [turned] to Him, till when that we have Him that we seek, in fulness of joy: that is, Jesus."*61

Sometimes our simple commitment to push forward into God past feeling and experience is the only prayer available to us, and this is not something to despise. It's very practical and honest. Don't feel Him? Join the club but keep on praying. *"And for profit of man's soul, a man is sometime left to himself,"* shrugs Julian.

For some reason, it's occasionally good for us — and pleasing to God — that we bullheadedly exercise faith muscles against the resistance of weariness or apathy or the worst feeling of all, his absence. The bite of fruity flesh will explode all the better for it someday, joy made full.

The grace of Jesus' presence doesn't always feel like grace. Or even presence at all. And this doesn't have to mean we're doing something wrong.

I imagine that ten thousand years ago, cavepeople re-enacted their hunting expeditions around campfires every night. With great flourish, the fathers threw buffalo-shaped shadows onto the dripping cavern walls, drawing out laughter from the little ones and eyerolls from the mothers. Then the mothers got up and re-enacted the snorts of the wildebeests that had been shooed away from the grains that morning. More guffaws.

People have always been hungry for dinner, yes, but they have also always been hungrier for story. And ten thousand years from now, humans will still be acting out scenarios in front of other human beings to connect over real and immediate sustenance in whatever theaters will have become by then — maybe with hologram technology and time travel elements. One thing Covid taught theater people is that the show must truly still go on, if not for the world's sake, then for ours.

A couple weeks before my surgery, I was invited to watch a Zoom reading of a play written by a colleague and friend at a theater where I had worked. The actors joined the call just like us audience members and then someone took all our little boxes away so we could watch them making a story together even while separated by thousands of miles. What struck me was how immediately real the whole thing seemed.

Even without costumes or sets or staging, even without physical proximity, there was something intimate and honest about these people — who were obviously excellent actors — in the way they connected to each other. The anger was real. The fear. The flirting. It almost felt like eavesdropping, which I think is one of the most generous illusions an actor can give an audience.

What we were sharing, despite the mind-blowing technology that lets us talk face-to-face with someone who is on the other side of the world, was a common experience of story in its most basic format, without decoration. Zoom had returned us to the dancing cave silhouettes.

And what we all want, I think, is not just story itself, but a *simple* story. Where there is a hunger for understanding, a storyline must be laid over the mess like a grid so we can see the spatial relationships between everything and possibly even make out a trajectory. We like point A to point B to Happy Ending. But art can only point to possible meaning, not promise it.

There's a hunger for the solace that comes with this certainty, and maybe therefore we prefer certain art because it mirrors the certainty that we all secretly believe must exist: that things are heading in a straight line to a definite conclusion, and that the ending is a good and satisfying one — not only for us and our little stories, but for the whole of everything and everyone we see. Does hunger prove that food exists? Does hope prove heaven?

Making art. Writing plays. Straining to see the pattern. These are also forms of bullheaded faith in the presence of darkness and the absence of trajectory.

I was called to the set in the late afternoon of November 16, 2020. The year prior, I had been cast in a scrappy thriller series in development that was shooting in Dallas/Fort Worth. The show hadn't been picked up or sold yet. It was a concept for which a trailer must be shot and scripts written in order to convince a major streaming network it was worth giving us $20 million and agree to air it. No small feat.

I was playing an abused wife and mother who must stealthily find a way to escape the clutches of her dangerous husband, protect her daughter's life, and perhaps solve a series of violent murders. (Observation: People on TV typically have worse thorns than the rest of us.) The scene we were slated to shoot was a hostage scenario where my "husband" would be holding my "daughter" and me at gunpoint, with the police just beyond the door. At the scene's climax, the detective would burst into the room with her Glock 19 drawn, screaming.

The assistant director went around to the actors showing us the guns, and opening their chambers to display their lack of bullets. When we had all acknowledged the guns were unloaded and ostensibly safe, it became time to pretend that they *were imminently lethal.* This was not hard. It is not difficult to act afraid when you have two real guns pointed at you at once and both people holding the guns are losing their tempers.

But still. It *was* fake. I knew this. I could see the camera lens glinting four feet away, and the guy with the red beard holding the fuzzy boom mic above our heads.

I could also sense the fake bruises on my arms and chest. They looked realer than real, but I had seen them scrupulously applied with a soft, feathery brush. I could see the tears streaming down my "daughter's" face, which was real in a sense — they were bonafide biological tears — but from a manufactured source. Real, though fake. Fake, though real. Fakery can indeed promote fear, which is quite helpful for an actor doing actorly things.

In real life, not so much.

I was carrying a real to life fear to the set that day but trying to fake that I wasn't. I was staring down a major surgery in three weeks which could damage my vocal cords, exacerbate my ongoing, now seven-month-long Covid symptoms, and result in months of radiation or worse. And yet, most of this was still incognito from my professional circles, kept close to my chest underneath my social media armor. My biopsy bruise had healed enough not to show up on camera. I came to set that day cheerful, ready to work, trying to look like I felt great.

My ebullience wasn't total fakery, but that didn't mean there wasn't a dark river running underneath my skin and flooding my thoughts about what a Trojan horse I had become. Here I was, perhaps about to be made unusable in just a matter of weeks and yet I was presenting myself as a good long-term investment, a team player. Because what if everything went OK? There was a chance it could all be fine — I could be *just fine* — and this was enough to justify the silence.

While I was afraid of letting the project down in the future, I was even more afraid of prematurely losing work now, of making kryptonite of my reputation if I came clean about all I was facing and enduring. I weighed these fears, weighed the cost of fakery, and found myself on set that day in the late afternoon, staring down the barrel of a gun.

The worst specter before me, however, wasn't the immediate fear of losing my part in the show. It was an image I had in my mind of the she-shed shriveling into something dry and dark and stuffy, collapsing back into itself, becoming once again an arena of cobwebs and useless old equipment.

I couldn't bear the thought of this, of stepping away from the light and into the shadow of the cave walls where all the stories are told.

The time is drawing close for me to leave. Julian would never evict me, but things are cramped, and the air is heavy with something indecipherable. But Julian is not going to let me go without this last thought, and I see she is trying to send me out into the night with something like an inner candle. *"And also to prayer belongeth thanking,"*[62] she says.

Thanking.

And what lever does thankfulness pull? I ask because I know she will tell me anyway.

*"Thanking is a true inward knowing,"* Julian continues — a real knowing of Jesus himself. To know Jesus is to thank him. And to thank him is to know him better. But this requires effort, too, something we must sometimes attempt *"with all our mights."*[63]

It could even be necessary to desperately *"rehearse [Jesus'] blessed Passion and great Goodness"* in order to re-ignite our hearts. There's a discipline in this, she's implying, something we do even if we feel blank, like a blinking cursor on an empty page. There's a sense in which we must take ourselves by the shoulders and remind ourselves, in specific ways, of our staggering belovedness in Him.

Persistence past feelings. Thankfulness past fears. These are the sometimes arduous, strenuous ways we can know Him, if not in the present moment, in preparation for a future encounter. It's good to take the desolate road if it's the only one you see.

Oh Lord, I don't owe the world a fake face. Give me the courage to acknowledge my fears, to own them, and to offer them in service in appropriate ways.

I bullheadedly seek You today, even when I can't feel You. The more I have of You, the more I can access the completeness I already have, and the more I can see and possess what is already mine.

I also thank You today, even though I'm scared.

## BLOOD

"Mom, you need to take Dad to the ER," we said. All of us McQuitty siblings were gathered around an iPhone at an outdoor table at a gelato place. It was the week of Thanksgiving 2020, five days before my surgery. Everyone was

"I WANT TO KNOW CHRIST—YES, TO KNOW THE POWER OF HIS RESURRECTION AND PARTICIPATION IN HIS SUFFERINGS, BECOMING LIKE HIM IN HIS DEATH,[11] AND SO, SOMEHOW, ATTAINING TO THE RESURRECTION FROM THE DEAD."
– PHILIPPIANS 3:10-11

now staying at our home since Covid had invaded my parents' house — nine people including in-laws and kids, sleeping on couches and cots everywhere, including the she-shed — swiftly upending the holiday plans.

Dad had been coughing. A lot. To the point, he really couldn't talk very well. His oxygen levels were also dropping, now at 89%. He had been isolated in his office, where mom would bring him plates of food. She would test positive for COVID a week or so later. Pre-vaccine, every Covid diagnosis came with a built-in black raven perched on your shoulder.

My sister-in-law, Katy, who is an intensive care nurse, had been seeing her share of Covid deaths among people who had waited too long to get to the hospital. We relied on her to throw the whole weight of her training and experience across town to catapult my parents to the Emergency Room. "Alice," she said to my mom via Facetime, all of our nodding heads behind her, "I think you should go."

Perhaps the scariest thing was that Dad actually agreed. He would only go if *he* were scared, as Dad is the sort who toughs things out as he did as a fifteen-year-old when the tip of his index finger was swiftly amputated by a whirring motorcycle chain. He had very calmly entered the house, the tip of his drippy red finger perched on a stick, to inform his parents that perhaps something should be done about this interesting development.

We ended the Facetime call and looked around at each other. This was probably the first time all the McQuitty siblings had been gathered without my parents present. Not in almost forty years had Julie, Elizabeth, Bonnie, Jonathan, and Jeff existed as a separate unit apart from our mother and father; yet here we were, a unique council of now-grown adults with a shared past and a newly emerging culture all our own. We looked around at each other like a team of people who had never seen themselves as a team before. Was I the coach?

The grim thought seized me that maybe this was why we were all together right now. Maybe mom was about to lose dad and would need us all close by, huddled over her. Maybe the timing had been orchestrated. How could we possibly do this? How could I? Even at my strongest and sturdiest, losing my dad would flatten me.

Dad had survived an unsurvivable cancer diagnosis for which multiple surgeries and months of chemo and the full brunt of thousands of prayers had been thrown. He had overcome a tumor you could hold in the palm of your hand, and now he was going to succumb to a microscopic virus? I hadn't even hugged him in six months. Would Zoom be how we said goodbye?

The week ahead looked like a colonnade in pre-eruption Pompeii, ready for a rush of rock and fire.

At the beginning of *Revelations of Divine Love*, Julian describes the first vision she saw during her illness. Suddenly, the crucifix that had been placed at the end of her bed began to bleed. Torrents of blood poured out and over everything, perhaps all over her bedspread and floor, but she couldn't tear her eyes away from the cross itself. The blood flowed *"hot and fresh and right plenteously"*[64] down from the thorns that ringed Jesus' head. It was suffering, liquified, and overflowing with pulpy excess.

In a later "shewing," Jesus said something surprising to Julian about the vision. Almost as though taking her face in his hands and whispering with all the tenderness of a thousand mothers, he said: *"It is a joy, a bliss, and endless liking to me that ever suffered I passion for thee; if I might suffer more, I would suffer more."*[65]

Perhaps this reminded Julian of pains in childbirth, of her own rushing blood and the burning and the constant crush, and of the glorious triumph of that first infant wail. Perhaps she had seen beloved friends die on their birthing beds surrounded by sheets saturated in red, their bodies still and white while their infants wailed in the arms of other people.

*"Our Saviour is our Very Mother in whom we be endlessly borne, and never shall come out,"*[66] Julian writes of Jesus. He is many things to us, as she will write later, but perhaps most of all he is the matriarch, one who delivers us painfully into true humanity. The cross turned on its back, becomes a cosmic birthing bed. And the pain he suffered *"seemeth him but little in comparison with his love."*[67] And he — she — would suffer more for us if she could.

The question in December of 2020 was: would she suffer the loss of my dad with me? Would she lie down next to me on the sunroom couch and shake with my fever? She bore my cross but does she also bear my Covid?

With that gentle insistence of hers, Julian might say that we must understand our own suffering cannot be the result of our Mother's indifference towards us. And our suffering cannot be her punishment, for she has taken the punishment and would take more if she could. Our suffering cannot mean she is powerless, because why suffer so much only to bring stillborn babies into the world? As we watch Mother Jesus suffering for us, there are ways not to interpret our own pain.[68]

But that is Julian's next point: we do not simply watch Mother Jesus suffer. Julian understood that *"we be now...in his Cross with him in our pains,"* and therefore we suffer with him together. We suffer with him, not because our suffering helps deliver us in any way — that's his labor alone — but because *"for this little pain that we suffer here, we shall have and high endless knowing in God which we might never have without that."*[69]

Our sufferings, in other feebler words, can piggyback on the sufferings of Jesus. Our sicknesses, our views from hospital windows, our despair when dusk falls pink behind the winter branches — all of this can be piled on the cross. And somehow, these sufferings, when joined with his, can result in greater, more mysterious joy for us and deeper knowing of God than if we had never borne them. There is something on ahead of us that will make all we have endured worth every drop of blood and tears.

*"For the soul that beholdeth it thus, when it is touched by grace, it shall verily see that the pains of Christ's Passion pass all pains: all our pains that is to say, which shall be turned into everlasting, surpassing joys by the virtue of Christ's Passion."*

If Jesus' pain was the pinnacle of pain-made-profitable, then we can know that for ours too he *"shall make well all that is less."*[70] Our victory is caught up in his, our relief part of his own great relief. Our consecrated suffering will receive an in-kind resurrection.

Whatever that means.

Specifics are shrouded.

Nothing seems worth the present crisis.

Sigh.

But this much seems certain: if prayer is meant for encountering Jesus, then almost nothing could be more intimate than bleeding together with him.


In the month that followed that gloomy December of 2020, two of my good friends would lose their fathers to COVID. I would not be one of them, thank God. I would make casseroles for one friend, and send helpless, heartbroken text messages to the other. What had become a thorn for me was turning into an axe for so many others.

You never knew who would be next. You held your breath at every ding of your phone.

Mama. Jesus. Help.

There are no words for the terror or for the pain.

The pain is making me bleed out.

Mingle my blood with yours as it runs down over everything. The red of mine matches the red of yours.


**FEAST**

Countdown to surgery: three days.

My friend Karen was hosting a prayer time at her house for me with several close friends and family. With thoughtful attention, she laid out gluten-free crackers with hummus and veggies and other delicacies that my diet would allow. The air was chilly and stealthy, creeping up open

"THE MASTER, JESUS, ON THE NIGHT OF HIS BETRAYAL, TOOK BREAD. HAVING GIVEN THANKS, HE BROKE IT AND SAID,

'THIS IS MY BODY, BROKEN FOR YOU. DO THIS TO REMEMBER ME.'

AFTER SUPPER, HE DID THE SAME THING WITH THE CUP:

'THIS CUP IS MY BLOOD, MY NEW COVENANT WITH YOU. EACH TIME YOU DRINK THIS CUP, REMEMBER ME.' WHAT YOU MUST SOLEMNLY REALIZE IS THAT EVERY TIME YOU EAT THIS BREAD AND EVERY TIME YOU DRINK THIS CUP, YOU REENACT IN YOUR WORDS AND ACTIONS THE DEATH OF THE MASTER."

– 1 CORINTHIANS 11:24-26

pant legs and
slithering down spines. Since it was the week of Thanksgiving, my sisters-in-law were there — Andie and Katy, whom I was hosting along with the rest of the McQuitty siblings while my parents fought Covid across town — and so were Schuyler, Lisa, and Alison.

Everybody asked me questions about what made me afraid, about what was going to happen in the operating room, and about when I would know my diagnosis or what the state of my voice might be. I shared what I could, holding court at the head of the table like Queen Elizabeth and memorizing the way their soft, open faces were illuminated by the porch light. They were regal, too, each in her own way; they sat there like a counsel of empresses in league to defy a common enemy.

In 2019, I was cast in a play called *Babette's Feast*, which was based on a short story by the same name by Isak Dinesen. The play is set in a small village in 19th century Denmark, where two spinster sisters, Philippa and Martine, serve their pious community in the years following their minister-father's death. With scrupulous attention to asceticism and self-denial, the sisters set about to live as righteously and temperately as possible while trying to heal the ill-will and divisions within their aging congregation.

One stormy night, their lives change forever when a desperate French refugee shows up on their doorstep with a letter of introduction from an old friend. Out of compassion, Martine and Philippa take the stranger in. Her name is Babette. For the next fourteen years, Babette serves as cook and housekeeper to the two sisters.

When she suddenly discovers she has a winning lottery ticket (a friend from Paris has been renewing it annually on her behalf), Babette declares she wants to use her winnings to cook a sumptuous meal for the village that for so long has been subsisting on a bland diet of cod. Over a period of weeks, the villagers observe suspicious crates full of ominous, exotic-looking ingredients being delivered to the sisters' home (is that a *turtle?*). When the night of the feast finally arrives, the villagers make a pact that no matter how delectable the food and drink might be, they will refuse to savor it and will remain silent as they eat so as not to put their souls in peril. Meaning Babette's Feast will be consumed politely but with as little enjoyment as possible.

This proves impossible, for it turns out Babette was once the head chef at a famous Parisian restaurant in her former life. Crusty bread, savory turtle soup, and the finest French wine gradually break down the resistance among the guests, like butter melting in a dish.

In our production of the play, when a tray of fresh grapes is brought out and set in the middle of the table at the very end of the meal, the villagers can't help but smile and giggle as the purple flesh explodes in their mouths. Something about the perfection of a simple grape crushed between molars was enough to break the last wall of resistance.

We held hands. We softened our irritable hearts. We had eaten our fill and were more human now.

Like any good Evangelical child, I was raised on monthly celebrations of The Lord's Supper in church services, never weekly and certainly never daily celebrations like my high-churchy friends. Communion was always a special occasion, the great round silver trays bobbing their way down the pew like gondolas on a canal, me vying for the plastic cup in the very center of the tray. It was the middle of the flower, the bullseye of the universe.

There was something special about that center cup, and if you took it the rest of the tray remained balanced.

This is his blood, shed for you. Do this in remembrance of me.

As the preacher instructed us, each person took a cup, threw it back, swallowed, then neatly stacked the little plastic thimbles one on top of another and placed the mini plastic towers carefully into the round-holed receptacles screwed into the back of each pew for that purpose. We sat in rows, like corn, lines of Sunday-dressed people quiet and attentive at eleven in the morning doing the one ritual that Bible church people still embrace from the old world of Julian and Augustine and Ignatius. We were not seated at tables on the floor, not laughing at stories or at lighthearted jabs, not refilling plates with hungry enthusiasm.

Our scene was very different from the one in which Jesus had initiated his sacrament, him glancing over the orange flames of lamps at his friends who were both hungry and thirsty, and who had no idea what was about to happen. They were his family and families remember your stories and your sacrifices. Families are most themselves, for good or bad, as they share a meal together.

If Jesus is our Mother who gives birth to us painfully and triumphally in a rush of blood and suffering, as Julian says, she is also the Mother who sustains us, feeding us with herself *full tenderly.*

Our little anchoress is referring now to the sacrament of Jesus' body and blood which she calls *precious food of very life,* an ever-available sustenance for hungry infant souls. Jesus' body is bread, his blood wine, and we are ever being sustained by their giving for us.

But how do we feed ourselves with these things, and how does this relate to prayer?

Where two or three are gathered, a feast can be celebrated, a grace can materialize and be ingested. We feed on Jesus as we prayerfully engage the eucharist, yes, but perhaps we also feed on him as we engage our brothers and sisters around tables of community, mutually bearing burdens. We feed on him as we feed each other. The grace of Jesus' presence can be savored among and between friends, and this can be a form of prayer even if we are not praying.

Then again, perhaps the power of Julian's metaphor lies in our constant need for sustenance. Other mothers may *give her child suck of her milk, but our precious Mother, Jesus, he may feed us with himself,*[71] she writes. Newborns feed every couple of hours, more often if they're hitting a growth spurt. Back and back again comes the baby's mouth, its whole being writhing and squawking towards the goal of filling up again, each feeding session a punctuation in the day. A pause for refreshment.

A Selah.

Are three meals a day enough to sustain me? How many times do I need to stop and pray, or stop and commune with friends, or just stop everything altogether to be attentive to the fact of Jesus' presence?

Karen and the other empresses could tell I was off balance, so they bowed their heads. They took turns speaking their prayers aloud, asking God for no cancer, for vocal protection, for the weird besetting Covid symptoms to finally wither away. They cried, whispered, and declared everything with boldness that rushed in like wind through a door. They also asked for my peace and my patience and my joy, which takes more faith to request than miracles of healing because contentment seems even more supernatural than recovery. Each one of the women brought my case before heaven like members of my spiritual legal team, making their appeals to God's character, to Scripture, to his mercy and grace. I figured it would be difficult for God to shrug off their petitions after such compelling arguments, especially since Karen *is* a lawyer by trade and isn't used to losing her case.

As my ship roiled forward into the night, I felt my sea legs starting to activate, mitigating more lurches, and giving me minutes of rest. I closed my eyes and breathed in the cold. I ate crackers off a cold plate, sipped red from a cold glass, and tried to say, "Thank you."

~~~

Lord, you steady me with the feast of Communion. You remind me in these elements that what you did for me was real, a flesh-and-blood actuality that took up space and time just like the flesh-and-blood realities I am facing today. The real liquid in my cup reminds me of the real blood that was spilled for me. The real food in my stomach reminds me of the real body you have, which you broke for my wholeness. The real faces of real friends nourish my heart as we encounter you together.

Stabilize me as I eat and drink to remember.

## RETURN

She bent her head down into my face. All I could see were gentle eyes behind glasses, the face framed by a light blue cloud of mask and hair cap. I had a mask on, too, and a hair

"FOR HE HIMSELF IS OUR PEACE."
– EPHESIANS 2:14

cap, so the nurse and I must have resembled two blue broccoli florets, one leaning down towards the other. She was searching my eyes for clues, making sure I was OK, asking if I had any questions. We were about to roll into the operating room.

Another nurse had made me take out my contact lenses and remove my glasses, so everything beyond the small perimeter around my mobile bed was only blur and movement. The IV had already been started in my left arm. My bed was stationed in the middle of a triage gallery with other patients lined up in other beds, all wearing identical blue masks and hair caps and gowns and ready to be rolled into various surgery suites for his or her different gallbladder/hernia/appendix surgeries and God knows whatever else. The environment felt sort of jovial and work-a-day, as though some huge ten-year-old girl was playing Barbies with us, her patients, and every doll had been assigned to specific surgeries. Maybe later we would all be mermaids in her lagoon.

"I'm a singer," I told the nurse, who turned out to be my nurse anesthetist, but what I really meant was, "Please be careful, for the love of God." Not only would I have to be intubated for surgery, but a second tube would have to be inserted down next to my larynx to serve as an alarm bell of sorts, to alert the surgeon if he was encroaching upon the vital nerve. Between the intubation, alarm bell, and threat of actual scalpel damage, it seemed like I should have said more, and expressed my fear more floridly, but "I'm a singer" was about all I could manage.

"We'll take good care of you," she said in a dear voice that made my eyes run rivulets down into my mask. It seemed like she should have said more, too.

Then I met the anesthesiologist, another very kind broccoli floret who materialized on the other side of my bed. The nurse anesthetist and her two assistants were to my right, the doctor was to my left, and they were all peering down at me with squinty smile-eyes as though evaluating an Ewok. "Do you have any questions?" the anesthesiologist asked. Yes. Will something go wrong during surgery related to my long-haul symptoms? Will Dr. D nick my laryngeal nerve? Will I be able to talk after this? Will the pathologist find cancer?

"Not really," I said. "I'm a singer," I repeated to him, then felt compelled to add, "And if something weird happens, or goes wrong in surgery, or seems off or whatever, it might be helpful to know that I probably had COVID back in April and haven't fully recovered and a lot of strange things have been happening in my body lately that people can't really explain, so. Anyway. That will be why." He (sort of) nodded.


The truth was, Julian had prayed to get sick. This wasn't her earlier prayer to die, but a prayer for a "gift of God" she described as *bodily sickness in youth.*[72] Her hope was that the illness should "purge" her and help her to *"live more to the worship of God because of that sickness."*

Well. She was an odd bird, that Julian. I'm not sure how much fun she really would have been in real life, but maybe that's what surviving two waves of the Black Death will do to a psyche. Or maybe saints are just born.

The illness would strike Julian when she was thirty-and-a-half years old. Many times during her illness she thought herself close to death, as did the people caring for her, who had arranged for last rites to be given in the room with the crucifix. She saw many disturbing, inscrutable visions during her near-death experiences, and would spend the next fifteen years processing and understanding the nature of them — with Jesus' help.

But what was the reason for all of it? She wondered later. After so many years of these extraordinary experiences and revelations, she finally had to ask, Why her? For what purpose? She had requested purging, for the ability to serve God better. And was this also God's ultimate reason for her illness and visions? Or had his intentions been different all along?

"*Know it well*," she heard the Spirit say one day. "*Love was his meaning. Who shewed it thee? Love. What shewed he thee? Love. Wherefore shewed it he? For Love...and in this love he hath done all his works; and in this love he hath made all things profitable to us; and in this love our life is everlasting.*"[73]

It wasn't to perfect her appearance, or her behavior. It wasn't to make Julian worthy of love, or even fit for service. The reason for her illness and her visions was to reveal the existence of God's already perfect, all-encompassing love for her. This love swallowed her whole, and she was wholly filled up with it. "*We are so oned*," Jesus had effectively said to her, "*that I am never out of you and you are never out of me.*" This was scandalous reality, that God, the very essence of love, had already made his home within her. He used her illness to show her that illness wasn't necessary to improve her lovability. This was the ultimate revelation.

And this all-encompassing love could manifest itself in almost any way a sentient being could love and relate to the ultimate sentient Being. "*And thus I saw that God rejoiceth that he is our Father, and God rejoiceth that he is our Mother, and God rejoiceth that he is our Very Spouse and our soul is his loved Wife. And Christ rejoiceth that he is our Brother, and Jesus rejoiceth that he is our Savior.*"[74]

God, Jesus, Spirit.

Father, Mother, Spouse, Brother, Savior.

All of God loves all of me in all the ways.

In another book he wrote, David G. Benner describes prayer as "Being in love — living our lives grounded in our being in God."[75] This reminds me of a muggy night spent at an outdoor play once, a Passion play where the actor playing Jesus sang lyrics that shot through the sternum and lungs of my eleven-year-old self, right to my red-hot heart:

*I am closer than a heartbeat, for my heart will be your home.*

I don't remember the actor's face or the set design or even the vantage point we had from seat to stage, but the words echoed around in me for days afterwards: My heart will be your home. Closer than a heartbeat.

Who wouldn't want to return to this reality, over and over again, all throughout an ordinary day? To stop and Selah, again and again, even all throughout a day in a sickbed? Return to being in love. Return to love. Return to Being.

Prayer is always a returning.


The team rolled me into a bright room that seemed unnecessarily large to be a surgery suite. It felt cavernous, like a rehearsal space before the set is moved in. A lone operating table stood off-center, floating in the white expanse like a random island. I was transferred from my rolling bed onto the table awkwardly, a blanketed manatee out of water. They adjusted my head in the neck groove so I would be comfortable for the few seconds I would be awake before the world went dark. Then the anesthesiologist held a giant syringe with a red cap in front of my face and asked, "Julie, where would you like to go on vacation today? I can send you anywhere in the world!"

"Hawaii," I said reflexively because it seemed like the answer he expected. I pictured glaring white sand and emerald water that was more my memory of Destin than of Maui. If I had had a split-second longer to think, I would have said Paris. A café on a Parisian side street at twilight, glasses alive with candlelight. A place of peace.

"Done," he said, as he pushed the medicine into my arm. "We'll see you when you get back."

Even in my last moment of consciousness, I tried to be a good sport. I waved my hand dramatically at the whole team as though I was bidding au revoir and boarding my flight. Or taking a final bow.

～～

Jesus, you are grace itself. You are love itself. You don't need to be asked to stay. You're just...here. Always here.

I am in you, and you are in me. I return to this fact now.

And because you are love itself, you are also peace itself.

You are

    Peace with myself

    Peace with my beloveds

    Peace in isolation

    Peace while waiting

    Peace while busy

    Peace while confused

    Peace while happy

Peace while successful

Peace in the quiet

Peace

In the cacophony

In my body

In the mystery

With my past

With my future.

Nothing is lost that you keep for me.

# CHAPTER 5

# BITE, CHEW, AND SWALLOW: THE HUMILITY OF HUNGER WHEN NOTHING GETS BETTER.

Beige. Beige, blank walls. White lights.

Quiet murmurs off to one side, perhaps about the woman in the bed — who is me — perhaps not.

Whatever my body was or wasn't capable of in that moment, I had no idea.

> "COULDST THOU NOT, MY LORD, HAVE ENDED [THE LORD'S PRAYER] IN A SINGLE SENTENCE, BY SAYING: 'GIVE US WHATEVER IS GOOD FOR US?'"
> – ST. TERESA OF AVILA

I had no idea I was a body or a person at all. I just knew beige, blank walls. White lights. Murmurs.

My eyes listed to the right. A young nurse was sitting on a stool at some sort of panel, a computer maybe, right next to my head. It felt as if she was waiting to encounter something, and then I realized she was waiting to see my eyes open.

"Soignwie dskhf kdjfsidhfh," I heard her say, but I understood her to mean, "Are you thirsty?" Or maybe she didn't ask that, maybe I felt it, but before I knew I was a body or a person or anything at all, I heard myself reply, "Can I have some water?"

I *said* it. With a voice I still had that worked well enough to ask a question.

And then consciousness surged in, like fizz. I had survived. Nothing catastrophic had happened while I was in Hawaii, that much seemed clear. I took in a deep breath through my nostrils. I was going to try that again. The talking.

"How are you feeling?" the nurse asked me, now in English.

"A little nauseous," I said, trying for more volume. It felt scratchy and phlegmy, but suddenly I was more worried about vomiting up through the surgically embattled trenches of my throat than I was about whether I could still sing Sondheim.

"I'll put something in your IV," she said. "How is your pain?"

"It's ok," I said, listening to every quiver and tone emanating from my larynx.

After five minutes, I said, "Can I have some pain meds?" because it really was starting to hurt, and I was also needing to hear my voice again. I had to try it out, push it farther, the way you put weight on a leg you hope isn't broken. Then try to take a step.

I wondered if I sounded like I was listening to myself more than I was trying to communicate with her. I didn't care. I wished she would ask me something new or that I could think of something new to ask *her*, but I was suddenly so tired. The swimming blur of sleep was lulling me fast towards oblivion and my goal was starting to feel unimportant somehow, the way certain things weirdly lack urgency in dreams.

When I awoke again, I was being wheeled back to my hospital room. Gordon was waiting. He smiled and bent down to say something to me. I replied without remembering that replying was not just a given and was once again jolted by: I *said* that. With a voice that worked well enough to *say* it!

It would have to be enough for now. It would have to be a little meal to eat, a bite of something sweet and small to tide me over. There would be no conversations today. No humming. No singing. Just a soft whisper — either the promise of a feast or the place where I would stay. Could crumbs like this sustain me?

The easiest memories to dig up and examine are the dramatic, bizarre:

My chin split open on the concrete suddenly, twelve-year-old me tripping in front of a group of cute boys.

The giraffe that had me by the shirt on a middle school field trip, thirteen-year-old me shot through with adrenaline and delight. (Those eyelashes!)

The starry sky over the Lake of Galilee in high school, the way the boat was steady on those disinterested waters, and the way I had leaned against the rail.

I was sixteen years old with my church youth group, visiting Israel. We hit the highlights. One day, we swam in the Dead Sea, bobbing like corks in the lake-brown waters. I sliced open my big toe on a glinting shard of salt that had crystalized on the shore. One day, we visited the Wailing Wall, where I resisted the urge to pull out one of the tiny white scrolls someone had stuck into the crevice with his prayer scrawled inside. One night, we took a bus to the Negev desert and slept in camel-hair tents, watching the smoke from our campfire disappear up into the blackness — black consumed by even deeper black.

Someone had brought a guitar on the boat the night we sailed Galilee, or maybe it was a 90s boom box, and we were singing contemporary worship songs of the mid-90s like "Shout to the Lord" and "All in All." The shoreline, which we could see all the way around in a 360-degree panorama, was ringed in golden dots of light, a bright necklace border. The hills beyond the shore were dotted sporadically with the same lights, though scattered. Those old hills were still rugged and grassy like they'd been for thousands of years, not altogether settled. At least they were in 1996.

Earlier in the day we had sat on one of those hills and looked down at the lake in the sunshine. There was a big tree and long grass, and we were perched up high where we could watch the small fishing boats resting on the water. They looked insignificant from a distance, floating like pieces of rice on an ancient pond. It was here on this hillside, our guide said, that Jesus fed five thousand people using only two loaves of bread and two dinky fish. Those people were hungry, he said, because they had walked from surrounding villages, sometimes traveling entire days on foot. You could see, from up here, how far that might be if you walked from the far side of the purple water.

One ordinary day, Jesus met a practical need for a lot of people using extraordinary power. And the people he fed, they completed the process in practical ways of their own: by taking the bread into their hands, putting it into their mouths, chewing, and swallowing.

I plucked a long narrow leaf from what was something like a weeping willow on the hillside and stuck it into my childhood Bible I had brought from home.

My youth group was led by a dynamic man named Scott. Scott was young, single, and blond. In his life right before becoming a pastor, he had worked in Hollywood as an actor with the stage name "Trevor Scott." We loved to look at his headshot whenever we could convince him to show it to us. Scott held devotionals for our group as we made our way across the Holy Land, applying spiritual truths along the way. The biggest impact of it all, however, was not the insights he illuminated for us, but the overwhelming sense of time and place and ordinariness that was inherent everywhere you looked: over on that side of the two-lane freeway was where Jacob had his vision of angels ascending and descending their heavenly ladder. Back over on this side of the road was where Jesus healed the lepers. Down that windy road up there, on the other side of the bend, is where David hid from King Saul, and see that mountain in the distance, the one rising up over that green pastureland? That's where Jesus was transfigured.

These were real places where the earth has been making its humdrum twenty-four-hour pilgrimage just the same as in Irving, Texas. These Bible stories took place where the air buzzed with grasshoppers, where your shoes got mud-spattered, and where the world was every bit as opaque and relentlessly real as the one I knew back home. Yet this is where Jesus looked up into the sky, said words of thanks towards it, ripped apart a pita, split it off, and gave it out as if by wizardry; impossibly real and crusty bread made of oil and flour that filled the real biological bellies of people who no more understood him and his power than they did the Scientific Method. The scraggly men, the foot-sore women, and the cranky kids were all full. That's what they knew.

Pastors like Scott and Sunday School teachers and youth group sponsors over the years were always teaching us practical ways for feeding our spiritual selves. They taught us models with handy names like the "5-and-5," which helped you remember to take five minutes a day to read your Bible and then another five minutes to pray. There were acronyms like ACTS, which stood for the four basic elements of prayer: adoring God, confession of sin, thanking God, and asking him for things ("supplication"). If you didn't know what to say to God, just start with ACTS. These were formulaic shortcuts into that realm between the dusty air of earth and the dimension where Jesus waited. They could also be mindless boxes to check if you were most interested in the comfort of routine.

The night in the Negev, after sopping up hummuses and wrapping meats with warm, pliable, gluten-y pita bread, we each retired to our sleeping tents. Something soon stirred me awake, or perhaps I never was asleep really, but something caught hold of me and brought me up to the surface of things somehow, in that eyes-wide-open state where you start to perceive another world layered perfectly across this one. I could see a light through an opening in the tent at my head, as though we were right underneath a freeway lamp. When I pulled the flap back, I could see the light was coming not from a lamp or from our fire, but from the sheer number of stars that had thrashed themselves across the black expanse above. Maybe the clouds had dispersed, or maybe the fire had died, to reveal them.

I took out a notebook. Words began to flow over the pages. It was joy, exultation, a mighty returning of praise. What had begun in my 9th grade class with Mrs. Hoerger was unfurling its wings to bear me up and away.

My pen was a fork and I feasted.

It was a shortcut I had discovered all on my own.


When I came out of surgery, my throat was sewn with sutures that held the swollen, fire-ant-red skin of my throat together. Below this incision, a drainage tube poked out of yet another new hole in my throat, which was, shall we say, an appalling discovery. The tube was fed down into a rubber pouch the size of a plum to provide drainage for the wound. Every few hours, I had the traumatizing task of *squeezing the pouch out into a measuring cup* and recording how much blood and fluid had been collected.

"What is your favorite color?" a friend named Kendra had asked me via Facebook Messenger a few weeks earlier. This was not a question I had been asked since maybe fourth grade, and in the intervening years between wearing training bras and becoming the mother of a teenager myself, it appeared my answer was no longer "hot pink."

"A lovely sage green," I typed back. I thoroughly enjoyed being asked and answering this question. It was such a different question from "How are you feeling?" and reminded me that I still had aesthetic preferences even though no one had been inside my house for almost a year. Yes, a lovely sage green. Or, more precisely, the color of my kitchen island, which was simply named "Artichoke." A lovely *artichoke* green.

Soon afterward, Kendra came over with a gift bag. We sat on the back porch, and I unwrapped a lush, textural marvel that unfolded to become a soft crocheted shawl. It was the perfect shade of lovely sage-or-artichoke green. The care and time it must have taken to knit it took away my voice and replaced it with a hot gurgle at the back of my throat.

"This is a prayer shawl," explained Kendra, when I opened it. "With every stitch, I prayed for you. When you wear this, remember that you are *still* covered in prayer."

Well. This couldn't have been more moving, especially since Kendra is not whom I would call one of my closest friends. We met while doing one of the church musicals together and remained friendly over the years. Her corgi, Phoebe, was a star on my Facebook feed. I could always relate to Kendra's obsession with her dog, being an absurd love slave myself of The Eyeballs. And just like Eloise would flop herself down on my abdomen because I am her obligatory ottoman, this prayer shawl would wrap me in love no matter where I was in the world.

Kendra is a rare sort of human, is what I'm trying to say.

I didn't take my lovely sage green prayer shawl to the hospital. I was afraid some horrifying substance would spill or leech onto it. But still, I felt Kendra's prayers as I lay in the hospital bed. Or maybe I was feeling the cumulative prayers of everyone who loved me, all radiating through the window and across my face like moonbeams.

I was still waiting to see what had become of my voice or how the Covish symptoms would behave. I was back in limbo, but it seemed I had avoided the worst extreme, even if cancer would soon be confirmed. People were praying for me. I could feel them. I could feel Him, I thought. Maybe he feels lovely, like shawls and pugs and corgis or even just the idea of them when they are absent. Maybe He's practical with the food he makes and multiplies for us if we have hands to reach and mouths to chew and throats to swallow, even if the food isn't dramatic or star born.

They had already dug her grave. It was just outside the thick stone walls of the convent. The hole was deep and murky, and there were shiny-back beetles just underneath the surface of things because their homes had been so recently disturbed. Perhaps it was drizzling or was just about to, or had just finished, but this would have been unlikely in the dry climate of Avila, Spain. One thing was certain: beautiful young Teresa was going to die.

≈

Lord, my life has been forced to slow down, small down. Small dreams, small expectations, small sustenance. Is this a good thing, Lord? Something I can dare to trust?

Lord, I pray so often for a word, a wink, a sign. But you don't just drop in occasionally to help me or to lead or feed me. You don't parachute down every so often and then blast back up into heaven like a Red Cross worker with emergency aid. I'm constantly in you, with you. The air I breathe is your word of love to me. Every beauty and pleasure is your nourishing love. Show me practical ways to take, pick up, bite, and chew.

## CRAZY

Saint Teresa of Avila was perhaps the most practical of the mystics. She planned, organized, and founded over fifteen convents, in which she instituted reforms during the tumultuous times of the Counter-Reformation in 1500's

"WHEN THEY CAME TO THE CROWD, A MAN CAME UP TO JESUS, FALLING ON HIS KNEES BEFORE HIM AND SAYING, "LORD, HAVE MERCY ON MY SON, FOR HE IS A LUNATIC AND IS VERY ILL."
– MATTHEW 17:14

Spain. She wrote books. Dealt with politicians and grumpy church administrators. Hid from the Inquisition. She did all the saintly things, too, make no mistake, conversing with Jesus himself and fighting demons, as one does.

We know so much more about her than we do about little Julian. She feels more solid and opaque, someone with the beginnings of gray hair sprouting at her temples, with hangnails and laundry, someone who would have lit the Candle of Learning and gone about her to-do list with gusto. This saint lived in twenty-four-hour increments.

She was asked to write some practical advice on prayer for the sisters in the convent she founded in Avila. While her contemporary Ignatius had developed his book of prayer exercises for lay people, Teresa was writing for a more spiritually educated audience.[76] Her efforts resulted in the nuanced, self-deprecating book called *The Way of Perfection*. But like Ignatius, Teresa was also prone to a good royal metaphor and took to calling Jesus "His Majesty" throughout, though also "true Spouse" and her Father, Brother, Lord, and Friend. Jesus would ultimately mean everything to Teresa, but not until after what amounted to a second conversion at about the age of forty. She had already been a nun for twenty years.

Teresa was a Carmelite, which back in that time meant living with lax rules about visitors, socializing, and other worldly comforts. It was quite the med-spa of convent living, perhaps even complete with servants and pets.[77] Teresa, who was born into wealth and a bougie lifestyle, was right at home. By all accounts, she was also lively and social, and in her words fell into great "wickedness" living and moving and having her being in indulgence and distraction even while wearing a nun's habit. But it's always more complicated than that, as are all stories of conversion and spiritual journeys because Teresa herself admits having a halting, up-and-down prayer life throughout the first eighteen years of her vows. She was always trying. (Except for that one year she stopped altogether.)

It appears she had a hard time sitting still, for instance, and she found using her imagination to engage with the life of Jesus difficult (sorry, Ignatius),[78] so she always had a book on-hand to help focus her mind. This focusing of the mind and heart was what she would later refer to as the "Prayer of Recollection" — the ability to walk around the rooms of your mind and heart and collect once again (re-collect) the parts and pieces of yourself that had gotten strewn across benches and beds and chairs throughout the day and put them back together into a unified whole with the help of God. A whole person, wholly in God's presence, wholly in the present moment.

By her own account, Teresa wasn't whole for the first half of her life. Not yet, anyway. She was fractured, diluted, a pixelated version of herself. Hungry for wholeness, yet unaware of her stomach growling and even more unaware of how to fill it.

Eloise, Her Highness, The Eyeballs loves to chew on tiny hands. Not actual people hands, but these little rubber toy hands that are ubiquitous around the Rhodes house. And while I am prone to step on Legos just like any other normal mom, I'm *more* likely to step on a random hand. I'll open a drawer and find a hand in there, or see hands stuck between the couch cushions. I've found hands in the washing machine and in the backyard and on the fingers of Maddie and Drew. They follow me around like groupies applauding me, these tiny rubber hands.

This hand-festation is all to blame on my friends Suzanne, Laura and Jill, who sent me a big box of them before surgery, which was also filled with other gag gifts and treasures — an Awkward Family Photos game, cushy socks, candy, tea, and prayer books. Suzanne ("Suz"), Laura, and Jill have been longtime friends since before we even had kids to produce Legos for us to step on. We were mostly all pregnant together and had made a pact to share our collective crazy with each other.

Somehow along the way, we ended up with multiple little babies that are now enormous and frightening teenagers. Nathan, Jill's firstborn (and the firstborn of our little posse), has always been referred to as "the blueberry" because, at the time we first learned of his existence, he was no bigger than a blueberry floating around inside of Jill. Jill pioneered the trail for the rest of us towards this idea that *we could carry human beings inside of us, too* — blueberries that would become grapes then plums then apples then cantaloupes!

During the dark days of 2020, Suz, Laura, and Jill patiently scrolled through messages I sent that were longer than newspaper columns and responded with hilariously inappropriate memes and soothing, cooing words. They hated any doctor I was hating on a particular day (see: motorcycle ringtone dude) and beat their own pillows on days I couldn't lift my head off mine.

They didn't mind getting pictures of my awful throat bag, either. Well, maybe they did and didn't show it, and this is another way in which they were heroes. They simply encouraged me to send whatever terrible thing I wanted to show them because true friends hold their breath, barrel through, and give you a hand — or eighty-four little rubber ones — with the load you carry.

And so, when I got the results from the thyroid surgery, I texted them.

I was mad. I was crying.

It was the week before Christmas when I received the news that makes most normal people rejoice: my tumors were benign after all. The nodules hadn't quite crossed the threshold into malignancy yet, which meant no more surgery, no radioactive iodine treatments, no PET scans. My long weeks of waiting and wondering were over. My family would be so relieved, and my friends would rejoice. My Christmas wouldn't have the shadow of the Non-Covid C-word cast over it. I could finally regroup and focus on the task at hand, which was to recover from "maybe COVID" and put the whole thyroid drama away like a novel on a shelf.

What I did was cry. I took a walk around Ward Parkway and sent angry texts to Suz and Laura and Jill and Schuyler and my family asking WHY I had put my body through hell and risked vocal cord damage for a big, fat zero reason, and why I now would require medication every day for the rest of my life.

I had also begun to plummet into a deeper Covid relapse: shaking, fevers, exhaustion, tight lungs. Why had I subjected myself to this when all along, my thyroid had been chugging along just fine thank-you-very-much and keeping its weird little goiters in check? I had already been through so much with no answers, and now I had gone through this for no reason.

Of course, these were not the thoughts of a rational human being who had just avoided cancer. These were the thoughts of someone on the path to madness after nine months of asking, "Why is my body hurting, damaged, and unwell, and nobody has a good explanation or solution for it?"

Justification and Answers: I was starving for them. Having cancer would at least justify why I had to get the terrible surgical gash along my throat. Having cancer would justify having to endure my flighty thinking and surges of emotion caused by plummeting T3 levels post-op now that my thyroid was wrapped up in an orange biohazard bag in a dumpster somewhere. Having cancer would justify accepting as collateral damage my racing heart, which had returned like the Ghost of Covid Past to reunite with my fevers and exhaustion.

There was a room in the attic of my brain where my rational self still dwelled and made herself soup in the microwave. She knew things down in the rest of the house were whacky. She knew she had friends who loved her, who had walked alongside her, who wouldn't leave her. But this rational self was just so quiet up there, biding her time while the toddlers and teenagers of my psyche went wild.

The worst part was that I knew I sounded a bit unhinged to everybody, knew my crazy was dripping out worse than the fluid in my throat bag, but I couldn't seem to stop, and even worse than that, I knew I sounded ungrateful. This was because I WAS ungrateful and I couldn't seem to become thankful, and that made me angrier still.

Ungrateful, unhinged. Unreachable by my oldest friends. Starving for reasons why and eating only ash.

David G. Benner has called prayer "the natural language of the soul,"[79] as though prayer is something nobody needs to learn how to do, that it's just something your soul is born doing, like a language no one needs to learn. In fact, he goes so far as to say prayer is as elemental to our moment-by-moment existence as breathing itself. Prayer is the "breath of the soul," which means, of course, that "it is essential that we pray, just as it is essential that we breathe." [80] If he is willing to switch metaphors to another life-sustaining function, I bet David G. Benner would agree that prayer is also food, the natural sustenance of the soul, and that it is essential that we pray just as it is essential that we eat. We are born to breathe and eat God in prayer. Without prayer, we die, because without God, we die.

But what if we don't feel hungry?

Mostly I feel independently hungry for things I'm craving more than for what's in front of me right here, right now. The hands of Jesus are empty of the specific relief I've been requesting, but his smile is broad, and his attention is riveted towards me. And yet this isn't enough to draw me to the table because I'm not hungry for *those* things — I don't think. I wanted the relief, the resolution. Him? Not so much.

I've heard that people who are starving to death reach a point where their hunger seems to go away, the gnawing of their stomach stopping as if the body has given up the fight. This is a bad, bad sign. This body has lost its sense and is now death-bound. It takes great humility to be hungry, and the only way it can start for some people is with great humiliation. If the ultimate experience of God's grace is the presence of Jesus, and prayer is the way to access, consume and digest it, then it takes admitting the need in the first place.

Losing your mind can be a way to start.

~

Lord, my life feels like such madness. I find myself in places that don't make sense to me, that invalidate my confidence in your plan. I'm bogged down in the what-the-hecks, struggling with circumstances out of my control that feel random, borderline tragic. My faith feels foolish. All the biblical symbolism is gibberish. I feel mistakenly snagged. I can't even thank you properly for objectively wonderful things. I'm reduced to babbling.

I'm starving for sanity, and I've decided sanity means living in a world where things make sense to me and resolve according to my felt needs.

Feed me something real.

## CONDUIT

It didn't take a moment of insanity for Teresa to realize her deep hunger for God, but she did experience a humbling. In those days when she was about thirty-nine

"AND HE SAID TO ME, "MY GRACE IS SUFFICIENT FOR YOU, FOR MY STRENGTH IS MADE PERFECT IN WEAKNESS." THEREFORE MOST GLADLY I WILL RATHER BOAST IN MY INFIRMITIES, THAT THE POWER OF CHRIST MAY REST UPON ME."
– 2 CORINTHIANS 12:9

or so, she described her soul as "weary" and "enslaved." It seems her strength and liberation — the apparently supernatural energy and daring that powered the second half of her life and made her an icon of faith — came only after tears. Well, and a statue. Or perhaps it was a painting. Nevertheless, it was an image of Jesus "sorely wounded," one she just happened to pass on her way to the convent's oratory that had just arrived at the convent. She looked at it, probably out of curiosity — what's this new piece of decor? — and the rest was history. It was one of those moments when you're walking along one day and then suddenly, you're falling off a cliff.

Was it something about his face? The contortion of his body? The way the light caught the nails drilled into his wrists? Something in Teresa's knees probably wobbled and broke, for she threw herself to the floor beside the image of Jesus, "*shedding floods of tears*"[81] for how her life had failed to merit all the suffering he had endured for her. It was a swift blow to the soul, out of nowhere, like she had been hit by a sniper in the bell tower.

It's so mysterious, why things like this happen to some people and not others, at some times, and not at other times.

Soon after this, Teresa read a book by Augustine — yes, our old friend Augustine with the pope-y hat! — specifically the story in *Confessions* from that day in his courtyard with the child singing, "Pick up and read, pick up and read," beckoning him towards the book and its writer. Suddenly, Teresa realized a parallel: it seemed the Lord had been "*speaking that way*" to her, too,[82] and that's when it really began the hunger pangs.

What she was feeling was a new sensation, a new urge, a new instinct towards Jesus: "*I began to long to spend more time with Him.*"

Teresa was starving for Jesus.

A mere three weeks after surgery and my bizarre outburst following the excellent, no-cancer news, I got a call from some People in Charge at our church. Could I read the Christmas story on stage for the Christmas Eve service? Most people would be streaming the service from the safety of home, but there would also be a group of us spaced out and masked, who would be in person. I had not been to in-person church in months, and now that my body was a shaking, feverish mess with no energy, no lung capacity, no thyroid, and with uncertain vocal ability, it seemed questionable to start galivanting around on a public stage. But the People in Charge were asking. I'd have a microphone, after all. It would only take forty-five seconds. And it was just reading a story out of a book, one I practically had memorized anyway. Ever the rebel, I replied with some version of, "You bet your bonnet I can!"

This was a novel assignment, a task unrelated to managing my upsetting physical state, and I was all for it. I poured over Luke 2 in the afternoons when all I could do was lie around, examining the nuances of different words in the passage that I had always glossed over every Christmas. What did "swaddling" entail? Who in the world *was* Quirinius? I thought about Mary and Joseph walking themselves slowly from Nazareth to Bethlehem, almost certain she would deliver along the way in some dusty enclave. What must it have been like for Mary to be so out of control of her body and her future as she plodded through that rocky, Mars-like terrain with this... man? Was *God* going to take care of them? This must have been a big question mark, especially after being turned out in the cold while waves of labor rolled through her torso.

I held my Bible in my lap and mulled the words over in my mouth like hard candy: "In those days, a decree went out from Caesar Augustus that all the world should be registered..." I practiced emphasizing one word or another to suggest different subtextual realities — "In *those* days, a decree went out" vs. "In those days, a *decree* went out" vs. "In those days, a decree went *out*" — just to see what might come to the surface and prove worthy of midwifing into a fuller expression. I pretended I knew Mary and Joseph, and that I was telling their story as a friend. I pretended I was telling the story as one of the angels who had been strung across the sky that night above the field. If I were an angel, it would color the way I said the names of these dear, weak, and wily human beings: "Mary." "Joseph."

When Christmas Eve came, I wore a green turtleneck to hide my incision and the awful drain tube hole that punctuated it. I slipped on high heels and wobbled around like an antelope.

When I got to church, someone fit a microphone around my ear. And when the moment arrived, I stood from the front pew and carried my childhood Bible up to the stage, the one with the leaf from the Galilee tree still tucked into Matthew. I could see the red glow of the camera at the end of the center aisle. It was steady, like a star. My family was to my left, on the front row. The orchestra was playing a soft carol beneath my amplified voice as I began, "In those days, a decree went out..." I looked down at the People in Charge who had asked me to do this and wanted to make them glad they did. My voice surprised me: it was full, resonant. This was the first time I had heard it through a sound system since illness and surgery. It rose and fell with the string section as though it was an instrument.

Selah. Everything paused.

For a weightless, zero-gravity moment I was free. Using face, voice, body, and breath, I was telling us all a story, a story I didn't make up, that no person made up, but a story of which we are all a part. This story was not about me or my problems, and it bore me up overhead like the Jetstream. This was only a bright flash of suspension, but within it was a world: I had gone from convalescent to conduit. I couldn't have sung a song or performed a tap routine. I couldn't have sustained a character through a two-hour show. My parameters were very small, but I still had a voice, a small and shaky voice, and the story I was telling was very big and very solid, and it almost seemed insistent on being told through a broken thing.

It was this moment of public fragility, and of this fragility being harnessed for something strong, that simultaneously raised me up and brought me low. I accepted this dichotomy the instant I wobbled to the stage. For some reason, I was the one doing this. Me. The Bad Luck Lady. And it didn't matter how shaky and small and quiet I was because there was a microphone and a camera and a whole orchestra to buoy me, along with the people sitting on the front row who loved me, along with that feeling of Him rising within me like a wave. My body was no longer a safe place for me, no room in the inn, but here I was somehow heralding good news with strong and reliable help on all sides. This nourished some invisible part of me that had grown thin because spiritual food is always on the bottom shelf, the one you stoop to reach.

Glory to God in the highest.

And on earth peace, goodwill to men.

～

Lord, you are on high. Lifted up, transcendent. Great.

I am on Earth. Time-bound. Lowly.

And yet you want peace and goodwill for me. You send me shepherds who bring proof of your love and attention like you did to Mary in her stall. You bring messengers to tell me I'm seen, that I haven't been misplaced, that I will be well used. Most of all, you personally infuse my wobbly stick-figure arms with sufficient strength for any love or service I need to channel toward others.

Help me walk slowly and confidently through my incomprehensible life, to mark the ways you have been personally good to me in the details. I treasure all these things and ponder them in my heart

## SOLIDARITY

Bernadette Peters once sang a song called *Time Heals Everything* in an obscure musical.[83] The song was written by the writer of the much more famous musical, *Hello Dolly*, and it's beautiful. It's a gorgeous, heartrending song, but is it a true song? Does time really heal everything, and is accepting the inexorable passage of time by gritting our teeth and sticking it out, the best way to thorn through life?

After her encounter with the image of Jesus in the hallway and reading Augustine's book, Teresa wanted to be known thenceforth as "Teresa of Jesus." Her identity had shifted

> "YOU PREPARE A TABLE FOR ME IN THE PRESENCE OF MY ENEMIES."
> – PSALM 23:5

totally onto the slab of his reality, and she was hungry for time spent dwelling in this reality. But how would they spend that time together? After all, if Jesus is like our nursing mother as Julian insists, what are the mechanics of satiating ourselves with him in prayer?

Teresa had some practical advice: spend your time intentionally, with focus.

Since she had such a difficult time concentrating during mental prayer, she recommends that beginners bring along a "good book,"[84] perhaps like the one you are reading, or some such devotional or passage of Scripture. Anything to corral the mind and heart in the same direction.

She also recommended getting out into nature, where you can see your Creator in the fields and waters and flowers[85], and air out your soul a little bit and find yourself to be part of the miracle of it.

She heralds the benefits of praying out loud vocally to focus the mind, even if the words are memorized prayers like The Lord's Prayer. (Oh, how she loved The Lord's Prayer like Augustine and Ignatius!) In fact, Teresa says she once knew a nun who couldn't pray in any other way other than vocally, and if the nun *"omitted saying her prayers, her mind wandered so much that she could not endure it."*[86] Vocal prayers are akin to my prayer form of choice: journaled ramblings, the ones that run across the page stream-of-conscious, fluid, the spirit moving by way of pen and paper and somehow keeping my mind on the tracks.

When it comes right down to it, Teresa promoted practices very much in line with the *lectio divina* of her spiritual ancestors: a little bit of reading, a little bit of opening to it and thinking about it, a little bit of responding.

The key to time with Jesus was focus, however you could get it.

Monks in the 2nd and 3rd century were way ahead of her. They used something called The Jesus Prayer to focus, placing a pile of stones next to them during prayer. With every repetition of the prayer – "Lord Jesus Christ, Son of God, have mercy upon me, a sinner."[87] – they would move one stone to the other side of their bodies until the pile had been transferred. The stones and repetition kept them single-minded and in place over a course of time, freeing the spirit while engaging the body.[88]

Focused, practical time, *lectio divina*-style, or otherwise, were all Saint Teresa-approved. But she also had another tip.

Ever the pragmatist, Teresa insists on something else for beginners: "cultivate friendships" and surround yourself with like-minded people who are also wanting to spend time with Jesus.[89] Cultivating friendships, as we all know, requires time, yet this time spent with special folks like this could exponentially increase the quality of time spent with Jesus. This is a mysterious dynamic. Teresa was convinced if she had had more such friendships throughout her life, she would have made much greater spiritual progress faster, and wouldn't have "fallen" so much during her long twenty-year dry spell.

Which is ironic if you think about it. Who else was Teresa surrounded by than with fellow nuns? Who else but nuns are expected to be seeking a prayerful life? Even those inside Christian circles might not be your best bet. It's the real pray-ers, the really ravenous ones you need to seek out for solidarity.

Many theories have surfaced to explain the phenomenon of Long Covid, or "Post-Acute Sequelae of Covid-19" (PASC). Some doctors suggest it is the virus persisting in some shadowy outpost of the body. Some say it is an inflammatory process that can't seem to settle down even after the virus has been defeated. Some say it's an autoimmune disease triggered by the virus. And some say it's a manifestation of "dysautonomia," a condition caused when the virus damages the parts of the nervous system responsible for heartrate, temperature regulation, and blood pressure. The tricky thing is that Long Covid could be not just one of these, but some combination of them in any Long-Hauler. Maybe by the time you read this, we will know more.

After nine months of taking all the autoimmune tests and healing my gut and doing a viral detox with Katie, I had fully convinced myself that dysautonomia was the holy-grail diagnosis I needed. It was January 2021. Things were getting worse post-surgery.

I read two books on the subject, including one on POTS (Postural orthostatic tachycardia syndrome), a sub-category of dysautonomia, which would explain my racing heart, fatigue, and fevers. I read blogs, too. One suggested an "at-home table test" that said if my heart rate jumped twenty beats per minute after simply standing still for ten minutes, I should be evaluated. Mine jumped by thirty, and my temperature jumped from 99 to 99.7.

Thus began my quest to find a neurologist. The Dysautonomia International website pointed me to Dr. V, a highly regarded physician who specialized in "autoimmune dysautonomia," which sounded like the very drain around which my symptoms were swirling. His waiting room would likely be the most terribly decorated one yet, I knew, but I fought to get a referral, wrestled to make sure the referral went through, skirmished with a nurse when there was a mix-up, and waged a scorched-earth campaign to get an appointment. The process took weeks. I had a paper printout of Dr. V's picture and bio sitting by my laptop. His face was warm, competent. "You'll show me a path forward," I said to him, stroking his face creepily.

His nurse called one morning to ask me a series of questions about my treatment and symptoms thus far. I was asked to list all the other doctors I had seen and all the tests I had run. I wondered what kind of square footage he might have on his desk for my archives. "I will present this to Dr. V and his team and will let you know if he is willing to give you an appointment," she said.

*Excuse me?* I thought.

I was under the impression doctors sort of *had* to see you if you wanted to see *them*. I began furiously texting my mom and my friends: PRAY DR. V WILL SEE ME. THIS IS THE END OF THE ROAD. THERE ARE NO MORE SPECIALISTS TO SEE AFTER THIS. I AM GIVING UP IF THIS DOESN'T WORK OUT.

"I'm sorry, Mrs. Rhodes, but the board of physicians at our office has reviewed your case and does not believe they will be able to help you," the nurse said to me the next day. She did sound truly sorry, and I tried to sound truly non-homicidal. "Thank you," I said. There was no arguing with her, and there was no arguing left in me.

I wasn't sick enough. That's what she meant. There were patients in much worse shape, with much worse prognoses, and these doctors have had enough experience to know which are which, and *you are not one of those patients.* This is what I heard in her voice, on the phone. But what I also heard was: *You're just being dramatic.*

Someone else will *always* have it worse. That's just true. It made me want to take my story home and stuff it under the bed like a tacky outfit I have been wearing all year and only just now realized was tacky.


"Hey Long-Haulers — "

That's how a lot of posts began in the Long Haul COVID Fighters Facebook group. I joined it about a month into my illness when it seemed someone had forgotten to flip the breaker switch back to "HEALTHY/ STABLE/RELIABLE" in my body. At the time, the group was for any COVID survivors who had been sick over 30 days, but the group quickly had to branch off into smaller groups based on when people became infected; too many thousands of people were trying to join at all different points in what would prove to be a longer-haul experience than we all thought was possible.

The "Long Haul Covid Fighters" soon became "Long Haul COVID Fighters – Round One (Onset of Illness prior to 4/1/20)." As of this writing, we are currently sitting at 6.2K members. I'm not sure how many are in all the other branches, but there are 176K members in Survivor Corps, another Long-Hauler group of which I'm a part. Not all of us have tested positive officially. Not all of us have *all* the Long-Haul symptoms (there are literally scores, perhaps hundreds, of symptoms). We are not any one race, gender, religious or political affiliation — though it does seem like a lot of us are middle-aged women.

The stories are varied, sad. Posts range from funny memes to cries for help from suicidal ideation.

"Hey, Long Haulers –

"Is there anyone out there dealing with long-term fevers?"

"You guys, I'm having one of those days where I'm terrified, anxious, and can't stop crying."

"I'm at my wits' end. This is so miserable. I can't catch my breath, feel like I'm having a heart attack because the chest pain and pressure get so intense, recurring headaches, and a fever for almost forty days."

"AMUSEMENT REQUEST! Give me your funny fatigue descriptions! I just realized today I have had to use my forehead muscles to open my eyes."

"I am struggling. I cry every day. I'm emotionally exhausted. I don't want to die but I don't want to live like this. If I'm not crying, I'm angry."

"Brain fog is a funny thing. Tonight, I asked my husband to 'circle the pan.' Luckily, he understood that I was asking him to stir the stir fry."

After Dr. D divorced me from my thyroid, I posted on the Long Haul COVID Fighters page asking about my COVID flare-up post-surgery. Almost sixty 'haulers wrote back with stories of wrangling their own bedraggled selves back up to hospitals to get pituitary glands out, spinal discs replaced, pacemaker procedures done, and hysterectomies performed, all while under the smothering blanket of fevers, fatigue, gastro issues, headaches, racing hearts, breathing problems, and brain fog. With the eagerness that only comes with boots-on-the-ground experience, this team of troopers armed me with earfuls of anecdotes to help set my expectations about what might await me in the weeks ahead. But mostly, they wanted to dote on dear old cute me.

"That's tough, I'm sorry you're going thru that little sister," said sweet Annette.

"May God bless and heal you, Julie," wrote Sue.

"Strong and brave — exactly what it takes to beat this. Get well soon," said Rob.

I had no idea where Annette or Sue or Rob were from. I didn't know how old they were or how much money they made. But I did know that they were safe people. In the dark winter mornings of deep, cold tiredness, when the fever would start shaking itself into existence first between my shoulder blades and then in my whole torso, I would think of them. Even as the last of my medical options sputtered out and died with the ringing in of a new year and the rejection of Dr. V, this group of internet people with their text bubbles and profile pictures had circled the wagons in the moonlight. Played songs. Swapped tall tales of hospitals and pulse oximeters. Lit a fire. There was meat on this fire, and I was learning to feed myself from it while the wolves watched from the inky perimeter. Solidarity was becoming sustenance.

~

Oh Lord, you were a man of sorrows and you lived among sorrowful people. You passed through crowds, healing as you went. Did you also heal their secret problems? The unspoken ones no one else knew about, the ones "too small" to make a fuss over? Maybe you even healed thorns too shameful to name.

Help me to be as gentle with myself as you are with me. You nourish me, and you do this through fellow thorn-bearers, my travel mates. Thank you for directing your sympathy, your mercy, your grace, through these diverse and ordinary mediators.

## STEADY

About eleven years ago, I met Schuyler (of the essential oils). She helped me meet my other friends Alison, Anna, and Kacey, who together with our husbands, formed Dinner Club. Every month for the past decade or so, one of us hosts the others in our respective homes or treats us all to dinner at a restaurant. Obviously, the pandemic had something to say about Dinner Club.

Schuyler had a solution: she would open her big sparkly garage to the outdoors and set out socially distanced card tables. We could still have somewhat normal

"KEEP ON LOVING ONE ANOTHER AS BROTHERS AND SISTERS."
– HEBREWS 13:1

conversations, and everybody would bring their own meals. We wouldn't go inside the house, except for bathroom breaks. The first month we tried this was July 2020, which is perhaps the most loathsome moment of heat in the state of Texas. Schuyler brought out big fans. We wore linen and prayed for the sun to go down. By August, I was on my anti-inflammatory diet, so I brought fish and vegetables. I looked longingly at the chips and queso, sandwiches, and pasta on the plates on the other card tables. I lusted for the cookies Schuyler had put on a plate in the middle of our table. I was running a fever and had to sit down before the others did.

When Alison got breast cancer several years ago, Dinner Club rallied around her, brought meals, gave gifts, and sat with her husband Chris up at the hospital. Now that I was sick, there wasn't a whole lot more Dinner Club could do for me. They had brought meals, but you can't bring meals to someone for a year, so they kept on praying and texting to ask how I was doing. I texted them my prayer requests. We exchanged funny memes. Sometimes I didn't want to bother Dinner Club with my complaints. Sometimes I did. Sometimes I wanted what we all want, I think, at Dinner Club and while dealing with thorns in general, and that is a place to talk about something *else*. Politics. Spiritual questions. Social quandaries. Hypotheticals. Ideas.

We want steady people, in the end. People to whom we can return, again and again, to feel like the best version of ourselves.

In January, six weeks after my thyroid surgery, I wore a high-collared shirt and sweater to Dinner Club to discreetly cover the bright slit on my throat. My Covid symptoms were still pulsating, fueled by my yet-to-be-regulated thyroid numbers. We were still in Schuyler and Clif's garage, this time with space heaters warming the cold floor underneath the card tables. We were bundled up in coats, laughing, exchanging stories about our holidays, ladling mugs full of the hot chocolate the Edwards brought in their Crock Pot. (Well, not me.)

"How are you doing?" they all asked at some point, in some way. And at some point, in some way, I said a variation of, "You know, I'm OK. Just one day at a time. Still trying to adjust. Still not sure what's going on."

And they all, at some point, in some way, gave me that look that says, "I see you. You don't have to say more if you don't want to."

And we all went home warm.

The famed Russian acting teacher Konstantin Stanislavski (and later teachers like Uta Hagen) taught a concept that has been helpful for me over the years: Public Solitude. This is the discipline of being in front of a large audience but feeling as if you are alone. It's important if you want to be natural. Assignments to acting students involve things like preparing a meal or clipping your toenails or making a bed — all done absent-mindedly, as these things are usually done in real life — in front of a group of fellow students, who are there to detect any pretension or self-consciousness in the performer. Over time and practice, the actor can inoculate herself against the dozens of eyeballs boring into her and relax into that almost robotic, guileless living we do when we think we are alone. It's a discipline, an intentional way to relax into the present moment of the scene at hand.

Teresa of Avila was also big on solitude, except she would have taken issue with the "public" part. She wanted real solitude for her sisters when they prayed, urging them to get away and alone so that they might come to the startling conclusion that Jesus had been right there beside them all along. They had to get alone to realize they were not alone. He was a steady presence both in crowded streets and empty caverns, and the only way to feel the truth of this was to find time to be by yourself.

Teresa was a Carmelite, a monastic order that traces back to a group of retired Crusaders in the 12th century who gathered themselves at the ancient Mount Carmel in Northern Israel. They looked to Elijah and his withdrawal from public life as their spiritual legacy,[90] so from the great prophet himself down to the 16th century, the Carmelites were one long stream of solitude-loving introverts (until they got lax, which is what Teresa ultimately helped to reform after her re-awakening). Teresa was not an introvert herself from what I can tell, so it's interesting to imagine her trying to break away. Did she gather up the skirts of her habit for hikes around the rocky hills of the convent, stepping over pits? Did she have a favorite boulder resting somewhere overlooking the Adaja river, where she would gaze down at waters flowing to places beyond the horizon?

Both Teresa and Julian saw the soul as a large, wide place — Julian's vision is that of a vast kingdom or city, Teresa's as an interior castle or the Garden of Eden — an internal expanse where each of us can walk with Jesus undisturbed.[91] It's a natural habitat, as David G. Benner might say, a built-in solitary place we carry within us everywhere we go. We can steal away inside of ourselves and walk with Jesus, and this can happen in public or private. I can walk with Jesus alone around the tree-lined ambles of Park Hill looking up at the red oak leaves, or while hooked up to an IV in my hospital bed, surrounded by friends. Solitude with Jesus can be public or private, if I have the discipline to break away and be with him, just him and me, alone in the depths of my being. But the practice of being alone, of taking the time to be by myself mentally *and* physically — away from my phone, in particular — is probably the best shortcut to that inner garden.

All of this takes intentional habit-forming, and Teresa doesn't apologize for saying so. We must commit to the practice of it, to the trying for it, to the steady stringing along of *Selahs* to break up our crowd-filled, screen-filled hours. Commitment to certain habits is necessary if we are going to keep ourselves on "an excellent road,"[92] filled at the source of spiritual nutrition.

Teresa even recommends the prayer of re-collection many times a day at first,[93] which is aided by the practice of alone time.

Selah. Selah. Selah.

Solitude. Solitude. Solitude.

Time spent with Jesus is good. Time spent with him alone is even better.

～

Thank you, Lord, that you don't change. That you're with me constantly, offering yourself to strengthen me. Thank you for keeping other things steady for me, too, even in this thorn, and thank you that many of these steady things are people. You are keeping people steady for me. Not every person — not the ones who don't try to understand, who won't take the time to bear with me, who have too much going on in their own lives. But the specific ones. There are certain ones you've provided to nourish me just by their reliable presence.

And most of all, you've provided yourself. You keep on keeping on right alongside.

I break away to break bread with you.

## CEASE-FIRE

By the time Spring of 2021 had arrived, I felt as though I looked like a different person. I was twelve pounds lighter since starting my diet the August before, but I was starting to gain it back. After losing my

> "YOU WILL NOT NEED TO
> FIGHT IN THIS BATTLE.
> STAND FIRM,
> HOLD YOUR POSITION,
> AND SEE THE SALVATION OF
> THE LORD ON YOUR BEHALF..."
> – 2 CHRONICLES 20:17

thyroid, I was placed on a synthetic hormone called Synthroid — now a lifelong necessity — and my body was having a hard time absorbing it in the weeks and months after surgery, like a breastfed infant who is resisting canned formula.

"We are seeing a lot of endocrine problems post-Covid, including insulin and hormone absorption," said Dr. L's physical assistant (PA), with a weary shrug of her shoulders.

I too had heard of people whose bodies had been trucking along fine accepting and appropriating Synthroid until Covid came along and whacked them in the kneecaps; for some reason, it seems to sop up the medication like a sinister sponge.

In response to my stalling progress, Dr. L kept bumping my dosage up every six weeks. I made only little improvements here and there. Once I was taking a high enough dose for two people, Dr. L asked, "Are you experiencing heart palpitations? Anxiety?", as though he expected me to be hurtling through space like a meteor on so much medicine.

"No," I replied. "I'm still pretty tired."

The thyroid affects basically every part of the human body, including metabolism, cell recovery, and immune support. These are helpful things, you understand, for fighting simmering Covid symptoms.

The thyroid also affects how you look. My hair started falling out. Great chunks began slithering out through my fingers in the shower, which I would wipe across the glass door. I bought hair thickening treatments and cut inches off every other month. One day, I was looking back at a photo album from a trip we took about ten years ago and was astonished at the two fat braids coursing down either side of my face like medieval extensions. All my life I've had mounds of horse-tail hair, and now it was almost half gone.

My skin was drying out, too, cracking trenches into the corners of my eyes and at the points of my smile. The magma within my thyroid scar was finally beginning to cool, but the scar was now the biggest wrinkle of all down at the base of my throat and looked as if it wasn't any happier about being there than I was. Everything from my neck up seemed suddenly ashamed of itself and twenty years older.

I took matters into my own (dry and craggy) hands. This sort of fast-forward aging is a complete nightmare to an actress, especially one as vain as I am, and who just got new headshots.

I made an appointment with a medical aesthetician named Amanda, who set me up with monthly micro-needling sessions. She roved over my face and neck with a wand that punched eleven small needles into my face repeatedly at a high rate of speed. I came out of her office looking like an extreme sunburn victim, and then my entire face would fall off for four days afterward. Amanda, who was blonde and fairy-like with a tiny pink braid undulating along the side of her face, was determined. "I'm going to ERASE this scar for you."

*YES, MA'AM, YOU SHALL INDEED.*

I also went to my dermatologist for Botox and "tear trough" fillers. I continue to stand by my vapidity.

I also wore turtlenecks, lots of them, so you *really* couldn't see the scar. I had all manner of them — furry cowl necks, tall wool turtlenecks that made it look like my head was resting on a tree stump, and even a few strategic mock necks.

I also started drinking a metabolism-boosting tea in the afternoon to stave off the weight gain, mixed in with collagen powder to regrow the hair and fill out the wrinkles.

I could feel the power that beauty had lent me leaking away, dripping down into drains, leeching out of the pores of my skin, and running down the backs of my legs. I wondered if there was any way to restock it even as I was frantically trying to hoard what I could, all the while feeling ashamed of how worried I was over this superficial, packaging part of myself. I couldn't replace what I was losing fast enough — the law of diminishing returns at work — and it felt like a cruel posture to take as I was also trying to coax my body into wellness. But it was a game of Beauty Pac-Man, chasing the next fix or tweak or product, and I couldn't pry my hands from the joystick.

Thorns leave a void where power used to be.

It turns out that suddenly converting from an active runner into a sluggish invalid also has its drawbacks in the joint department. One day, my left hip decided it would not allow me to put a shoe on my left foot anymore or sit cross-legged on the floor. It seemed to have grown itself a little ice pick for stabbing important nerve endings.

I knew I probably needed to stretch and strengthen every muscle I had but wondered what the balance between rest and activity should be. One theory about Covid Long Haulers is that they suffer from a form of chronic fatigue — CFS — which exercise could make even worse (though rest does little to help). But it had been almost a whole year now of the new normal, which was now a normal of being sedentary. I needed to at least *try* to move my body again.

I started with yoga.

On the first day, I wore a blue tank top and black leggings and posted a picture of my flimsy self in the Long Haul COVID Fighters Facebook group so they could all wish me luck. The forty-five minutes that followed felt archeologic; I was the mummy of Nefertiti trying to raise her crackly skeleton up out of her sarcophagus from under three feet of sand. It turns out it wasn't just my hip that refused to let me do things (even the yoga Child's Pose!) but my elbows and wrists, ankles, and knees were all aching and quivery like a hatchling's. I groaned like I was about to break apart.

A couple of weeks later, a joint doctor told me I now had arthritis and bone spurs, and cartilage tears, and that physical therapy was the first order of business. A pony-tailed physical therapist gave me exercises to do every day at home, then laid me flat on a table once a week to move my leg around and see what progress had been made. She would press her body weight against me in various poses, asking me to breathe deeply until the muscles and ligaments gave up more ground.

My yoga teacher, Cara, did something similar. She was always telling our class to move with our breath, and then to hold the poses long enough for a change to be made to our bodies — a dogged evolution towards stronger, stretchier muscles. Up through a sun salutation we would go, arms reaching overhead (inhale), then down we would plunge (exhale) into a forward fold, then up halfway with a straight back (inhale), then down into plank (exhale). Then chaturanga, and into Warrior Two where we would remain, tailbones tucked, shoulders back, chin down, core tight, right knee bent, left foot planted. Breathe. Breathe. Breathe, sinking further into the work of holding still. Holding still is especially hard work for an embodied person with so many other options available to her, especially when the holding hurts. "Three more breaths," Cara would say, so we all knew we could do it.

I couldn't always do it. I'd break out of a pose, gasping, shaking out a cramping foot or an immolated hamstring. With gentleness, I was encouraged to try again. Sometimes I would, but often I would just sink down into a modified Child's Pose that didn't tear at my hip flexor, feeling my heaviness on the mat. It turns out that this type of surrender is also a form of stillness. I could still rest attentively, breathing, breathing, breathing, even when I wasn't working at all.

I soon discovered there were many modes of stillness that can produce a change. There were days when my body told me we couldn't push ourselves to walk, and some days my body told us we needed Cara's class in the morning. Some days my body reminded us it was OK to lie still and let the warmth pour into the sunroom while we looked through the arched windows up into the infinite blue. Whatever posture we took, my body and I were learning to hold the position until some sort of new strength or flexibility had been achieved. Being still — being *positioned* — is a way to fill up: with air, with strength, with resolve. Despite my thinning hair and climbing scale, this shared work was helping us to begin a tentative cease-fire. This shared work between my body and me began to nourish both flesh and feelings.

As 2021 blossomed into spring and I began anticipating the one-year anniversary of my illness, an idea was unfurling. It was not a conscious realization, nor something I understood in a momentary thunderclap, but it was a felt truth beginning to bloom along with the daffodils of March: perhaps what stretched ahead of me was more than an endless timeline of illness, but also an endless table of food.

They had already dug her grave. It was just outside the thick stone walls of the convent. The hole was deep and murky, and there were shiny-back beetles just underneath the surface of things because their homes had been so recently disturbed.

Teresa was young and beautiful, but she was very sick. Long-term, chronic illness would come to be part of her life in the years that followed, and its effects can mostly be traced to this day. Some people think it was malaria ravaging her body, but decades afterward, she would endure terrible attacks of heart pain and ongoing, relentless morning sickness. She would have no respite after twenty weeks as I had with Drew when Easter had lifted the curse and the narrative was tidy. When she didn't die that day, she was sent home to recover, only to return to her convent where she spent three years in the infirmary. The illness was prolonged and awful, but so were the various remedies that were tried and failed.

There was blood. And tears. Writhing in the middle of the night, staring at ceilings. Fetal positions. Vomit? Probably vomit.

Ever practical, Teresa had advice for those enduring illness while trying to pray — give yourself a break. Be gentle with the rhythms you're trying to achieve because people in this state must *realize they are ill and make some alteration in their hours of prayer.*[94]

We must *realize we are ill.* This is hard when you're doing all you can to unrealize it, to make the illness unreal. Realization can be the greatest work of beginning because it requires a stopping and a momentary stillness, a held position. Realization is the first spark of humility, which leads to hunger, which leads, ironically, to a new kind of nourishment and health.

Teresa suggests changing it up if your body isn't allowing you to concentrate because of illness, mental or otherwise. If prayer is too hard, perhaps other forms of "spiritual recreation" are a good idea, like reading a good book or having spiritual conversations with like-minded people or doing "works of charity." But she's careful to acknowledge that the body can't even do these things sometimes and that all we can do is all we can do: "*Sweet is his yolk, and it is essential that we should not drag the soul along with us, so to say, but lead it gently, so that it may make the greater progress.*"[95]

Soul and body must be carefully, tenderly held together, a whole person, wholly in God's presence, wholly in the present moment. We can't drag part of ourselves down the road and leave the other half behind. That's not true progress. That's the definition of being *uncollected.*

Teresa would live to the ripe old age of sixty-seven, having lived almost fifty years with chronic health struggles. She would ultimately succumb, some people think, to uterine cancer, the C-word I had mercifully avoided. In a world without morphine and hospice, it's difficult to imagine what a death like that entailed. Was she alone? Surrounded by fellow nuns whom she had taught to pray? Dying could be a terrible business back then.

It's natural to try to draw a direct line from Teresa's chronic health thorns to her spiritual insight, but it is not a line she draws in her writings. Although her acute initial illness did inspire a brief spiritual awakening, after which she began the practice of prayer, the ongoing physical torments didn't seem to keep the spiritual magic alive. It didn't seem Teresa learned to leverage her lingering illness for closeness with God in any sort of deliberate way over those long years, as Augustine had suggested the widow Proba do with her thorn.

What Teresa does emphasize is the mysteriousness of prayer as a gift, as a grace — which, of course, is very Julian-esque — that no matter what your situation, God grants closeness to Him in his time, by his means. We can be pragmatic, practical, methodical, and committed, picking up our spiritual forks and knives for three meals a day with our Bibles and our acronyms and our shortcuts — but, as Julian would say, Jesus is the Ground, the initiator of the nourishment. He can use thorns to instigate the meal, but he doesn't have to. He can use enormous blessings to do the very same thing. Thorns are necessary for spiritual sustenance — unless they aren't. Jesus is unpredictable. He can even use a statue in a hallway. As practical as we can be trying to feed ourselves with His presence, it's ultimately a mystery and a great gift when it happens, something we don't have to strive and claw and fight our way to achieve. Every person is different, and he treats us with profound specificity. Therefore, we can't take pride in our blessedness, and we really can't take pride in our thorns. Thorns themselves don't make us spiritually exceptional.

We can only take a seat, pick up a fork, and hold still.

∿

Lord, I resist fighting today. Fighting involves so much activity, so much effort, action, and energy. Let me listen to the rhythms of my life and my body. Let me know what posture to hold today to achieve the kind of change or healing you have in mind. Let me breathe you in, and exhale thanksgiving.

Sustain me with every sunrise, pouring strength into my weak and withering parts. Help me put away the empty calories of self-given glory I consume to try to satisfy my hunger in my own way, on my own time.

People who fight can't be filled. I surrender and sit for supper.

# CHAPTER 6

# STILL FOR NOW:
# A SONG TO SING
# IN THE MEANTIME.

Crunch, crunch, crunch — up a steady hill, plodding deliberately through snow, I turned around to look. I could no longer resist the view I knew had materialized during my brief pilgrimage: the stark white of the Sangre de Cristo mountains set against blue skies, rolling along the horizon like they planned to just keep going on like that forever without anyone's permission. I stood in the roadway and breathed. Watched. Waited for something new to happen, but there is nothing new that happens in the woods. The pine trees

"BLESSED ARE THOSE WHO ENDURE IN PEACE, FOR BY YOU, MOST HIGH, SHALL THEY BE CROWNED."
– SAINT FRANCIS OF ASSISI

overhead moved together with what might be called a breeze, though it couldn't be heard or felt. Perhaps it was more the ghost of a breeze, or just the determination of the trees themselves to keep from falling asleep. I lingered there beneath them and before the mountains, feeling some kind of roots plunging from the soles of my boots down into the pavement and on through to the center of the earth. It might have been possible to stand there forever, but then my body reminded me why I was there in the first place.

If a pilgrim to the Holy Land likes to walk and wants to keep on walking, she can visit Jerusalem and traverse the Stations of the Cross along the

Via Dolorosa, following Jesus' meandering path to the hill of crucifixion. Hundreds of years ago, Franciscan monks began to lead devotional walks through the Old City, pointing out the various places of significance during Jesus' last hours: the spot where he was condemned, the places he fell under the weight of his cross, the place where he was stripped of his garments. A couple hundred years ago, official markers were installed (though the historicity of the exact spots have been disputed for centuries), and many churches around the world today feature their own versions of the Stations, including my Evangelical childhood church back in Irving, TX. It's a popular prayer exercise, especially during Holy Week, when the air is hot with approaching summer and the eggs are being dyed and decorated and sought after by pugs.

On my trip to Israel in high school, Scott walked us to several of the Stations. I remember the trek in vibrant flashes: the crush of crowds, tightly packed vendor stalls, glint of copper pots, cinnamon and cumin meandering in and out of breezeways, and the music of fast-tempo Arabic spoken in surround sound. The Stations did not provide a serene, contemplative environment for our little group that afternoon, which appropriately mirrored the day of Jesus' actual crucifixion. His world was chaos, too, all heckling and blows, the dripping of blood onto stones. There was no dignity in it. No measured pace. No stillness.

The Franciscan tour guides trace back, of course, to an Italian named Francis, who was born around 1181 in the Tuscan town of Assisi. One of his biographers, Bonaventure, paints a picture of a man completely, unwaveringly in love with the Cross of Jesus. In fact, Francis' moment of conversion happened one day when Jesus himself appeared "under the form of a crucifix" and *"so deeply was the memory of Christ's Passion impressed on his heart that it pierced even to the marrow of his bones."*[96] From that day forward, nothing in Francis' life was the same, much as Julian's life was changed after her bedridden vision of Christ's passion. Whatever may be said about Francis' famous love of poverty and of the natural world, what must be said first is that whatever he would do and become was set into motion the day Jesus stretched out his arms in sacrifice. *"All his life long,"* Bonaventure writes, Francis *"ever followed the footsteps of that Cross."*[97] His life was a one giant loop around the Stations.

Francis even wore a costume of sorts by way of tribute, apparently, which I can appreciate. After his youth of privilege and fine clothing, the newly converted Francis took on a "poor mantle"[98] tied with a simple cord and marked it with white chalk down the front of his chest: a stick-figure cross. He never wore much more than that until the day he died at about age forty-four. He even signed his name with the Greek letter Tau, which resembles a cross in shape. This was not a man of subtlety. Francis' birth falls about halfway between the crucifixion and our present day, and I wonder if God has considered sending reminders in the form of prophets or saints every 1,000 years to reinforce the centrality of Jesus' cosmic act for humanity. It's hard to imagine anyone as theatrical as Francis, and I mean "theatrical" in the very best sense of that word.

Although the cross was heavy for Jesus, it seemed light for Francis. He would come to earn the nickname *Poverello* — "little poor one," yet he was rich in love. Francis was known as a chronically hungry, destitute, and sick... and joyful and generous man. Mostly, his cross carried him. Francis sought out crosses to carry, *and to be carried by*. He seemed to be in a constant cycle of asceticism and manic productivity. This man seemed incapable of sitting still, despite his terrible physical state, except when it came to spending time in the presence of Jesus. He was forever going off into the elements for weeks at a time to fast and pray, and then re-exploding onto the scene with spiritual guns blazing, preaching or traveling or giving alms or giving away food or instructing his followers or rebuilding (literally, stone by stone) dilapidated churches. He bent down to pick up his cross, then shot up straight and fast, like it had a jet engine blazing out behind it.

During a turning point in his life, Francis was deciding if he really should go out into the world and preach or lead a quiet life of prayer. He loved prayer so much — he "had the gift of it"[99] — and was tempted to stay in that place of quiet surrender until his last breath. With the help of other prayer-loving, discerning friends, Francis decided Jesus was asking him to convert this stillness into service. Just as Jesus had submitted to stillness, to the immobility of having arms and feet nailed to a tree, Francis had also found a practiced surrender. And just as Jesus, by his stillness, achieved the greatest work for mankind, so Francis also became cosmically productive in his own practiced stillness. Francis was so identified with radical humility of Jesus' Cross, that it powered all the different versions of his greatness, both when he was at rest and when he was in motion.

Francis was a rare sort of human, is what I'm trying to say.

In 1996, the same summer we camped in the Negev under the show-stopping stars, our youth group traveled to Penza, Russia. Of the many service projects we planned, the dramatic re-enactment of the Crucifixion — set to Queen's "Bohemian Rhapsody" — was going to be the highlight. Scott, being the actor and director that he was, had an ambitious vision. For months, we rehearsed the moments of Christ's passion as they aligned with the raucous ride that is that song. (Yes, it is in fact true that the Stations of the Cross can be set to a Queen song, though I seem to lack the video evidence at the present time.) Somehow, we found ourselves on an outdoor stage in a Soviet-era city square, a gargantuan tray of concrete where tens of thousands of Russians stood shoulder-to-shoulder for a political rally. I'm not sure what politician was running for which office, or even that it was an election rally at all, only that we were surrounded by an undulating wave of young Russian faces who had been only children a few years earlier when the Iron Curtain came down. They seemed interested in participating in something new and democratic for their generation. Or they just didn't want to miss the biggest event of the year.

Inexplicably, our youth group was the opening act to this spectacle. I'm not sure how this was arranged, but perhaps the display of ten American teenagers wearing their Massimo shirts and GAP jeans was a no-brainer to the event organizers who saw us as a good prelude to the pageant of freedom that would follow. (This was before Putin came to power, of course.) We climbed the steps and looked out over a would-be 90s Russian Woodstock.

The audio system was blaring. The crowd pressed themselves in closer to the stage. It was about 3 p.m. and the sun was bright, but not Texas hot; it was *Russian* bright and *Russian* hot. As the music started, I felt the crowd's recognition of the song rise and zing back and forth across the square. This amazed me since I had never heard one single Queen song in all my life (see: the homeschool years, circa1986-94) until Scott played it for us on the first day of rehearsal. The crowd was at first thrilled to be hearing Queen and then immediately perplexed at what we were doing. Clearly, we were not re-enacting the music video. Clearly, something serious and sad was being pantomimed. One of our guys, perhaps Shaun or Joe, made the motion of hammering nails into Justin's wrists, who was Jesus. (This happened during the driving, head-bangy guitar bridge). I can't remember my exact stage directions, but I seem to remember portraying Mary or one of the women kneeling at the foot of the cross with my head bowed, a helpless woman who was also about to be a helpless actor.

Suddenly, a *plink* hit the side of my arm. And then I heard another *plink* land next to me, and then over my head. *Plink. Plink. Plink.* Bottle caps. They were throwing bottle caps. The threat was beginning to rise almost from the hot concrete itself. Never before had I faced the prospect of being heckled off a stage. Fortunately, there were enough people not throwing things to warrant staying up there for the last twenty eternal seconds until that fateful lyric closed us out: *nothing really matters to me...*

We stayed until the bitter end, which was, of course, the Resurrection of Justin/Jesus. There's always a resurrection if you hold still until the bitter end. Even if your play isn't good.

We were in Angel Fire, NM in March of 2021 to ski, really, but there are some things that are incompatible with skiing: fatigue, shortness of breath, and fevers. I was a few months out from surgery and still cycling through Covid symptoms in addition to the added lethargy of thyroid-less-ness and insufficient medication. But Spring Break waits for no man, especially those with energetic teenagers who can only be tamed by sun-streaked slopes and hikes to the snack bar. Drew was thirteen now, Maddie eleven. Gordon had taken charge of the kids' ski education and found out quickly that he was not the man for the job. A pigtailed instructor named Kristi would eventually take Drew and Maddie by the shoulders and show them how to snap into their skis without an unnecessary homicide, and soon they were wedging their way down the mountain like the athletes Gordon envisioned them to be. I stood at the bottom of the slope with my iPhone, my face freezing into white marble, taking videos of each child's arrival as if they carried Olympic torches. But then it was too cold, or I was too tired, and I would find myself back in the room, lying on the bed, looking out of the window.

But there was too much to see out there in the chilly, beginning-to-thaw beauty, too much sun and sky to let slip past. When my energy meter had risen back above absolute zero, I pulled my boots back on, stuck my arms through my puffer coat, put my hat and gloves on, and made my way back out into the chill. Instead of turning right to the slopes, I turned left up a roadway heading into the trees, as though I knew something was up there for me to find. I took my time, trudging deliberately to save what little I had in the metabolic reserves, opening my eyes wider to take in wildness on every side: tight piney cloches that rose from the road and ascended forever into the distance, the sugary waves of snow covering indecipherable things beneath; the distant call of some great bird. There were mountain homes, too, nestled into the camouflage of branch and shadow.

I stopped, finally. I stood still. Out beyond me was the quiet grandeur of mountain peaks, also unmoved and immovable.

What descended on me then was not snow, but a freeing calm that wriggled off the weight on my shoulders. My spine decompressed. My jaw slackened. The heaviness of fatigue and discouragement was pulled up and away like a velvet drape and replaced with a gossamer wrap: the twin elements of focus and curiosity. It was the fullness of the present moment coming to bear, demanding to be entered and lived.

It was simplicity, lightness, breath.

I stood transfixed before the everlasting range of Sangre de Cristo, the Blood of Christ mountains, waiting for the next thing to happen, whatever it was. All was suspended in quiet. And with the quick subtlety of a glance, an invitation: to be a human being again, one who could take her body back down to bed carefully and with attention. I was invited to do this without leaving any of the beauty behind. I could carry myself without adding any weight at all.

~~~

### Station of the Cross: Jesus is Made to Carry His Cross

Oh Lord, you bent down and hoisted it up. It only took a moment. No time like the present. You bore its weight to lighten my shoulders.

The idea of giving you my whole life — of taking up my cross alongside you — is daunting. But I can give you this humble moment, this little ordinary sixty seconds in which nothing seems to be happening, in which no progress seems to be in motion. This chair I'm sitting in. The way my lungs take air in, then breathe the air out and away. The tick of the clock on the wall. Surely, I could give these humble things to you. Surely, I could endure this instant of the thorn with your help. Surely, right now, I can be still. If I string enough of these surrendered seconds together, I've turned over a lifespan. You can be trusted with lifespans and lightyears, but also with little breaths and little-to-nothing happening.

You are Lord of Right Now, of the long calm in this moment I'm living. Even if the Now is difficult, incomplete, or confusing, its saving perfection is that you've teamed up with it.

Now is when I can be light on my feet.

**SILENCE**

Drew was learning to play the cello. In all his fidgety thirteen-year-old glory, he would settle into his chair to work exercises for his orchestra class at school.

"ABOUT THREE IN THE AFTERNOON JESUS CRIED OUT IN A LOUD VOICE, "ELI, ELI, LEMASABACHTHANI?" (WHICH MEANS 'MY GOD, MY GOD, WHY HAVE YOU FORSAKEN ME?')."
– MATTHEW 27:46

This was like watching a rubber band about to snap — great pent-up energy straining against the tension of will. Because he is hyper-obsessive over anything he happens to have latched onto in a given season, Drew had been intensely googling YoYo Ma, digging up old performances on YouTube and trying to emulate them at home. (Eventually, Drew discovered that the theme song from *Jaws* was a lot easier to replicate than "The Swan.")

Ever in desperate search of ways to be slightly less mediocre parents (and Santa Clauses), Gordon and I had stuffed Drew's stocking with tickets to see YoYo Ma in person when he was scheduled to play for the Fort Worth Symphony Orchestra's gala on February 20th. The tickets were pricey, so we decided that I, being the musically inclined spouse, would take Drew on a mom-and-son date despite my unpredictable physical state. It would be a whole thing: a black-tie event preceded by a nice dinner. Then the news came: YoYo Ma had canceled because of Covid. He wasn't sick, he was only just being careful. The Pfizer vaccine had just been released only eight weeks before, and it was still winter.

As I lay on my couch and recorded another one of my fevers, I released YoYo in my heart and sent him gently on his way. *You do you, YoYo.* Drew, however, took the whole thing as a personal offense. The idea that YoYo would give him the cold shoulder even in the face of disease and death was a very deep betrayal. Some other lady was performing now, some pianist, whatever.

I convinced Drew we should still get dressed up. *Let's go!*

When the night arrived, women in long evening gowns glided around the atrium of the concert venue like figure skaters, some with bedazzled masks strung across their faces. I was proud of Drew as he shook hands with the soon-to-be mayor. He was my sparkly little penguin, like a Judith Lieber handbag with dimples. Because the event had been moved from a smaller venue to a giant arena where we could space out safely, Drew and I found ourselves way up in the nosebleed section looking down onto a stage flanked by giant screens. Out came the beloved Fort Worth Symphony conductor, Miguel Harth-Bedoya — the audience cheered him with a verve that had been pent up for months — and then a small woman in a glittery dress made her way into the spotlight. She had short black hair, platform sandals, and a smile you could see from the stage without having to look at the screens. She had taken her mask off. She sat down on the bench of the piano.

Rachmaninoff: Dark. Complicated. Roiling. The muscles in her back were hard pistons of steel, powering a forceful yet somehow intricate performance. She was all arms and fingers and back, flashing like lightning in a dress that seemed more and more illuminated by electricity from within. Her smile somehow stayed fixed, even though she was putting forth enough effort to birth a baby. The orchestra welled up behind her, like a wave of sound carrying the piano's song to a crest before crashing it down upon us.

Tears were running down my cheeks and into my mask. Drew was very still. We were so far away from the musicians and from the other patrons, stuck up there like bats in the rafters, yet you could feel the entire crowd had been gripped with a common hand around the throat. There was a shared constriction of breath, rigidity of spines, and heaviness of water gathered at the corners of eyes. What a drought we had all survived, I thought, after months of Covid shutdown. A drought of sharing a communal tempo and a collective audio beauty that language itself had abdicated. Suddenly, we were more at home in our bodies; the music was a tuning fork realigning us with each other to such a degree that it was almost embarrassing to make eye contact afterward as we streamed back out to our cars. Somehow, now we knew each other's secrets. We had been told the truth in a mutual way, soaked in the same indescribable color. It was not the lifting of Covid. It was not the lifting of my symptoms. But it was still the lifting of a curse, if only temporarily, by something wholly outside of ourselves. Seated and listening, we received it.

The idea of silent listening as a vital prayer practice goes back to the ancients and their *lectio divina*. But really, it started with Adam and Eve, who were friends with a God who walked through Park Hill with them during the cool part of the day. (It must be noted here that God is the inventor of taking walks.) God, Adam, and Eve walked and talked together sometimes, presumably, and if one of you is talking, the other one is listening.

If prayer is like breathing, as David G. Benner says, then reading God's word might be the inhale. Meditating on that word silently is that millisecond before the exhale when we respond with words of our own and then with the action of our daily lives.[100] In the process of breathing you must take that quiet moment to absorb the oxygen before expelling the $CO_2$ in words or sentences of your own. That vital pause is key because silence is "only good manners since God is already communicating."[101] To not listen quietly as part of a two-sided conversation is just plain rude.

The acolytes of Saint Francis, who went on to become the order of the Friars Minor, were given very simple instructions. When the order was just starting out, they didn't have prayer books from which to read or study, and so they were instructed to devote their time "*to continual prayer*," more specifically, to "*contemplate the Cross of Christ continually*."[102] Although Francis would go on to write many helpful prayer guides and prayer services (even a paraphrase of The Lord's Prayer!), the contemplation of the Cross was his order's incubating practice.

Francis himself was a man devoted to the persistent prayer of all types and varieties, "*whether walking or sitting, at home or abroad, laboring or resting, he was ever intent on prayer, so that he seemed to have dedicated to it not only his heart and his body, and all that was in him, but also his work and his time.*"[103] If prayer is truly a conversation with Jesus, then Francis apparently did a lot of talking *and* a lot of listening. His life was a continual conversation, a gentle cycle of silence and speaking, a running back-and-forth openness that took different forms depending on what he was doing on a particular day.

This is a total inversion of Selah-praying. We must stop now, dead in our tracks, and observe this fact. Instead of stopping frequently throughout his day to pray, Francis made prayer his life. Instead of his life being punctuated by prayer, his life was prayer itself, punctuated by sleep. Francis had learned to breathe God in and exhale him out.

What is the Cross saying that must be contemplated to foster such a living, breathing connection to God?

Francis spent many days and weeks alone answering this question for himself. Perhaps, as he sat at the base of some mossy rock with the Tuscan sun at his back and the shadows cast longways down a slope, he pictured Jesus crying out to the one who had rejected him in the worst way possible: by going silent. For the first time, Francis ponders, Jesus was having a one-sided conversation with his Father. His own walking-and-talking companion was suddenly gone. The gentle cycle of openness between God and the God-man had been cut down to one speaker, and when you've been left in silence, you yell even louder and squirm even harder.

Jesus screamed out a Psalm, but even that didn't get God's attention.

Francis, absorbing this reality, was perhaps quiet. Maybe he sat there in stillness until his shadow bled all the way to the bottom of the hill as the sun sank behind him. Maybe he lost himself in the melody of this thought, letting it work through his fingers, down his throat, and to the tips of his toes, until some cursed part of him was healed.

~~~

### Station of the Cross: Jesus Falls the First Time

Oh Lord, you stumbled under the weight of it. Were you anticipating the searing pain of silence, of unsurvivable ghosting? You endured alienation so we could have proximity. You suffered cosmically painful abandonment so we could enjoy chronically intimate presence.

And yet, I am rarely silent before this startling love.

My Word Factory is never shut down or turned off. Even if my body is lying prostrate, my words run full-tilt through my brain or through my lips.

I choose to sit and listen to your music, even if the melody is faint today.

It's *your* turn to speak. Your cross speaks louder than words.

## POOR

Apparently, the People in Charge at my church thought I did a good-enough job reading the Christmas story in the service that they believed I would be able to sing Broadway for

"FOR YOU KNOW THE GRACE OF OUR LORD JESUS CHRIST, THAT THOUGH HE WAS RICH, YET FOR YOUR SAKE HE BECAME POOR, SO THAT YOU THROUGH HIS POVERTY MIGHT BECOME RICH."
– 2 CORINTHIANS 8:9

an upcoming concert, a regular offering the church provided free to the community. The rational adult inside of me should have raised her manicured hand and asked, "Now, tell me what exactly makes you think your voice is capable of this right now? You're still going to a speech pathologist to monitor your vocal cords post-surgery. You don't KNOW if you can really sing like that anymore. Have you, in fact, tried? Have you spent any time even attempting to sing basic warm-ups or have you been too afraid to explore what's possible because of what you might find? And there's also the small matter of you continuing to run fever and having no energy and needing inhalers to breathe. What part of Broadway singing is even one percent compatible with any of these things?"

My "rational adult" voice talks at a very high rate of speed.

And the answer to her questions were really very simple: I would be singing Fantine from *Les Miserables*, my ultimate dream role, one I'd never gotten to play. Since a key to success in the performing arts is being able to borrow the confidence someone else has in you, and since the People in Charge wanted me to sing *I Dreamed a Dream*, I was working under the assumption that I must be capable of it.

I started practicing the song. I sang it constantly, trying to gin up more power, and more vocal presence, but it was like jumping rope underwater. Essentially, I could sing the song one time through before needing to lie down and wouldn't be able to sing it nearly as well until twenty-four hours later. I could get a single pretty-good one in per day. This scared me because I'm a big believer in drilling a performance down into the DNA of your cells before you take your darling self out onto a public stage. I pushed. I sent videos of my song to Katti, my wise and wonderful vocal coach, who helped me wade through.

The night of the performance, I stood onstage in a black velvet dress, microphone in hand. My thyroidectomy scar was slathered in concealer and a layer of powder as thick as cardstock. A full orchestra, the same glorious one from Christmas Eve, swelled behind me as I began to sing.

What I should have steeled myself for was what happened when the oboe lifted her solo line above the strings. It was a rush of fire, a hot sparkly geyser of emotion shooting up through my throat to strangle me. I didn't croak, exactly, but my voice was uneven, strained, weak. I was an overwhelmed, tired Fantine, one with too much heartache to convey and not enough physical infrastructure to sustain and channel it. The journey of the past year was coming down upon me, amplified by the excruciating beauty of music.

I cringed when I heard a recording later.

I sat back down in the front pew, buzzing with adrenaline and a vague sense of defeat. The rush of performance energy was loud in my ears, but I could hear the words, as if shouted from the mezzanine: YOU BOMBED THAT.


Saint Francis would have hated being called a Saint. "Mister" would do just fine, thanks. He was so identified with his Savior on the Cross that the idea of being somebody important, anybody of significance, outside of this, would have been repulsive. One way he expressed this total union was through poverty, and this is where all the famous old stories of Saint Francis come quickly to mind, of the way he would give away clothes and food almost the moment they were given to him for his own meager survival. He never had much to give away, but whether it was a cloak or a dime or a crust of bread, he always offered it quickly and totally. He called poverty "Lady Poverty," and desired her ardently, like a lover. Eighty years after Francis' death, our old friend Dante was so captured by this that Lady Poverty and Francis together make an appearance in his famous work.[104]

It would be easy to see Francis' commitment to extreme generosity as some sort of unattainable example that you might follow in a more reasonable gear for your circumstances, but he would have hated that, too. Francis' first motivation in poverty was not to be an example. It would also be easy to see his generosity as an extreme act of service done to attain divine favor. Again, Francis would balk. He was not trying to make God an offer he couldn't refuse. Francis' biographer paints a man motivated by only two things in his lifestyle of abdication: to identify with Jesus and to serve Jesus.[105]

Jesus, after all, was also a man of, shall we say, self-imposed boundaries. If you accept the premise of the incarnation, Jesus abdicated unspeakable eternal grandeur to confine himself inside of a respiratory, digestive and circulatory system. He traded infinite abundance for a life of hardship, of sleeping out in the elements with nowhere to lay his head under the very stars he flung into being. He emptied himself of the perfect love-connection he had enjoyed from eternity past with God to be rejected by Him and then mutilated by people he had adored since before they were born. Jesus exited the eternal for the time-bound. He constrained himself into a tired body that could stub its toe or have its beard pulled out. Even if Jesus had been born to infinite human wealth and extraordinary human acceptance, he still would have experienced an unimaginable poverty compared to what he had left behind. Jesus' whole life was one giant thorn, not just the twelve awful hours of his rejection and crucifixion. Jesus was poor in every sense a person can be poor, and for all of his life.

In the faces of the poor, then, Francis saw the face of Christ. There was Jesus in the corner of that doorway, huddled and sick, with nothing to eat. Here is Jesus, begging for alms under the eave of some dripping roof. As he took off tunics and emptied pockets to give to Jesus, Francis *"was thus restoring to him what was rightfully his own."*[106] While prideful people wandered restlessly in the past or in the future — how much money they had at one time, how much they might have someday — prayerful people like Francis dwelt in their present poverty. They could sit in it. Relish it, even. Be nourished by it, even as they nourished others who beforehand had felt unseen and neglected. For Francis, poverty was the "food of humility."[107] Because if Jesus is beside you, within you, and before you, what other wealth do you need?

It seems extreme to willingly pierce oneself with the thorn of poverty. Unattainable, and even somewhat perverse, this is totally at odds with our culture's revered idea of self-care. But the more you read about Mister Francis, the Poverello, the more it seems like he had found a shortcut to a wildness of joy and a freedom of spirit that can only be described as indulgent spiritual decadence. Pondering the cross in prayer was leading Francis somewhere open and free, somewhere wonderfully enriching for those around him.

Is it realistic (or healthy?) to embrace the various iterations of poverty we have been given — our thorn — and then to offer whatever crumbs we can?

I sat down on the front row pew. The next song was up, and I watched the concert until the end. Three older, rather fabulous ladies were seated behind me and kindly congratulated me when the program was over. I visited with them a while and came to realize a very startling fact about two of them: they had just lost their husbands to Covid. This was their first time out of the house to an event.

I suddenly felt conspicuous and squirmy. Something gripped my wrist as I replayed the words of my song in my head as they might have heard it. There were lyrics about dreams dying, of the living hell that contradicted everything Fantine once imagined for herself. She was now living a killed life, one separated from her beloved and all he represented for her. It wasn't witches or demons that had killed her life. It was life itself. Life was the faceless killer, as is so often the case when we are randomly impaled by thorns: out of nowhere, without explanation, vicious.

Strangely, whatever had bunched up inside my chest on the stage smoothed out, like a knot slipping back into straight rope.

I hadn't given the performance my ego had wanted. It wasn't the thing I wanted to offer the world, but maybe it was what these particular ladies needed to receive. They didn't need alms, but maybe the cracking of a voice, the rattle of a chest, the stranglehold of grief — maybe they needed these from me. Maybe these meager offerings of mine could alleviate a molecule of their emotional destitution. Maybe, as paltry as it might be, my song was a good mirror to hold in front of people who up to this moment had felt unseen.

It seemed like a miracle, that what little I had might have been enough.

The next day, I picked up my prayer journal. I hadn't visited it since August of 2020, six months prior. Something inside me was ready to pick up her fork and relish the time at hand like a gourmet delicacy.

"Help me to accept my boundaries so I can revel in the Ocean of You," I wrote.

~~

**Station of the Cross: Jesus is Stripped of His Garments**

You gave it all. Not just your time and your blood, but the very clothes on your back.

Lord, I sit quietly before you, unconcerned about how and when you want to use me. I accept that you have purposes and plans that are far beyond my ability to comprehend right here, right now. I accept that maybe I was given a little bit so you could make a lot and that offering my weakness and inadequacy is good and noble and should be done freely, without shame.

Bless the world in your way, not in mine.

## BE

Mister Francis had a habit of going out into the middle of nowhere for extended times of prayer and fasting. Perhaps it is clear by now that this is not something the great saint and I would ever have in common given

"I WILL STAND AT MY WATCH AND STATION MYSELF ON THE RAMPARTS; I WILL LOOK TO SEE WHAT HE WILL SAY."
– HABAKKUK 2:1

my tortilla dependence, but it's undeniable that fasting would quickly bring a person to standing smack dab in the center of her being-human. The immediacy of hunger brings you into the immediacy of Now. And before we can offer our poverty to be of service in the world, we must offer ourselves. Before we *do*, we must *be*. Being...with God. Another possible definition of prayer to try on for size.

Somehow or another (spies?), Bonaventure, Francis' biographer, was aware that Francis would go out into the woods and fast in this way, and that he would "beat his breast" before God, relating to him on a lot of different levels —much as Julian and Teresa would later practice — *"[discoursing] familiarly with his Lord. He made answer to Him as judge, besought Him as a father, conversed with Him as a friend."*[108] Of course, this sounds like the opposite of silently contemplating the Cross. This is clearly the other side of the conversation, the responding part that Francis was in charge of, and he was very comfortable just being himself in all of his largess (never have I ever beat my chest while praying). The man could own his feelings when he had big feelings to feel. Perhaps he contemplated Christ crying out to God from the Cross — "Why have you forsaken me?!" — and felt permission to follow suit. The cross was harrowing and awful and big enough to absorb smaller crosses, and Francis could trust it to provide a sturdy framework for his own.

If God loves us as a friend, as a spouse, as a father, as a brother, wouldn't it delight him for us to engage him prayerfully in these modes of being, even in our crucifixion turmoil? What would it feel like to express my frustration as one married to God? How does that change if God is my brother? If he's my best friend? If he is my Creator and Judge?

David G. Benner suggests employing the use of something others have called the "Welcoming Prayer," where we are to welcome difficult, troublesome emotions "into the home of our self" to surrender our total selves to God — the good, the bad, and the ugly — and let go of things that might stand in the way of greater trust and openness to him.[109] It takes a great deal of grit to admit how powerless we feel, how choked by grief, how violently angry, or how bewildered we are with God's action, or inaction. Owning our emotions — not just owning them begrudgingly but welcoming them eagerly — feels dangerous. Perhaps if we ignored them, they wouldn't trouble our spiritual life so much.

At any rate, what's clear is that Francis was both great at silence and great at stating the facts, whether he took time to welcome his own unsettled, wild-animal emotions or not. He was a true conversationalist in that sense, someone in an actual relationship with another sentient being. He was being himself and being with another Being at the very same time.

"Unwelcome circumstances...are not gifts," writes David G. Benner, of thorns, and of praying through them honestly with God. "But they may contain a gift. Don't simply ask, therefore, what you are supposed to learn from the circumstances. Rather, pray that the Spirit would help you discern the gifts of God that the circumstances contain. The core of that gift is God's presence."[110]

Perhaps this is what Francis was always trying to get at out there alone in the woods, hungry, past all the grime and the tears: that being, and having your being in God, is the golden center of all heartache.

Maybe the heartache is worth reaching that center.


March 14, 2021 was sneaking up quickly: my fortieth birthday. It had been almost a year of illness, a year of total societal upheaval, and now I was about to have a birthday that people buy tombstone-decorated napkins to celebrate. Because it was still pre-vaccine for most people, no big party was in order. I would ring in the day quietly with my family and reflect on all I had overcome to achieve such a ripe old age. I wouldn't be taking it for granted.

In the McQuitty house when I was growing up, my dad instigated a tradition of sharing "Words of Wisdom" with the rest of the family on your birthday. After candles had been blown out and presents opened, the birthday boy or girl would reflect on what he or she had learned the past year, which of course meant ruminating on things he or she was only now just beginning to get an inkling about and practice. The more years that pass, the less wisdom I seem able to process, package and share in a concise way. It seems I'm only able to offer the scroungy beginnings of wisdom, maybe, the mere whiff of wisdom that makes me want to follow its scent out the back door and down the alley. It's really a dreadful, wonderful tradition, one none of us ever seem to remember is coming until almost the moment it happens.

My turn came inevitably a few days before my actual birthday when my parents came into Fort Worth to have dinner with us and my in-laws. They had both fully recovered from Covid (thank God) and we figured it was probably safe to meet. I looked at them sitting across from me, their dear faces regal and pale with the navy wall of my mother-in-law's dining room behind them. People looked more solid in real life. The Zoom boxes couldn't diminish them for long.

"It is now time for Words of Wisdom!" Dad declared ceremoniously, as though I was turning nine. We all giggled, and for once in my life, I was not caught off guard that this moment had come. "Julie, I'm sure you have a lot of wisdom to share after *this* year," he said.

Later, I couldn't remember what I had said, and I blamed this on my incessant brain fog. I asked Gordon about it, and he suggested I had said some version of what *he* had said during his Words of Wisdom in October, which was something like, "I'm learning the importance of releasing control."

"The importance of releasing control?" I asked, liking the idea.

"Actually, I think that's what *I* said. I think *you* said something about just *being*." It appeared the brain fog was contagious.

"Just *being*?" I repeated. I liked this idea, too. *Being* was more of just a single word, not exactly Words (plural) *or* Wisdom. But it sounded like something I would have said in my shaky state, when nothing else in my life was possible for me to manipulate or rush. Sometimes we must decide to just *be*. Sometimes we get to choose just to be a person living in a particular moment, and sometimes that can be enough. In this way, *Being* is a quiet form of heroism. It stares down something that can, at times, be even scarier than danger or death, and that thing is drudgery. Perceived meaninglessness. Monotony. The long swaths of afternoon where nothing changes, and nothing seems to be about to change, and possibly you've been forgotten. *Being* under these circumstances is harrowing. But since even a bedridden person can have the sovereignty of deciding to be, this brand of heroism is also very democratic. Anyone can wear the cape.

"I'm sorry I didn't remember what your Words of Wisdom were," said Gordon. We both shrugged.

On my actual birthday, a few days later, Gordon told me to sit down on the couch. He pushed play on the TV, and suddenly there were the faces of friends and family, one after the other, saying all kinds of wonderful things about me and what our friendship has meant to them. They were using more "being" words than "doing" words; more words about what it's like for us to spend time together and less about ways I had impressed them with what I had performed or achieved. The words tasted so good. The words poured over me and through me, but after a few days, I couldn't remember what any of them had said, either; words just had a way of falling away out of my ears and onto the tile. I couldn't remember their words, just the way it felt to sit and watch the faces of my beloveds and hear the timbre of their voices.

Words and maybe even wisdom couldn't last, but I was beginning to feel safer in my skin somehow and for longer periods of time.

～

**Station of the Cross: Jesus Meets His Sorrowful Mother**

What an awful, beautiful moment: eyes locked with her. Fully terrified, entirely beside herself, Mary met your gaze. Made a last true connection.

Lord, today I stand at my post. I inhabit my body. I look for your face, and I listen for the tones and inflections of your voice. I choose to accept this moment as it is because you are in it, and that makes it good.

I allow my true feelings to come to the surface of my awareness. I express them to you, speaking them aloud so we both can hear them.

It's freeing to be myself around you.

**OPEN**

A few days before my first installment of the Moderna vaccine, I was scheduled to shoot the last scene for the *Beneath The Trees* trailer. It had been six months since my last time

"WE LOVE BECAUSE HE FIRST LOVED US." – 1 JOHN 4:19

on set with the project, where I had feigned wellness and confidence despite my illness and impending surgery. So much had been overcome, so much avoided — the threat of cancer, the loss of my voice — and my improvement with energy, breathing, and endurance was clear. Yet key symptoms hung on like barnacles: I still felt foggy in the head, especially in the afternoons when my temperature would gin up to 100 degrees and leave me shaking.

The fatigue still stalked me like a bear who preferred to lie across my chest instead of eating me. I was worried about remembering my lines and how to be an actor in general, all the old familiar risks that had plagued my work life for a year. We would be shooting in the late afternoon, my witching hour.

My scene partner, Sam, and I had never worked together before. She was about a decade younger than me, with long black hair and a wide, open smile. Our scene took place in a gazebo overlooking a placid pond. The occasional duck floated by sending aloof, disinterested looks in our direction. I was playing "Shannon," and Sam was "Pilar." We held glasses of "wine" and ran through our lines before the cameras were set up, or the scene was lit. We began settling into the pace of the dialogue and making choices about the intentions of certain moments. I got used to Sam. She got used to me. We established that trust between actors that says, "I will take care of you. I will give you what you need to play this scene."

There is a lot of time on a set to sit and watch other people do their jobs for forty-five minutes so that you can do your job in thirty seconds. Sam and I soon started talking about real-life things, and I found myself unzipping the bag of 2020 to show her my souvenirs: my Long Covid journey, my cancer scare, and my thyroidectomy. I pulled the collar of my shirt down to reveal where I had covered my scar in concealer and powder. There was something in me that had to confess everything like she was a priest sent to my holding cell.

"I've been worried about today," I said. "My mind isn't what it used to be when I don't feel good like this."

She leaned in. It turns out that Sam was a safe place to park all this information. She didn't bristle. She seemed unconcerned about having to share a scene with someone still fighting a lingering illness, who might drop a line or space out at any moment. This ability of hers to hold her face in the right configuration to appear generous and full of grace was all the encouragement I needed.

I knew how to be Shannon — lost, bewildered, determined — with Pilar, partly because Julie knew how to be herself with Sam. I felt the crisp zing of oxygen that fills your lungs when you are finally telling the truth. It was the energizing shiver of being open, like walking past a door flung wide on a cold day.

As a homeschooled Evangelical kid, I was unfamiliar with the idea of Patron Saints. We collected Christian CDs with the faces of DC Talk and Audio Adrenaline band members on the covers, and these were the extent of our revered spiritual icons. We did not possess a mental stable filled with disembodied heaven people all waiting to intercede on our behalf. But those Catholics. It turns out those Catholics have a nuanced selection.

There's even a Patron Saint of Theatrical Performers whose name is Saint Genesius. (He also covers Epilepsy, which is not totally unrelated.)

Legend has it that Saint Genesius was a little too honest, a little too open and vulnerable on stage one day when he was performing in front of the bloody Roman emperor Diocletian in the late third century. Apparently, he was in a play mocking the new sect known as "Christians," who had invented a creepy new ritual they called "baptism." While re-enacting the rite onstage, Genesius had some sort of vision that led to an immediate, real-life conversion. He became the first consummate Method actor who was never able to get out of character. He apparently stopped the whole performance and began preaching that everyone there should follow Jesus, too, even the mean old emperor. It slowly dawned on Diocletian that this actor was not acting anymore. Genesius lost his head, and then he lost his head.

What Genesius lacked in discretion, he made up for in humility. It takes great humility to be open and transparent about anything, especially publicly and in front of any random person. The best actors I know are the humblest. They are willing to be uncomfortably real in front of total strangers. This is a function of courage, yes, but mostly it's a function of humility. Acting is a trick of deep virtue, a celebration of and a submission to reality. Genesius must have had some measure of acting talent because even under the gaze of so many eyes, he was able to jettison the innate human tendency to avoid, downplay or suppress reality when the biggest truth of his life made itself evident. If something was real, he wanted to connect with others over it, no matter how it made him look or how it interrupted his agenda.

If you've lived in Western culture for any length of time, you are aware that Saint Francis of Assisi also had a peculiar openness to deep reality and that he expressed this by wanting to connect with everything that lived, even with birds and sheep and wolves. He was so humble that he had a natural inclination to commune with everything God had created, even addressing animals and stars and sun as his *brothers* and *sisters* because they "had all one origin with himself."[111] He preached to birds. He taught a sheep how to kneel at Communion. Francis had a sense of what Jesus would reveal to Julian two-hundred years later: that we are all part of the hazelnut resting in the palm of God's hand.

And the beautiful thing was that Francis not only elevated the natural world in dignity, but the natural world elevated him as well in a self-sustaining cycle. Everywhere he looked, he saw doorways to little rooms of reality. One day, even the chirping of a grasshopper was so poignant that it compelled Francis to worship God. He asked the grasshopper politely to continue its song every day for a week afterward, which, apparently, it did.[112] Francis learned to draw near to God by any means possible, and usually, it was by the glint of a wing pushing against wind or by the song of a bug.

There was something about Francis' engagement with the Cross that seemed to give him this great openness to everything else, and this openness of his, in turn boomeranged him back to Christ on the Cross in a continuous exchange of self-giving attention. Just as Jesus spread open his arms to be nailed, so his Francis could remain open himself, and maybe this is a general characteristic of those who pray in meditative gaze on the gospel. True vertical connection (prayer) brings a broader horizontal connection (creation, people).

And if you wanted to call this connection something else, you might pick up that old word we so often fumble and drop on the ground: "love."

~~~

### Station of the Cross: Simon of Cyrene Helps Jesus Carry His Cross

Lord, your cross intersects the real world. Your cross brings reality to bear on everything it touches. Because of your sacrifice, all creation is compelled to bear the weight of it. We cannot live in a world that doesn't pulse with what happened that day. Trees, sky, sea. They exist in the world where you loved and died, and so can I.

Today, I repent of the ways I've tried to avoid reality or suppress it around others, either by minimizing my thorn or by blowing it out of proportion. Neither is truly loving. I remain open to them, to myself, to everything that is.

## SECRET

Getting the COVID vaccine was — and still is — a point of debate among Long Haulers. Some of them rush back from their shots delirious, posting in the online groups about finally feeling normal for the first time in over a year mere hours after getting the first dose. They're like the leper who was healed and came back from the FEMA tent rejoicing. Then there are those who sit in dust and ashes, completely relapsing post-shot.

"THE SECRET THINGS BELONG TO THE LORD OUR GOD, BUT THE THINGS THAT ARE REVEALED BELONG TO US AND TO OUR CHILDREN FOREVER, THAT WE MAY DO ALL THE WORDS OF THIS LAW."
– DEUTERONOMY 29:29

My general practitioner, Dr. G, sent me an exclamation-point-laden message begging me to get the vaccine. Although my fever rates had been down overall, I had been running four straight days of fever that week, and I was struggling with how to check the box on the form that asked if I had been feeling sick. "Just check the box *no!*" she wrote. "It's looking like 40 percent of Long-Haulers are improved by receiving the vaccine!!!"

Of course, this meant MOST Long Haulers either stayed the same or got worse, but still. It seemed like a bet worth taking. My other consideration was how strict the Actors Equity Union was becoming on their standards for returning to live performance. Unless I was fully vaccinated, I wouldn't be allowed to perform at an Equity theater. Even though requests for exceptions could always be made, why would I make myself more of a hassle for a theater to cast? It's hard enough to get acting work anywhere, any time. I could read the hastily scrawled writing on the wall. I held the risks in a heavy palm, weighing them.

Ultimately, April Fool's Day 2021 seemed like a good day for the Bad Luck Lady to get her first dose of Moderna. A cute firefighter jabbed my arm with the needle for which the world had been waiting.

The vaccination center to which I had been assigned was in Trinity Park, a massive public park with winding trails that funneled thousands of cars through the FEMA tents. I spent two hours inching past trees and bike racks, and playground equipment. Finally, a FEMA officer approached me, had me roll down my window, and took my forms. "I like your perfume," he offered, unnecessarily. Leave it to me to get dressed up for a vaccination. He pointed me to a specific lane where a firefighter was stationed with a red cooler full of shots. I eased closer.

I could hear the rushing of my blood. I could see the drop-off coming. What *would* this do to my body? I was forty-five seconds from the plunge. Then twenty. Then ten. Then came the sharp prick, stomach-in-throat, over the edge and down, followed by the firm press of a Band-Aid and the instruction to pull my car into another line to wait for a reaction. I did as I was told. I took deep breaths, willing my heart rate down, massaging the place on my arm where a year of history-making science and political turmoil had converged.

Nothing happened, is what happened. I was released to drive home. I went to Maddie's soccer game an hour later. Made dinner. Slept well. And when the next afternoon arrived, I realized: I hadn't run a fever in over twenty-four hours. In the four days before my shot, I had been pushing 100-degree temps, but now there was nothing out of the ordinary. It was indeed exclamation-point worthy!!! I was quiet and hopeful, not wanting to jinx it. Gordon, who had gotten the same brand of vaccine, had run almost 104 for two days after his shot. I sat around in chairs with a clenched jaw.

But I didn't run a fever the next day either. Or the next. Easter Sunday came on April 4, 2021, three days later. It was Easter Sunday exactly one year prior that my illness had begun, the fatigue and fever sinking me down into the couch after the ham and scalloped potatoes. Here was Easter all over again, but I was more awake, somehow, more aware of my surroundings. Was this the answer to how the narrative resolved, a thorny year bookended by Easters?

Saint Francis was drawn to lepers. Leprosy is probably world history's kingpin chronic illness, not only wasting the body but wasting the social capital of its victim, who would be forced to leave his or her community to suffer alone. Jesus famously healed lepers in the gospels, and the first thing they did was to find a priest to reinstate them as bona fide human beings once again. Lepers didn't have the luxury of Pac-Manning their way from specialist to specialist to gobble up whatever medical care they could find. They were written off as the walking dead, and the only belonging they could claim was to their own sad and ailing zombie colony.

Francis was naturally attracted to them. Death always attracts resurrection because death is the aberration, not the rule. Bonaventure writes that Francis, *"in his deep love of humility, [went] among the lepers and remained with them, serving them diligently for the love of God."*[113] He *remained* with them, the most mind-blowing verb of all. He didn't just give money or drop off clothing, but he stayed, wearing that rough tunic with the chalk-scrawled cross down his chest. He washed their bodies, dressed their wounds, and even kissed their wounds,[114] a visual assault on the imagination. In later years, after Francis had died and the lore of his life was already at a fever pitch, rumor had it that his name could be invoked to heal leprosy. [115] What might have appeared quirky or eccentric about Francis' openness to animals and the natural world unveiled itself as true splendor in his openness to the terminal debris of humanity. It's one thing to commune with squirrels. It's another thing to kiss lepers.

It's no surprise that someone who had spent hours reflecting on Christ as the "man of sorrows" given for us would be able to find brotherhood with lepers in this way.[116] In the Cross, Francis saw his own chronic need for grace. Just as Jesus was ever present with him, a sinner who required a Cross, he could be present with the leper who needed a friend. Francis loved those who could not pad his ego with triumphant before-and-after stories, much as Christ had served him when he had nothing to offer but vanity and selfishness. If you don't believe in sin as a wasting disease, it's hard to believe in the Cross as the great cure.

For Francis, the Cross was the great equalizer of men and women, of classes and creeds, of ages and abilities. Christ had gone to the cross for the well and for the sick, the rich and for the poor, the beautiful and the ugly — all of them fundamentally marred and totally loved. Serving lepers wasn't stooping down to their level. It was reaching over, not straining up or bending down, to serve equals for whom Christ had died. When thorns seemed to stratify people into levels of lovability, the Cross had come to prove that chronically sick still meant chronically valuable. And so, whatever the "reasons" might be for someone contracting and dying from leprosy, it was not because God didn't love them. It was not because they were less than. It was a great mystery, not a tidy penalty.

A God willing to stoop down to live in our own human zombie colony to experience its horrific pain and crushing poverty could be served wholeheartedly, even dangerously. A God like this could be trusted with the secrets he wasn't telling.

Gradually, as though an old crime syndicate was reorganizing within my vascular system, my temperatures began to increase the week after Easter Sunday. In fact, the temps were higher than they had been in the past six months. In the month that followed my first shot, I would only have three days of normal temperatures and fifteen days of temperatures above 99.5. The fact was: I was worse. I was not in the privileged 40 percent of improved Long Haulers. I had humpty-dumptied off the wall.

My Functional Medicine nutritionist Katie seemed sad on our video call. "You did better when you were on the MegaViron," she observed, referring to a viral suppressant supplement I had taken back around Christmas. "Let's get back on that." She went on to adjust a few other dosages for various vitamins and detox supplements to prep me for my second shot, which would happen on June 12.

For the first time in nine months, I sensed a certain hail-Mary-ness about her approach, which made me jumpy. I felt camped on the edge of civilization, zipped inside a canvas tent with a dead cell phone. Whatever alchemy had bewitched my body from that little needle had run its course, and we couldn't guess at the reason or its meaning.

And yet, somehow, I wasn't particularly distraught. There was confusion, to be sure, and disappointment. But more than anything, a new and unexpected feeling began to bubble to the surface, one I hadn't felt in so much of the past year, and it began to wedge a beam of light between myself and my thorn. This feeling was curiosity.

I was just so curious about the whole thing, from the science of mRNA to the possibilities that might await me that summer as new research and treatments and insight would surely roll down the mountain from the CDC and the National Institute of Health (NIH) and the World Health Organization (WHO) and the Food and Drug Administration (FDA) and whoever else. I was also curious about what God might be doing — or purposely *not* doing — in the middle of it all. My curiosity itself also made me curious. "Curiouser and curiouser!" cries Alice in Wonderland. When curiosity drapes itself momentarily over bewilderment and fear and restlessness, even for one shaky second and even if the veil is very thin, you know it's possible to transition genres from horror to adventure. At least for that moment, you've held still long enough to wonder about it.

"Let my hope be defiant today," I prayed in my journal on April 5, the day after Easter, before my fever ratcheted up. Another open-ended year had stumbled through the door.

∿

### Station of the Cross: Jesus Meets the Women of Jerusalem

What a communal shock. Grabbing each other's hands, reaching for your arms, your face, the women were trying to comfort you. But also asking you why? Why this? Why now? You couldn't answer them then.

Oh Lord, help me to let you set the parameters of my thorn. I've insisted on benchmarks, but you have not agreed to my terms. I've insisted on progress, and you've said to wait. Do I trust that you set its boundaries as you do for the oceans, that you set its intensity as you do for the storms, that you set its duration as you do for each season?

Help me to trust your good intentions towards me. Help me to trust that you are committed to my final and everlasting happiness.

Meanwhile, I'll go about my business today. I'll let you keep your secrets.

I'll make myself a cup of tea. Plan for dinner. Feed the dog and wipe the counter. My curiosity will not bring my confidence in you into question. Not today.

Or for this hour.

Or at least for this moment.


## CHILD

Christmas in Paris, TX, was always twinkly, and full of fairy whispers. Grandmama and Grandaddy put the tree up in the sunroom where the old multi-colored building blocks sat next to the couch, but the real festivities happened in the living room

"MY HEART IS NOT PROUD, LORD,
MY EYES ARE NOT HAUGHTY;
I DO NOT CONCERN MYSELF WITH
GREAT MATTERS
OR THINGS TOO WONDERFUL FOR ME.
BUT I HAVE CALMED AND QUIETED
MYSELF,
I AM LIKE A WEANED CHILD WITH ITS
MOTHER;
LIKE A WEANED CHILD I AM CONTENT.
ISRAEL, PUT YOUR HOPE IN THE LORD
BOTH NOW AND FOREVERMORE."
– PSALM 131

in front of the fireplace. It was there I would conscript my younger siblings into grand nativity plays. Backstage would be the dining room, just off stage right, from whence we would set the entrance of the magi or the offstage bleating of a sheep.

Oh, the joys of a captive audience! It is truly the great unappreciated privilege of childhood performers. It's hard to say how many hours my parents and grandparents and aunts and uncles were confined to the salmon-colored couch in the Paris living room for improvised rock concerts, nativities, and puppet shows. My younger sister Liz and I were never deterred by their earnest, wrap-it-up applause. No, no! The good part was just about to come! Hold on, just one more costume change! Just one more song! Holding their gaze was our lifeblood. It was all about being at the center of things for one minute longer before the dessert got served or the baths got drawn. Our reason for being was to keep the adults engaged by any means possible, but especially by frenetic action: flitting this way and that, hamming for a laugh, yelling for a reaction, whispering in loud *sotto voce* for them to lean in. It was the most selfish form of theater imaginable and should not have been called theater at all. It was politics, at best.

Only the humblest person can hold still on a stage, say her lines truthfully, and then leave the stage willingly.

Only the still can be of real service.

Admittedly, there are things about the old mystics and church fathers and mothers that bother modern-day, Bible church me. (Of course, there are things about modern-day, Bible church me that bother me, too.) The gender inferiority lens through which Julian and Teresa saw their world agitates this educated American female. The saints' over-obsession with purgatory and hell seems incongruent with Scripture, let alone with their professed reliance on the grace of God. Their sometimes-disturbing desires for suffering feel more like mental illness than piety. They came from societies that largely did not value human rights. They didn't know about penicillin or gravity. Their views on sex could get dicey. But in the same breath, I must concede that 500 years from now, there will be things about me that seem ill or offensive to modern-modern-modern-modern-day readers of that era, and I don't think this means those future people-bots shouldn't listen[117]. Surely there will be something good and beautiful sticking up out of my mud. If someone has suffered, she earns the right to a fair trial. That's my story, and I'm sticking to it.

And here we come to the more outlandish of church history lore, the much debated, often revered account of Saint Francis receiving the Stigmata — the wounds of Christ — in his physical body. According to Bonaventure, Francis was on one of his extended prayer fasts on a desolate mountain, when a winged creature came and pierced him in his hands, feet, and side. For the next two years before his death, Francis would suffer *"from so many infirmities, that there was scarcely one of his members but was tormented by immense pain and suffering."*[118] He had so identified with the Cross of Christ that his body had manifested this reality physically, a phenomenon that was broadly reported by many witnesses and affirmed by Pope Gregory IX, who canonized Francis almost immediately after his death.

Whether or not you believe the full extent of this account, it seems clear Francis was suffering terribly and incapacitated, forced into a stillness he hadn't anticipated. What's most miraculous, after all, isn't the miracle itself but, once again, Francis' reaction to it. Here was a man who at every turn had joyfully given every penny and thread away, who had led a thriving new sect of monks to do the same, and who regularly ministered to the dregs of society — lepers. This is how God repays him? With constant, chronic pain? Ah, but Francis did not have a transactional relationship with God. Theirs was a relationship of *identification*. Francis had become "so oned" (to use Julian's phrase) with God, that he took on God's will and God's suffering as his own glad occupation. Jesus' ongoing presence in Francis' psyche and physical body was a constant infusion of steel. Francis was joined with the ultimate love in the universe and was intent on bringing that love to fruition by way of sacrifice, which is how the greatest loves prove themselves in the real world.

And Francis loved until the end. According to his biographer, Francis asked to be carried from village to village (he couldn't walk because of the wounds on his feet), so that *"he might thus encourage others to carry the Cross of Christ."*[119] He referred to his "grievous torments" as his "sisters" because they made him more useful for serving God's family.[120] By simply enduring the wounds of Jesus, he drew many Italians to faith, and by extension, untold millions in Europe and the world across centuries. He held still, like a caterpillar in a chrysalis, and let love do its work.

The first nine verses of Francis' famous *Canticles of the Creatures* were probably written during this time of great physical suffering and infirmity.[121] It's here we see him invoking God's role as Creator of a great big family. We meet "Sister Moon" and "Brother Wind," "Sister Water" and "Brother Fire," and "Sister Mother Earth." It's almost as if Francis has gone back to the book of Job and latched onto the litany of questions God asks his horribly afflicted would-be servant: Where were you when I laid the earth's foundation? Were you there when the morning stars first sang together? Did you make all of this or did I?

In Francis' worldview, we are not the parents, the originators, of anything. We are the children, the kids, the babies. We are mere siblings to all that is, even siblings with Sister Bodily Death itself. All things serve us, and we serve all things. All things can bring us Home where our great Parent waits.

In our long-term angst or pain or turmoil or grief, Francis would likely agree we should talk to Jesus himself in prayer (like Julian), according to the Bible's revelation (like Augustine), and with the power of our imagination (like Ignatius), and the help of daily prayer practices (like Teresa). And then Francis would admonish us to pray and work and rest in the shadow of the Cross. To think and operate under its implications, and then to spend life open to this Crucified God as the core posture of our hearts[122].

But the Cross is only the beginning. It has to be. Just as surely as Francis lived his life in its shadow, he must have surely been looking past it to the sun. After all, this was how Jesus saw it, who didn't die just for dying's sake but to come back from death and set up a new creation where "every tear will be wiped away." In that world, all his children will see his face in a place so bright it doesn't need the sun. In that world, we won't carry trauma. In that world, pain from the past will only be a trace memory of his enduring presence. Of grace itself.

The glaring, red all-caps text jumped out at me from the screen of my phone: "POSITIVE." Maddie and I were at the pediatric Urgent Care center, in a little waiting room with neon tiles on the floor. One of the *Trolls* movies was playing on a small screen above the examination table where she was curled up like a baby spider. The afternoon before, she had returned from summer camp and was beginning to wilt with fever and fatigue. I had been involved with a play reading at a theater in town and was just making sure Maddie didn't have COVID before I returned for the afternoon performance. *Surely,* she was just worn out from her time at camp. Surely, *surely,* she hadn't finally caught COVID after all this time?

But she had.

Thankfully, her fever would eventually lift and take her fatigue right along with it. Maddie's taste and smell would return. She would never have heart or lung problems, diarrhea, or brain fog. She would not be a Long-Hauler.

I called the theater in a daze of worry and stayed home that afternoon from my last performance. Because the theater was conscientious and employed union actors, they offered free COVID testing to the rest of us who might have been exposed. I wasn't concerned for myself because I had received two doses of the vaccine by then, but I went anyway out of solidarity.

"The world is getting stranger and stranger," said the theater's managing director when he called my cell the next day. "Your test also came back positive for COVID."

I was in the sunroom looking out on the bright July day. Everything was so warm, buzzing, and alive with summer energy. Bees and mosquitoes hummed around the boxwood bushes that bordered the front of our house; kids rode bikes down the sidewalk under the 90-year-old red oak trees that are the only blessed shade from the Texas sun. Whatever else was true, so was this: that morning, I had awakened with a vague trickle down the back of my throat. It could have easily been allergies, but there was no denying something had felt even more off than usual. I stood at the hot window with the phone at my ear, awash in confusion, trying to say things that sounded coherent and calm to the theater's managing director while trying to process the idea of receiving my first positive COVID test in over a year and a half of symptoms. After being vaccinated. After being a Long-Hauler.

My General Practitioner, Dr. G, sent me to the ER the next day for an antibody infusion. Given my history and the antitrypsin deficiency, she didn't want to take any chances. By then my normal afternoon fever was markedly higher, and I was even more fatigued. My sinuses were beginning to close. I kept waiting in dread for the awful airlessness to constrict my lungs along with the dry cough. I wondered if my heart would start running for the hills again. I braced myself for the onslaught of gastro issues. These were the symptoms that had blessedly lifted after months of good diet, supplements, rest, and detoxes. The fatigue, fever and brain fog had been the only hangers-on. With feeble sighs, I stared down the prospect of starting back to square one.

In the ER, I sat beside an older, dark-haired lady in the quarantined section for Covid patients. We were taken together for X-rays, and swapped exposure stories outside the X-ray theater, or whatever it's called (a studio? It has a certain feel of drama.). A nurse gave me a warm blanket for my fever. I laid down on the couch in the waiting room across from my new co-Covid friend, and we both waited a grand total of five more hours for our monoclonal antibody prescriptions to be made, filled, and administered.

Finally, the dark-haired lady and I were ushered back to a ward of upright chairs that looked like a chemo lab. She was hooked up first to my left. A man in his sixties was seated to my right. He and I got to talking, as much as sick people can get to talking in a pandemic triage, and we eventually made the connection that we both attended the same church.

The dark-haired lady, overhearing this, said, "I knew I recognized you! Weren't you Mary Poppins?" Our church had put on a production of *Mary Poppins* about five years before.

Yes, I was.

The three of us got to talking.

It turns out we had all been fully vaccinated and were among the first breakthrough cases our hospital in Fort Worth had seen in the summer of 2021. The man had endured Covid back in February and had received an antibody infusion then as well. "You should have super-immunity!" I said with sharply exhaled exasperation, but he just shrugged his shoulders. We watched the clear liquid dripping down the tubes and into our veins.

The man hadn't seen me in *Mary Poppins*. "So, you sing?"

I made a sheepish sound.

"My granddaughter loves *Frozen*. Do you think you could sing *Let It Go* for her?" he asked.

I blinked at him. "Right now?"

Instead having a captive audience, I was now a captive performer. I was literally hooked up by my veins to an obligatory center stage.

"I could text her mom a video?" he urged.

A split-second of hesitancy, and then: "I'd love to." There didn't seem to be any other words I could have possibly said in the universe or in any parallel or potential universe.

I looked up the lyrics on my phone and found a key that fit my voice, whatever was left of it. The man had just been unhooked from his drip bag and was able to stand to shoot the video on his phone. I had no makeup on from my Blushed Nudes palette, no perfume or bangles, and was every bit as tired and feverish as I had been the whole year. My lungs, however, were still placid within the storm.

The man made a little introduction for me so his granddaughter would know I was there with him and that all of us were having a good time, despite the tube sticking out of my arm and snaking up to a hanging bag. I leaned forward into the iPhone camera and said her name.

"This is for you, and I hope you enjoy it! Can you sing it with me?"

I mostly whisper-sang it, shaky and sickly, without all the blazing power and beauty the song requires. I had no cool moves. No flourishes. It was simple, light, breathy.

The lyrics, of course, are about the release of perfection, of riding the storms and the freezing temperatures of life with a sense of power and adventure — all very ironic given how trapped I must have appeared in my chemo chair. I certainly wasn't standing in my power. I was singing in my weakness, unable to throw off the fetters of tubes, fevers, or fatigue. Some things you just can't let go of, as much as you want to.

Some things, you can.

I pictured the child on the other side of the camera, a little one who would love to hear her grandfather's voice and know that he was thinking about her even in such a scary place. In my mind, she was wearing a blue Elsa dress and a blonde, braided wig. She probably loved putting on plays in her grandparents' living room surrounded by tinsel and empty eggnog mugs, the center of their universe.

She knew all the lyrics to the song, the man had told me.

She knew all the lyrics, and now so did I.

Selah.

~~~

## Station of the Cross: Jesus is Nailed to the Cross

The pain held you in place until the work was finished. You held still for me. For my flourishing, now and always. You held still, did what you came to do, made your exit. And then came the Encore, a civilization upended by Easter.

Oh Lord, not only the Cross, but all creation points to your love. The fact of pugs. The sunshine. The staggering swath of stars behind black mountains. Songs to sing and lungs to sing them.

I sit in wonder at it all. I am only a child, a baby, so new to the scene. I don't have the language yet to process so much of reality. And like a baby, I wail at the discomfort and pain I cannot understand.

But not today. Today I nestle into the love that's detectable anywhere and everywhere, wherever and however, I can find it. I look for ways to lay hold of it and splash around in it and drink it down my throat.

You have nurtured me. You have satisfied me. You are holding me. You will cradle me close, and you will grow me up to glory.

# EPILOGUE

Pain, illness, hurts, and hang-ups can be chronic, but there's a force every bit as persistent. Less of a force, really, and more of a Person.

I'm writing in January of 2023, in a world that feels very much like a pre-pandemic flashback — masks are scarce, the news isn't aflame with Covid death numbers, and theaters are open again. That doesn't mean Covid isn't continuing its rampage, as we are now watching China grapple with its swift about-face in virus policy.

Also, I just found out last week about another friend who just recently contracted Covid and has begun experiencing Long Covid symptoms. It's Kendra, actually — Kendra of the artichoke prayer shawl.

I wish I could crochet her something.

There are others, too, still slogging through each day, posting on the Long Haul COVID Fighters Facebook Page asking for encouragement as they have been doing week after week since the spring or summer of 2020.

But not me.

Apparently, I'm well now.

*Well?*

Yes, I'm well.

It feels almost boastful to say it because it never seemed possible.

My recovery from probably-Delta-but-definitely-Covid was very much a study in anti-climax. After a couple of days of high fever following my infusion, all the congestion and fatigue dissipated and blew away in the hot summer wind.

But sure enough, the fevers, brain fog, and fatigue began cycling again. The Alpha Variant (or whatever OG bug assaulted me in April 2020) had evicted Delta and reasserted its dominance. After all, Alpha had been the one hanging curtains and painting accent walls in my body for the past year and it wasn't planning to leave.

A few months later, as I continued with symptoms, my intrepid Functional Medicine guru Katie ran a series of tests that tested for tick-borne disease. The test was a bit of an outlier, given that I didn't have any of the major markers for Lyme disease. It was literally the last test on Katie's Fatigue Protocol after systematically ruling out nutrient deficiencies, mold, Candida, SIBO, and other common problems. Lo and behold, I tested positive for three bacteria.

After a months-long detox on sophisticated capsules and droppers of dark liquid that tasted like distilled char, my remaining symptoms gradually began to lift. The last of my fevers petered out in February of 2022, almost one year ago.

It's likely the bacteria (along with my other previous health issues) was in my system before the mysterious respiratory virus (Covid, probably) attacked my lungs and heart, making it so very difficult to heal.

Long story short: I have my life back. And I can't tell you how grateful I am.

There's been no more turning to stone on the sunroom couch. No more dragging myself up the stairs on all fours to kiss the kids goodnight. No more rabbit heart threatening me with unconsciousness. I don't even have to take naps every afternoon anymore. There is no doubt that I could not have written this book in the state I was in for so long.

I've also been working steadily doing commercial and theater gigs and not taking a moment for granted. My mind is sharper now, and my feet are swift for most tasks. I even like wiping countertops now.

Although this health thorn of mine is no longer pricking, I'm aware yours might still be. And Lord knows thorns will always be a part of life and at varying levels of intensity because this is the nature of a world that began as a garden and dried into a desert. (I'm sure there's another one heading my way soon enough.)

Deserts can be beautiful, though. I know this now because I am now forty-one, and because what hair I *have* been regrowing is coming in grey, and because of the words of a particular Person to us in John 16: "In this world, you will have trouble."

But take heart.

In 1999, as a senior in high school, I had the privilege of performing in a play about a Holocaust survivor named Alexandra. She was fifteen years old in 1945 when she escaped a slave labor camp. After brutal months at

Dachau, she was moved to a labor camp where she spent a year breaking her back over railway construction projects and enduring atrocities like medical experiments — even an unanesthetized tonsillectomy. Before her imprisonment, Alexandra had been an orphan. After her captivity, she became a refugee.

Alexandra's whole tween life was an ongoing nightmare, not just a basically good life pricked by a thorn or two. One night, while lying on her top bunk in the labor camp's putrid barracks, she prayed for God to take her life. She wasn't brave enough for suicide, so she begged for a divine dismissal. The following day, however, she woke up. Her prayer had been denied.

Inexplicably, in place of her brutal nighttime despair was now an irrational daytime joy, a yellow rose in a nuclear wasteland. It wasn't that Alexandra had sensed a promise of deliverance or any specific reassurance at all. It was a matter of feeling settled, of having a supernaturally acute sense that God himself was with her. This was enough, more than enough to keep on living. And with that strong and wildly absurd invigoration, Alexandra went out into the sunlight and worked her job that day. She cared for the other girls in her barracks. She planned a daring escape.

In the wee hours one morning sometime later, she led nine other teen and tween girls past a guard and his dog under a barbed wire fence to freedom. The guard didn't flinch. The dog's ears didn't twitch. It was a slow-motion miracle, akin to shutting the mouths of lions. Deliverance happened, freedom was wrought and ratified, and lives were reclaimed for the future: for future husbands, children, grandchildren, vocations, and legacies. But deliverance was not what brought the joy. The joy is what first broke the jail.

I will never forget lying on the top bunk, the stage lights rising. Alexandra had coached me on what she had felt in those moments, about her options, and where her rational thoughts had ended. To this day, in a very diminutive, fractured way, I remember her memories of that fateful night and magical morning. They still play along the screen of my mind like a dream I can't forget.

At the time, I was responsible for sharing her pain — and pleasure — with an audience. On opening night, Alexandra sat in the front row and relived the experience with about 300 people with no such extraordinary personal histories.

She approached me afterward with eyes twinkling, with a gladness that hadn't been diminished by the years or the nightmares of the past.

"Wonderful, Julie," she said in her still-thick Russian accent.

I suppose it is likely her joy has only grown over time and in defiance of the nightmares. I say this because Alexandra has helped over 250 families adopt children from Russian orphanages with the adoption agency she founded. Bitterness doesn't affect that kind of change. Alexandra hasn't merely left the past behind. She has plundered it for better use. I guess you could call her a saint.

Grace is like that. It keeps up right alongside pain and can then surpass, override, and convert pain's effects — eventually. And, very frequently, grace does this *immediately* as well, even before circumstances improve. Grace has that kind of preemptive authority and that kind of ongoing alpha-and-omega toughness. If pain is bronze, grace is steel. Both can last and last, but one is ultimately stronger in the present moment and over time.

One way I have defined grace in this book is the abiding presence of Jesus himself, the felt proximity of a person so big and yet so available he can meet with a fourteen-year-old in a German prison camp and not only help her escape her captors but first and finally, her despair. When I think of the better days of my illness, they too were marked by that sense of him there with me and of the fizzy and surprising discovery that "in his presence, there is fullness of joy" (Psalm 16:11). He was with me in my jail, and it made all the difference.

The late, great Tim Keller was always so fond of quoting George Herbert, the English 16th-century poet, who once wrote, "Death used to be an executioner, but the gospel has made him just a gardener." And the sweeping gospel-good-news of the Bible is that this jail-breaker Jesus went down into that death to raise us, alive and free and forever united to him, which makes death only the beginning of a great bloom.

Bewildered, restless, fearful, or hungry, we are invited to sit in the sun of this warm, invigorating news. There's a spot for you here, too, thorn-bearer. Let's nestle in together.

# ABOUT THE AUTHOR

PHOTO CREDIT: DANA PATRICK

JULIE K. RHODES lives in Fort Worth, TX, with her husband Gordon and two teenage kids, Drew and Maddie, plus the pug Eloise ("The Eyeballs."). She performs on stage and in front of the camera when people will let her.

Visit juliekrhodes.com to connect.

# APPENDIX

# PRAYERS
# BY TOPIC OR NEED

**Prayers for the Bewildered** (Chapter 2)

For Prayers for the Restless, Fearful, Hungry and Still,
scan the QR code:

# NOTES

1  https://www.cdc.gov/nchs/covid19/pulse/long-covid.htm
2  https://www.tandfonline.com/doi/full/10.1080/03007995.2022.2081454
3  The Ruthless Elimination of Hurry, John Mark Comer
4  https://www.ignatianspirituality.com/ignatian-prayer/the-examen/rummaging-for-
   god-praying-backward-through-your-day/
5  Exercises, p. 21
6  https://www.theway.org.uk/back/s042Torrens.pdf
7  Exercises, p. 122
8  Exercises, p. 122
9  Exercises, p. 123
10  Exercises, p. 99
11  https://www.ignatianspirituality.com/st-ignatius-and-community/
12  Exercises (end notes, p. 153)
13  Exercises, p. 81, 84
14  https://www.britannica.com/biography/St-Ignatius-of-Loyola
15  https://www.pillarcatholic.com/p/ignatius-the-soldier-saint
16  The Spritual Exercises of Saint Ignatius, edited by George E. Ganss, S.J., Loyola
   Press, 1992
17  https://www.historytoday.com/archive/death-st-ignatius-loyola
18  https://www.theway.org.uk/back/s087Clark.pdf
19  Confessions, p. 39, translation by Henry Chadwick, Oxford World's Classics, 2008
20  Confessions, p. 40
21  Confessions, p.152
22  Confessions, p. 153
23  Opening To God, Benner, p.48
24  Benner, 48
25  https://www.thegospelcoalition.org/article/saint-augustine-on-prayer/
26  https://www.newadvent.org/fathers/1102130.htm

27  https://www.newadvent.org/fathers/1102130.htm (Translated by J.G. Cunningham. From Nicene and Post-Nicene Fathers, First Series, Vol. 1. Edited by Philip Schaff. (Buffalo, NY: Christian Literature Publishing Co., 1887.) Revised and edited for New Advent by Kevin Knight.)

28  Desiring God's Will, David G. Benner, Invervarsity Press, 2015, p. 77

29  https://www.newadvent.org/fathers/1102130.htm

30  Wittgenstein in Translation: Exploring Semiotic Signatures, Walter DeGruyter, 2012, p. 118

31  Exposition on the Psalms, Augustine of Hippo: https://www.newadvent.org/fathers/1801004.htm

32  https://www.newadvent.org/fathers/1102130.htm

33  https://www.newadvent.org/fathers/1102130.htm

34  "Babette's Feast" (Conceived and Developed by Abigail Killeen, Written by Rose Courtney, adapted from the short story by Isak Dinesen)

35  https://www.tertullian.org/fathers/possidius_life_of_augustine_02_text.htm#C31

36  https://www.tertullian.org/fathers/possidius_life_of_augustine_02_text.htm#C31

37  Amy Frykholm, Julian of Norwich: A Contemplative Biography, The Paraclete Press, 2010

38  Julian of Norwich, Amy Frykholm, Paraclete Press, 2010

39  Revelations of Divine Love, Julian of Norwich, Ixia Press, ed. Kaya Oakes, 2019, p. 9

40  Revelations, P. 10

41  Frykholm 50

42  Frykholm, 12

43  Revelations, p. 12

44  Revelations, p. 12

45  Revelations, p. 20

46  Revelations, p. 12

47  Revelations, p. 79

48  Revelations, p. 80

49  Frykholm, 22

50  Frykholm, 26

51  Revelations, p. 140

52  Revelations, 137

53  Revelations, p. 79

54  Revelations, p. 121

55  Revelations, p. 79

56  Revelations, p. 81

57  Revelations, p. 79

58  Revelations, p. 82

59  Revelations, p. 83
60  Revelations, p. 77
61  Revelations, p. 78
62  Revelations, p. 78
63  Revelations, p. 78
64  Revelations, p.7
65  Revelations, p. 43
66  Revelations, p. 125
67  Revelations, p. 44
68  I must here credit Tim Keller, who has frequently used this line of logic in his many sermons through the years.
69  Revelations, p. 42
70  Revelations, p.55
71  Revelations, p. 132
72  Revelations, p. 3
73  Revelations, p. 180
74  Revelations, p. 110
75  David G. Benner, Opening to God
76  The Spiritual Exercises of Saint Ignatius, p. 165 (endnotes)
77  https://www.ncregister.com/blog/5-important-lessons-from-st-teresa-of-avila
78  Way of Perfection, Ch. 4, p. 24
79  Opening to God, p. 15
80  Opening to God, p. 37
81  Autobiography, Ch. 9, p. 54
82  Autobiography, Ch. 9, p. 56
83  "Mack & Mabel" book by Michael Stewart and music and lyrics by Jerry Herman
84  Way of Perfection, Ch. 26, p. 178
85  Autobiography, Ch. 9, p. 55
86  Way of Perfection, Ch. 30, p. 199
87  Opening to God, Benner, p. 119
88  Opening to God, Benner, p. 119
89  Way of Perfection, Ch. 7, p. 46
90  https://www.britannica.com/topic/Carmelites
91  https://www.jstor.org/stable/20716965?read-now=1&seq=5#page_scan_tab_contents
92  Way of Perfection, Ch .28, p. 184-185
93  Way of Perfection, Ch. 30, p. 195
94  Autobiography, Ch. 11, p. 69
95  Autobiography, Ch. 11, p. 70
96  The Life of St. Francis of Assisi, Bonaventure, p. 5

97  The Life of St. Francis of Assisi, Bonaventure, p. 164

98  Life, p. 10

99  Life, p. 87

100  Opening to God, Benner, p.57

101  Benner, 49

102  Life of St. Francis, 24

103  Life, p. 81

104  Writings of St. Francis, p xiv, Fr. Paschal Robinson

105  Life of St. Francis, p. 53, 66

106  Life of St. Francis, p. 66

107  Life of St. Francis, p. 54

108  Life of St. Francis, p. 83

109  Opening to God, Benner, p. 155

110  Opening to God, Benner, p. 154

111  Life of Saint Francis, p. 67

112  Life of Saint Francis, p. 70

113  Life of St. Francis, p. 11

114  Life of St. Francis, p. 11

115  Life of St. Francis, p. 157

116  Life of St. Francis, p. 75

117  Again, I must credit Tim Keller for this line of reasoning. He used it frequently in sermons over the years.

118  Life of St. Francis, p. 116

119  Life of St. Francis, p. 115

120  Life of St. Francis, p. 115

121  http://franciscanseculars.com/the-canticle-of-the-creatures/

122  Opening to God, Benner, p. 156

**ELOISE "THE EYEBALLS" RHODES**

Printed in the USA
CPSIA information can be obtained
at www.ICGtesting.com
LVHW012015181123
764304LV00031B/175